American Oracle

American Oracle

The Civil War in the Civil Rights Era

David W. Blight

The Belknap Press of Harvard University Press
Cambridge, Massachusetts, and London, England
2011

Book Design by Dean Bornstein

Library of Congress Cataloging-in-Publication Data

Blight, David W.
American oracle : the Civil War in the civil rights era /
David W. Blight.
p. cm.
Includes bibliographical references and index.
ISBN 978-0-674-04855-3 (alk. paper)
1. United States—History—Civil War, 1861–1865—Historiography.
2. United States—History—Civil War, 1861–1865—Influence.
3. Warren, Robert Penn, 1905–1989. 4. Catton, Bruce, 1899–1978.
5. Wilson, Edmund, 1895–1972. 6. Baldwin, James, 1924–1987. I. Title.
E468.5.B55 2011
973.70072—dc22   2011006653

To
John and Pamela Blum
historians and beloved friends

Contents

Prologue. "Five Score Years Ago"
Civil War and Civil Rights   1

1. "Gods and Devils Aplenty"
Robert Penn Warren   31

2. A Formula for Enjoying the War
Bruce Catton   81

3. "Lincoln and Lee and All That"
Edmund Wilson   129

4. "This Country Is My Subject"
James Baldwin   183

Epilogue. "The Wisdom of Tragedy"
Ralph Ellison Had a Dream   251

Notes   261
Acknowledgments   295
Index   301

And so the Civil War draws us as an oracle, darkly unriddled and portentous, of personal, as well as national, fate.

—Robert Penn Warren, *The Legacy of the Civil War*, 1961

· PROLOGUE ·

"Five Score Years Ago"
Civil War and Civil Rights

A BREEZE eased the intense heat of the late August afternoon as the huge crowd, weary but peaceful and jubilant, leaned forward to listen. All along the reflecting pool of the Washington Mall, people steadied their sore feet and peered up at the steps of the Lincoln Memorial, the unofficial secular temple of the United States. Martin Luther King, Jr., a Southern Baptist minister who had become the preeminent face and voice of the Civil Rights Movement, stepped to the microphones and delivered a short, transcendent oration to the world on the meaning of the unfinished American Civil War, and thereby on the meaning of America.

On August 28, 1963, King gave what should be considered the most important speech marking the turbulent and divisive commemoration of the Civil War Centennial. As American society engages the Sesquicentennial of the Civil War in 2011–2015, King's famous address demands a hearing or, better, a reading. In what will always be known as the "I Have a Dream" speech, the "dream" metaphor emerges late, and extemporaneously. In the second sentence, King announced the text of his sermon, suggested the historical weight of the moment, and began to employ other unforgettable metaphors:

> Five score years ago, a great American, in whose symbolic shadow we stand today, signed the Emancipation Proclamation. This momentous decree came as a beacon light of hope to millions of Negro slaves who had been seared in the flames of withering injustice. It came as a joyous daybreak to end the long night of their captivity. But one hundred years later, the Negro still is not free. One hundred

years later, the life of the Negro is still sadly crippled by the manacles of segregation and the chains of discrimination. One hundred years later, the Negro lives on an island of poverty in the midst of a vast ocean of material prosperity. One hundred years later, the Negro is still languishing in the corners of American society and finds himself an exile in his own land.

No one at the event, or watching on television, or for that matter who reads or hears the speech in its entirety today, can miss the significance of "Five score," a clear and poignant reference to Abraham Lincoln's use of "Four score and seven years ago . . ." in his Gettysburg Address.[1]

As Lincoln implied in that brief address at the Gettysburg cemetery in November 1863, the Civil War, the outcome of which was still far from determined, necessitated a new founding, a redefinition of the United States, rooted somehow in the destruction of slavery and the reborn, ill-defined principle of human equality. In the "Dream" speech, King argued the same for his own era: the civil rights revolution heralded yet another refounding in the same principle, one hundred anguished years after Lincoln's promise. The Civil War and civil rights have been forever intertwined in American history and mythology. The Reconstruction era forged a permanent, if forever contested, bond in national memory between the war's results and the American tradition of civil rights reform. But in the period of the Centennial, from the 1950s to the mid-1960s, the two phenomena were too often like planets in separate orbits around different suns. For seventeen magnificent minutes the power of King's rhetoric broke down the segregated gravitational pulls of the two planets and brought them into the same orbit. But befitting his role as leader of a radical, if nonviolent, protest movement, King's arguments were hardly mainstream in the Cold War political culture of 1963 America.

In the year of the assassination of John F. Kennedy and worldwide exposure of vicious racism and violence in the civil rights crisis in the

South, as before and since, the meaning of the Civil War was the most divisive element in national historical memory. By the early 1960s, some Americans had learned and accepted the idea that the war had been, in one way or another, caused by slavery and that its principle result had been the emancipation of four million slaves and the preservation as well as recreation of a new Union. Indeed, the idea of "Union" as the war's purpose and the North's "victory" as the grand result had flourished in the century since 1865, especially in periods of intense American nationalism, such as the World Wars and the Cold War. The centrality of slavery and emancipation, bound up with the preservation of the Union, emerged as a consensus in the new scholarship on the subject.[2]

But that story was yet to find consensus in public memory. What may seem relatively settled understandings among scholars, even in the midst of rich debate, rarely means that anything is settled in the broader world of social memory. For the majority, especially of white Americans—even as they watched TV images of civil rights marchers being clubbed by police and bitten by dogs in Birmingham, Alabama—to claim the centrality of slavery and emancipation in Civil War memory was still an awkward kind of impoliteness at best and heresy at worst. In 1963, the national temper and mythology still preferred a story of the mutual valor of the Blue and Gray to the troublesome, disruptive problem of black and white.

As we contemplate the memory of the Civil War during its one hundred and fiftieth anniversary season, we might best do so by going back to listen to King's refrain—"one hundred years later"— and then explore how American writers and readers were searching for the meaning of their history during the Centennial commemoration. Their questions and interests, their conclusions and arguments, their metaphors and stories may or may not reflect our own. But the best historical understandings often emerge from a probing behind, into, and through how other thoughtful people have done the same before us.

• • •

In his book *The Great War and Modern Memory*, Paul Fussell argued that for the Anglo cultural world, especially among British poets and writers, World War I obliterated assumptions and ideals that had been honed into settled values for generations. As millions were slaughtered or maimed in the "troglodyte world" of the trenches on the Western Front, British survivor-writers tried in verse, fiction, and memoir to find access through "tragic," sometimes "preposterous" forms of *irony* to represent their experience, to make sense of senselessness. "Thus the drift of modern history domesticates the fantastic and normalizes the unspeakable," wrote Fussell. "And the catastrophe that begins it is the Great War." In America, that modern history began with the Civil War, fifty years before the Battle of the Somme, in the trenches of Petersburg and on the killing fields of Shiloh. Americans, both the survivor-writers and the three or four generations that followed, would sometimes face, but normally deflect, even deny, the fantastic and unspeakable in their own first "great war"; they found myriad ways to sidestep its disillusioning tragedy in a grand story of greatness emerging out of mutual sacrifice and sectional reunion. Cups of wrath could be converted into cups of sweet sentiment on Decorations Days, as stories of the Blue and the Gray made a new nationalism easier and more palatable than just solutions to the enduring American dilemma of black and white.[3]

But the trenches and the bones and skulls of the dead were still there, protruding from the ground in the 1860s and 1870s in the American South, just as they did for decades over hundreds of square miles of ruined French farmland after 1918. Writing in the early 1970s, Fussell described the landscape of the Somme:

> To wander now over the fields destined to extrude their rusty metal fragments for centuries is to appreciate in the most intimate way the permanent reverberations of July, 1916. When the air is damp you can smell rusted iron everywhere, even though you see only wheat and barley. The farmers . . . collect the duds, shell-casings, fuses,

and shards of old barbed wire as the plow unearths them and stack them in the corners of their fields. . . . The mine craters are too deep to be filled and remain much as they were. . . . Lurking in every spot of undergrowth . . . are eloquent little things: rusted buckles, rounds of corroded small-arms ammunition, metal tabs from ammunition boxes, bits of Bully tin, buttons.[4]

In 1869, Russell H. Conwell, a twenty-six-year-old Union veteran writing for the *Boston Daily Evening Traveller,* made a three-month journey to the Civil War's battlefields of the South. Beginning his tour in Arlington Heights, Virginia, at the former residence of Robert E. Lee, which had been converted into a massive federal cemetery, Conwell dwelled on the irony that the Confederate general's estate had been turned into "one great graveyard" of the Union dead. Stunned at the "shattered and ruined" landscapes of Virginia, he remarked that the war had "transformed the 'Garden of the South'" into the "Graveyard of America." The dead seemed everywhere to Conwell. "Scarcely a day passes," he wrote, "when the plow of the farmer tilling the soil, or the spade of the Negro hunting lead, does not disturb in their secret resting-places the bones of Union soldiers." At the Cold Harbor battlefield in Virginia, Conwell observed the "surest and saddest prompter of memory." He "met several Negroes with large sacks, collecting the bones of dead horses which they sold to the bone-grinders of Richmond." When he reached Charleston, South Carolina, and while visiting the remains of Fort Wagner on Morris Island, Conwell met an "old darkey soldier" wearing his blue cap, "digging for old iron in the sand." "The products of his industry," wrote Conwell romantically, "reminded us of the stacks in a New England hay field. He sells it by the ton and is putting his money in the bank." As Conwell strolled over the sand along the shore where the famous charge of the 54th Massachusetts black regiment had taken place six years earlier, he saw "old haversacks, belts, bayonet scabbards, and shoes" strewn along the beach. In the surf at his feet, human skulls and bones "lay grinning upon the shore and filled us with sad sensations, which still haunt our dreams. The sad and the beautiful, how strangely combined." As he mused over this extraordinary sight, he observed skulls embedded with seashells "in their ears, mouth, and eyes," as though "set in frames of diamonds." As he contemplated this scene of war's human and metal refuse, Conwell felt the "inspiring sensations which the traveler feels as he treads the Plains of Marathon."[5]

This nineteenth-century American combination of the macabre and the romantic would have no place along the Somme. Modern memory of the Civil War and that of World War I developed differently in the two cultures, for a host of reasons. Both carried the sense that war had become what Fussell called "the permanent condition of mankind." It is impossible to imagine, however, a relatively informed tourist describing Fussell's "boneyard" of the Somme as Conwell did the sands on Morris Island: as a living memorial to "the cause of human freedom."[6] For reasons explored in this work and elsewhere, the American Civil War has been forever an event that fiercely resists popular consensus about its causes and consequences; despite voluminous research and overwhelming scrutiny, it remains the mythic national epic. As a broad culture, Americans seem incapable of completely shucking this event from its protective shells of sentimentalism, romance, and pathos in order to see to its heart of tragedy. It might be argued that this is rightly so with national epics—they should or can never be utterly deromanticized. Or it might be argued that such epics are also dangerous to national self-understanding, to a healthy, informed confrontation with the meaning of the most important elements of our past, and therefore the imperatives of the present. Modern nations are and always have been built upon their narratives of origin and development, and in this case, of destruction and rebirth. This study of the Civil War's literary and intellectual history, as well as its popular memory, engages the compelling question of how the United States, to an important degree, *is* the stories it tells itself about its Civil War and its enduring aftermath. Throughout the

generations, up to this historical moment of the war's Sesquicentennial, those stories have had lasting consequences.

. . .

In this book I examine the works, and to some extent the lives, of
four of America's most important writers on the subject of the significance and legacies of the Civil War during the 1950s and 1960s. I
have chosen each of the four writers—Robert Penn Warren, Bruce
Catton, Edmund Wilson, and James Baldwin—for particular and
representative reasons. Many other writers might have been selected
had I attempted a much longer and more comprehensive study of
novelists, poets, historians, and journalists who treated the Civil War
era during this period.[7] One of those other writers, Ralph Ellison, is
the source and subject of my epilogue. Instead of a comprehensive
survey of how various kinds of writers used, interpreted, and rewrote
the Civil War, I have drilled deeply into the work of four especially
important ones.

Each of my four chosen writers left a profound imprint on American letters generally, and on our understanding of the Civil War
epoch specifically. Each had a compelling sense of history and was
in his own way engaged in an unending quest to know the purpose
of the past in life and art. Three of the four can fit well into the vast
category of "modernist" writers, while the fourth, Catton, defies such
a literary label as a narrative historian. Above all, each was a serious
American writer, and each in his distinctive way wrote at least one
work we might deem a classic of the Centennial era. In nonfiction
and fiction respectively, Warren's *Legacy of the Civil War* and *Wilderness: A Tale of the Civil War,* both published in 1961, brilliantly
represent that multiple-genre writer's nearly life-long effort to comprehend the indelible impact of the events of 1861–1865 on his family,
on his own imagination, on his native South, and on the American
nation. Bruce Catton was by far the most popular and widely read
American historian of the Civil War from the mid-1950s to the mid-
1960s. Among his fifteen or so books of narrative history, perhaps

Stillness at Appomattox (1953) and *The Coming Fury* (1961) stand as his most lasting, although his exquisite talent for prose and storytelling, formulaic as it might be, did not fail him in any of his books. Edmund Wilson, widely regarded as America's preeminent literary critic of the twentieth century, spent nearly twenty years discovering and reading writers from the Civil War era and published his massive *Patriotic Gore: Studies in the Literature of the American Civil War* in 1962 to both great acclaim and consternation. And as the Civil Rights Movement took hold and began to reshape America forever from the late 1950s to the mid-1960s, James Baldwin, by choice and circumstance, transformed himself into perhaps the greatest essayist of the era, in the collections *Notes of a Native Son* (1955) and *Nobody Knows My Name* (1961), but especially in his bestselling manifesto, *The Fire Next Time*, of 1963.

Three of these authors were born within the same decade around the turn of the twentieth century, Wilson in 1895, Catton in 1899, and Warren in 1905. Baldwin, born in 1924, was from the next generation. Warren and Wilson began to write in the 1920s and matured as prolific artists in the 1930s. Catton spent almost twenty years as a journalist in the 1920s and 1930s, and then nearly a decade as a federal government servant in the World War II era. He did not begin writing books until nearly the age of fifty. Baldwin started writing reviews, short fiction, and articles when he was barely past twenty, in the late 1940s, and came into his own as a novelist-essayist in the 1950s. All four men were still at the peak of their literary powers as the Centennial era arrived.

I have also chosen these writers because they represent divergent backgrounds, genres, and points of view. Warren (1905–1989), born and raised in Guthrie, Kentucky, near the Tennessee border, was a white Southern poet-novelist who was originally imbued with the Lost Cause tradition—Southerners' claims that in the Civil War they had fought nobly only for home and states' rights, and never for slavery, arguments that by the turn of the twentieth century also became an ideology of white supremacy—but who lived the final forty-nine years of his life in the North at universities where he labored to overcome the racial worldview of his youth, and wrote all of his most important works. Catton (1899–1978) was born in Benzonia, Michigan, a small town in the northern reaches of the Lower Peninsula, attended but dropped out of Oberlin College, and served in World War I in the U.S. Navy. A Yankee who was determined to write the story of the Union common soldier and his cause, Catton lived most of his adult life in either Washington, D.C., or New York City, where he edited *American Heritage* magazine and maintained an astonishingly productive research and writing schedule. Wilson (1895–1972) was born in Red Bank, New Jersey, went to a private boarding school, and graduated from Princeton University. During World War I he served in the U.S. Army in France as a hospital orderly, burying the dead and caring for physically and psychologically wounded soldiers. A multilingual, thoroughgoing cosmopolitan critic who wrote about French, Russian, English, and many other literatures, Wilson was a Yankee with relatives in Virginia and with a complicated array of Southern sympathies that sometimes burst through his attempt at a philosophically antiwar and nonpartisan approach to the Civil War. And Baldwin (1924–1987), born in Harlem, New York, amid most of the ravages of urban poverty and racism, but educated in good schools, did not go to college, for lack of money. Baldwin was, in the parlance of the time, a Northern Negro; he did not travel to the American South until he was thirty-three years old. There he saw the land of Jim Crow, where his parents had grown up, and there he discovered many of the most compelling issues and historical legacies that animated his art.

All four writers might be seen as sharing, to quite different extents, the masculine preoccupation with war that characterized the post–World War II years and the Cold War era. Yet only Catton might be said to have appealed to the perennial male fascination with military history, with the drama and the contest of the traditional, triumphalist

American "war story." Catton did so, though, with thorough research and an enviable prose style applicable to nearly any genre of history. Wilson was personally a fierce opponent of war from a philosophical perspective, although he became enthralled with its enduring influence on history, on human values, and on literature itself as crafted by women and men. Baldwin was gay and one of the first American writers to successfully write fiction about homosexual life; he hated war, but learned to embrace the political and rhetorical uses of conflict and famously warned that violence was a just reaction of the dispossessed to oppression. And Warren, though endlessly intrigued by war and violence, and a student of the idea of manhood achieved in warlike experience, sought understandings in his art of broader questions of good and evil, of the character of history itself, and of mankind's moral and political nature. All four had an intense interest in the power of epic events, in the role of myth in shaping how people gain a sense of history, and in the consequences of human strivings, with their residues of violence, failure, and possible renewal. Each in his own way deeply probed why men make war in its many forms, join armies, commit great violence in the name of causes or nations, organize systems of exploitation against their fellow humans, destroy as well as build societies, and live and die with the divided heart at the core of the human condition. None of these writers can be reduced to their gender alone, although it surely helped to shape their experiences, their questions, their worldviews, and their imaginations. Each possessed the poet's faith in language. Above all, the four would have agreed with Warren's proposition. The Civil War, said the Kentuckian, gave Americans an "awareness of having a history."[8] How we comprehend that history, and act upon it, is the problem at hand, and the essential subject of these writers.

· · ·

To various degrees, each of these writers wrote with an awareness of the public dimensions of the Centennial commemoration, though all of them pursued their art for its own sake. In 1957 an unsteady coalition of people and interests emerged that culminated in a National Civil War Centennial Commission (CWCC), established by Congress and President Dwight D. Eisenhower. One of the four writers, Catton, was a member of that commission and played a key role in it. State Centennial commissions, especially in the South, where they often took on a distinctly Confederate viewpoint, also planned many events to reap an expected bonanza of heritage tourism in which Americans would visit historic sites by car. As a broad, public cultural and political phenomenon, the Civil War Centennial has been well documented and its story recently well told.[9] Its general reputation and legacy are, as historians have pointed out, troubled: it became largely a series of public rituals and events mired in conservative, sometimes pro-Confederate, racially divisive, and Cold War impulses. By and large, African Americans either avoided or bitterly criticized the tone and substance of the official Centennial; they often felt offended, or even threatened, by a consensual evasion of the story of Emancipation in favor of efforts to forge national unity in an era of heightened anticommunism and tensions with the Soviet Union. Put simply, the official Civil War Centennial could never find adequate, meaningful ways to balance Civil War remembrance with civil rights rebellion. Indeed, its early efforts were defeated by racism, by a perception that the commemoration should serve only the ends of reconciliation and patriotism, and by the urgent needs of the Kennedy administration to sustain support among segregationist Southern Democrats.

The early, ill-fated leadership of the CWCC included Karl S. Betts, a successful Kansas-born businessman who lived in Maryland and who was media-savvy and enthusiastic for battle reenactments that would draw patriotic audiences; and General Ulysses S. Grant III, great-grandson of the famous Civil War general of the same name, and a staunchly conservative superpatriot and racist. Twenty-five people were appointed members of the commission, including some distinguished historians such as Catton, Allan Nevins, and Bell

Wiley. But initially, the historians' voices took a back seat to the aims of Betts and Grant, who promoted patriotic pageantry and obedience to the wishes of Southern segregationists. The commission leadership also promoted a brothers' war vision—a view that the conflict had been between men of equal valor and purpose, North or South— potentially pleasing, they thought, to all sides and memories. Betts promised that the CWCC would not "stir up hatred and passions out of the past." And Fred Schwengel, congressman from Iowa and a commission member, told the *New York Times* in 1957 that this commemoration would be unique in history because it was "the first time that winners and losers ever had joined in remembering a major conflict."[10] Such a dubious, parochial American point of view reflected a broad sentiment across the majority white society.

The official Centennial opened in 1961 with several particularly regrettable events from which the larger commemoration never fully recovered. In February in Montgomery, Alabama, where the seven seceded states of the Deep South had gathered to create the Confederacy one hundred years earlier, the city and state organized a massive, week-long celebration. White men dressed as "Confederate Colonels" and women as "Confederate Belles"; a crowd estimated at fifty thousand attended a parade, a fair, and a pageant that told the dramatic story of secession and resistance to federal power. The parade passed directly in front of the Dexter Avenue Baptist Church, the home pulpit of Martin Luther King, Jr. Four years after the Montgomery Bus Boycott had launched the Civil Rights Movement, stores, corporations, and every level of government joined in a thoroughgoing demonstration of white supremacy and states' rights. A carefully detailed reenactment of the swearing-in of Jefferson Davis, who was played by a local attorney, highlighted the week. Speeches, as well as press reports, were full of the intended lessons of past and present. Judge Walter Jones, a leader of Alabama's campaign to destroy the National Association for the Advancement of Colored People (NAACP), said white people had gained "a deeper appreciation of the things the Confederacy fought for, and helped them to realize that unrestrained federal power is destroying this nation." And as mob resistance to court-ordered desegregation continued across the South, one commentator in a Montgomery newspaper voiced the neo-Confederate sentiments that never seem to die in our political culture: "Today the South is facing many of the same problems it faced in 1861. Federal dictatorship is literally being stuffed down our throats. . . . The battle is not solely one of segregation versus integration, any more than the Civil War was one of slavery versus freedom of slaves. . . . We should stand up and fight as our forefathers did so we can lick this ever-present battle with the federal government as it continues to usurp rights delegated to the states."[11] In the entire previous century, Jim Crow had rarely been so dressed up for a celebration—or federal authority, increasingly the agent of civil rights enforcement, so openly scorned.

In April in Charleston, the hundredth anniversary of the war's opening salvo at Fort Sumter was to be a national affair. But the various state Centennial commissions included one black member, Madeline A. Williams of New Jersey, and the headquarters hotel in Charleston, the Francis Marion, with the blessings of Betts and Grant, refused to open its doors to Negroes. An enormous controversy, in which several Northern state commissions announced they would boycott the ceremonies, achieved a compromise only with the intervention of President Kennedy. Civil rights intruded over and again on the Civil War. Kennedy had been in office a mere two months, and his general preference was to avoid any public confrontations over race relations, but in this case he chose to make a statement at a news conference: he told Grant and the CWCC that "a Government body, using Federal funds, should hold its meetings at places free of racial discrimination." The CWCC's executive committee at first resisted, but the impasse was bridged when alternative housing in integrated "barracks" was found for Northern commission members at a naval yard across the bay from the city of Charleston. Today, the absurdities of racial segregation may baffle younger generations of Americans; but in the spring of 1961, this issue all but derailed the Centennial, caused it enormous negative publicity in the national press, and led to the eventual resignations of Betts and Grant from the CWCC.[12]

Race was surely the thorniest problem for the official Centennial commemorations. But the spectacle of battle reenactments, and their commercialization, caused nearly as much turmoil and criticism. In late July 1961, a crowd estimated at seventy thousand people paid as much as four dollars each to sit in bleachers and witness a mock staging of the First Battle of Bull Run in northern Virginia, near Manassas. Produced at a cost of $170,000 by the First Manassas Corporation, a combination of the CWCC, the National Park Service, the Defense Department, and the Virginia state commission, the well-rehearsed event involved some three thousand reenactors, including civilians and National Guardsmen in Civil War garb. The printed program, which sold for twenty-five cents, included this statement of purpose for the spectacle: "There was a curious thing about the men who came against each other here a hundred years ago. Whether they wore the blue or the gray they were all deeply in love with their country. *And the country they loved was America,* though they saw America in segments then. Now it is wonderful to know that out of the misery of their differences came the magic and miracle of Union . . . as one wide, majestic land of infinite opportunity for all." A more saccharine and spurious expression of the orthodox reconciliationist spirit, devoid of any awareness of current events in race relations, could hardly be imagined.[13]

That year, events threw the irony of that "wonderful" reunion into bold relief. In 1960, the Supreme Court decision *Boynton v. Virginia* had declared segregation in interstate bus and rail stations unconstitutional; and in early May 1961, the Congress of Racial Equality (CORE) organized the first Freedom Rides to test that decision. When the interracial group of young bus riders reached Alabama, one of their buses was burned at a stop near Anniston. Large mobs savagely beat the Freedom Riders in Montgomery and Birmingham, without police intervention. Publicity surged across the front pages and on network television news, and by the end of that summer similar civil rights protests had spread to train stations and airports all across the South.[14]

With such a backdrop, the Bull Run reenactment was staged as a patriotic festival and the contradictions between the Blue-Gray Centennial and the Civil Rights Movement could hardly have been starker. The merits of reenactments made headlines both before and after the playing-out of the Confederates' victory at First Bull Run. An editorial in the tourist industry's major magazine, *Holiday*, in July 1961 (in which many Southern state commissions had advertised heavily), attacked Southern mob violence and the Centennial's general "holiday mood . . . cheered on by gleeful commercial interests, and blessed by sentimentalists who prefer to forget . . . that some of us even now are being brutally denied certain personal freedoms." And though it is clear that thousands of Americans were awed and fascinated by reenactments (and still are), the Northern press had a field day pillorying the Bull Run entertainment. The *New York Herald-Tribune* said it was "not enough to condemn this puerile show" and maintained that "the issues it [the war] was fought for are still scars across our body as a nation." A commentator in the *New York Times* labeled the reenactment "a grisly pantomime" and "a grotesque evasion of the more challenging task before us at this juncture in history." And the prominent black journalist J. A. Rogers, who wrote a regular column in the *Pittsburgh Courier* entitled "History Shows," complained that "right now enemies of the Negro, the Ku Klux Klan and others, are feeling especially cocky. They are celebrating the Civil War Centennial, when for two years the South defeated the North shamefully. . . . The reenactment of the battle of Bull Run, where Northern troops ran like frightened rabbits in July, 1961, gave a big boost to Southern pride." Rogers, a Civil War buff in his own right, demanded public recognition of the pivotal role of black troops in the war, and published an illustrated pamphlet of facts and stories about their service. He printed thirty-five thousand copies, gave away many free, and charged fourteen cents for the rest, to "supplement," he wrote, "the splendid work of the Freedom Riders." Rogers sustained a campaign of awareness and activism for the Civil War anniversary, with emphasis on Emancipation and African American soldiers, for a black readership he believed too reticent in countering the Confederate Lost Cause fervor emanating from the South.[15]

In October 1961, in an effort to restore respect and legitimacy to the reeling federal Centennial Commission, President Kennedy accepted Betts's resignation as chairman and replaced him with the two-time Pulitzer Prize–winning historian Allan Nevins. The historian and Virginia native James "Bud" Robertson assumed the job of executive director. A group of historians, led by Bell Wiley of Emory University and to some extent by Catton, had organized a coup and driven Betts out. Nevins, a committed Democrat and close friend of former presidential candidate and Illinois native Adlai Stevenson, brought much-needed prestige to the commemoration planning. In the following year, the Centennial staged far less patriotic celebration of the war, and provided more of what Nevins called "attention to its darker aspects." This was all for the better and initiated more serious projects, events, and publications. Still, in a policy statement for the CWCC, Nevins could "discourage" all "cheap and tawdry" observances and at the same time reach, "above all," for a Cold War consensus aim of "unity . . . out of a brothers' war . . . a firm union of hearts instead of an uncertain union of jarring political elements."[16]

But merely urging the jarring elements to be silent proved ineffective. As the anniversary of the Preliminary Emancipation Proclamation approached in 1962, even the best of intentions on the part of the historians now in charge of the federal commission failed to provide a robust and racially inclusive commemoration of Lincoln's edict. Deeply suspicious of Nevins and the new CWCC leadership, some Southern state commissions feared that the September 22 ceremony planned for the Lincoln Memorial would be converted into a new "civil rights–emancipation proclamation." Black journalists and some academics had advocated just such a proclamation by President Kennedy, their apparent new ally. A Chicago-based coalition, the American Negro Emancipation Centennial Authority (ANECA), pushed for a new presidential executive order about civil rights and planned a major exhibition for 1963.[17]

Most important of all, on May 17, 1962, Martin Luther King, Jr., as head of the Southern Christian Leadership Conference (SCLC), sent President Kennedy an open letter entitled "Appeal to the Honorable John F. Kennedy, President of the United States, for a National Rededication to the Principles of the Emancipation Proclamation and for an Executive Order Prohibiting Segregation in the United States of America." In this remarkable and little-discussed document, in which King appeals deeply to history and memory, and in which he may have modeled some of Bruce Catton's own language, the civil rights leader astutely mingled 1863 with 1963: "The struggle for freedom, Mr. President, of which the Civil War was but a bloody chapter, continues throughout our land today. The courage and heroism of Negro citizens at Montgomery, Little Rock, New Orleans, Prince Edward County, and Jackson, Mississippi is only a further effort to affirm the democratic heritage so painfully won, in part, upon the grassy battlefields of Antietam, Lookout Mountain, and Gettysburg." Moreover, on September 12 the New York Civil War Centennial Commission hosted an elaborate dinner at a Manhattan hotel, at which King, Catton, and Governor Nelson Rockefeller, keenly aware of blacks as a voting block in his state, were the speakers. Again, King did not mince words in his tone and argument about the meaning of the Centennial. The states of the old Confederacy, King declared, still exercised "a veto power over the majority of the nation." They retained powers as if they were "an autonomous region whose posture toward the central government has elements as defiant as a hostile nation." Although he might have privately agreed with King's historical point, Kennedy was unwilling to alienate Southern Democrats before the congressional elections of 1962, and he ignored this and other demands for a new Emancipation Proclamation.[18]

The CWCC strove, against all odds, to keep "social contentions" and "political" issues out of the September 22 ceremony at the Lincoln Memorial. Many white Southerners and their commission members threatened not only to boycott the ceremony but to secede from the national Centennial altogether. Their own coalition, the Confederate States Centennial Conference, announced that they considered any commemoration of Emancipation nothing but "propaganda . . . to reopen the wounds of the war" and contrary to the "true events of history." James Robertson struck a tenuous compromise by promising that the CWCC would allow the Lincoln Group and the Civil War Roundtable of Washington, D.C., to be the primary sponsors of the ceremony and that racial issues would be firmly downplayed.[19] In effect, the CWCC told the professional neo-Confederates who ran Centennial commemorations in the South that the federal body was not in the business of promoting civil rights, and gained their guarded cooperation.

Initially, Nevins and his staff planned an Emancipation celebration with no African American speaker, though President Kennedy would be in attendance, along with Governor Rockefeller of New York, where the state archive contained one of the original copies of Lincoln's proclamation. But under a storm of protest in the black press and from civil rights leaders, as well as under the threat of a church-led boycott within Washington, the CWCC opted for some late-hour tokenism on the platform. A young black composer, Ulysses Kay, had already been invited to produce an original piece of music, entitled "Forever Free"; and now, hastily, Mahalia Jackson was invited to sing as the soloist, and federal judge Thurgood Marshall was added to the speakers' list. Nevins and his staff had wanted the event to be as internationalized and as anticommunist as possible, drawing attention away from America's domestic racial turmoil. Originally, platform guests included the president of Colombia, the prime minister of Nigeria, and the ambassador from India, but no African American civil rights leader. In the booklet produced for the occasion, Southerners had demanded that "no modern-day problems" be discussed. So the CWCC prepared a collection of documents without any commentary or interpretation of the Emancipation Proclamation or its historical context.[20] This astonishing acquiescence to racism and blatant avoidance of the present when commemorating so pivotal a moment from the past can be grasped only if we remember the character of Cold War liberalism that the Kennedy administration embodied. In the year after the erection of the Berlin Wall, and as tensions rose to fever pitch in Oxford, Mississippi, over the admission of James Meredith to the University of Mississippi, the Kennedy White House practiced a type of racial stereotyping and tokenism nearly unthinkable in the twenty-first century.

At the last minute, a major event in near shambles was made worse when President Kennedy announced a scheduling conflict (he planned to attend the America's Cup yacht races), and sent a video address. The U.S. ambassador to the United Nations, Adlai Stevenson, was abruptly made the keynote speaker. The event came off without incident; approximately three thousand people attended, with Thurgood Marshall delivering brief remarks, Archibald MacLeish reciting an original poem, and Stevenson giving an essentially Cold War address about the significance of America's fight against communism, rooted in "the globe-circling spread of our spirit of national independence and individual freedom." In his video address, Kennedy extolled the abolition of the "evil of human slavery," and, even more poignantly, declared that "much remains to be done to eradicate the vestiges of discrimination and segregation, to make equal rights a reality for all of our people." The event ended with Mahalia Jackson's stirring rendition of the "Battle Hymn of the Republic."[21]

What the well-meaning and sympathetic Nevins and his friends throughout the Kennedy administration had not taken into account—

indeed, seemed unaware of—was the intensity of African Americans' resentment over the character and intent of the Centennial generally, and the Emancipation anniversary ceremony in particular. At the very time of the September commemoration, James Baldwin had begun to write his most vigorous statement on the Centennial season. In *The Fire Next Time,* he left a warning that the CWCC leadership would have benefited from reading: "The sloppy and fatuous nature of American good will can never be relied upon to deal with hard problems. These have been dealt with, when they have been dealt with at all, out of necessity—and in political terms, anyway, necessity means concessions made in order to stay on top. I think this is a fact, which it serves no purpose to deny, *but, whether it is a fact or not, this is what the black population of the world, including black Americans, really believe.*"[22]

And believe it they did. The black press, as well as many African American intellectuals, had been brutally critical of the purpose and tone of the Centennial from its beginning. "The South may have lost the Civil War," announced an editorial in the *Atlanta Daily World* in February 1960, "but it is sure going to win the centennial." Addressing the "hoopla about the Civil War Centennial," Eric Springer, in the *Pittsburgh Courier,* asked: "What in the world are we celebrating and who won the war anyway?" Roscoe Lewis, in the *Norfolk Journal and Guide* (of Norfolk, Virginia), lampooned the opening plans of the federal Commission and accused the "ex-Confederacy" of "still attempting to win the peace" by "bringing the Lost Cause before the nation," packaged ideologically in the "same stupid southern self-centeredness." Charles Wesley, a distinguished historian and the president of Central State College in Ohio, blasted the Centennial Commission in November 1961 for its "preoccupation with the glorification of the drama of the war," at the expense of serious history. The original leadership of the Commission, Wesley said, wished to give the public merely "an ancient Roman holiday in an amphitheater." In a Negro

History Week radio address in March 1961, the historian Dorothy Sterling complained that the South had "captured" the CWCC. She demanded that more attention be given to the black experience in the war, and lamented: "The Civil War we hear about today is a fight of brave brother against brave brother, with both separately but equally righteous in their causes. There was an underlying issue in the war— slavery. The leaders of the Confederacy were fighting to perpetuate a slaveholding, slave breeding, slave driving society, based on the shameful belief that one man could own another."[23] Such a claim about the costs of the reconciliationist vision of Civil War memory could nowhere be made in official Centennial activities. It could find solace only in the apocalyptic metaphors of the official performances of the "Battle Hymn."

Contempt, satire, and even demands for inclusion were hardly the only black responses to the official Centennial. As early as March 1961, the NAACP national headquarters warned its local chapters to beware of how the Centennial could "strike a hard blow at our present day movement toward equality." The organization's executive secretary, Roy Wilkins, asserted that Southern state Centennial commemorations would be exclusively Confederate affairs for the purpose of "repudiating the great moral issue which lay at the bottom of the Civil War." He urged local leaders to draft statements of "resentment" when they felt threatened by public Confederate remembrance. Some black papers even warned their readers to be on guard against the "rapid recurrence of the Confederate flag" at public functions in the Southern states.[24]

As readers, collectors, and authors, many African Americans did participate in the Civil War Centennial.[25] But officially, and on a societal level, the process by which the nation and the states remembered the struggle of the 1860s enhanced and exploited the racial divisions of the 1960s more than it helped to alleviate them. In scholarship, those "darker aspects" that Nevins alluded to found their way into many books, and eventually into new paradigms of publishing, historiography, and teaching. But that process would require time and would cause great turbulence in schools and on college campuses.

. . .

The favored American conception of the nation's history—a story of uniqueness, special or divine destiny, and progress—has had countless advocates of all kinds and in all eras. In blessed, redemptive America—as the master of grand narrative in the nineteenth century, George Bancroft, put it—"the order of time brings us . . . a persistent and healthy progress."[26] In this enduring vision, the United States was born essentially perfect, and then began a career of improvement. Against this vision of progress, a genuinely tragic sense of America's past has always struggled to gain traction. Within a narrative of order and betterment, where does one place and how does one explain a civil war of such destructive proportions? Somehow, no matter how dark or bloody our experience, American innocence seems to rekindle itself. For many decades, scholars, novelists, poets, and playwrights have written against this progressive grain and produced much of our best art and history. Even in the era of the "American Renaissance"—the 1840s and 1850s, when Bancroft himself began his writing career—writers such as Nathaniel Hawthorne and Herman Melville offered a thoroughgoing, genuinely tragic "counterstatement" to the American myth of progress and righteousness. But in the bend of the popular imagination, public culture in America still tends to resist tragedy, of classical or modern forms. This has been particularly true of the Civil War's place in national memory, despite all that William Faulkner, Flannery O'Connor, Richard Wright, or C. Vann Woodward, among many others, have told us about the South as a repository of tragic or satiric lessons for the rest of the country—lessons to be drawn from the extended consequences of the defeat of the Confederacy.[27]

Warren, Catton, Wilson, and Baldwin were not alone, but they may have been the best at imagining a tragic sensibility from which to understand the Civil War and its legacies for a people and a culture unaccustomed to such a conception of the nation's master historical narrative. Academic history preceded, fueled, and ultimately benefited from the work of these four artists, although it is the rare popular historian who can garner the kind of readership that flocked to Warren's *Legacy of the Civil War*, Catton's *Stillness at Appomattox*, Wilson's *Patriotic Gore*, or Baldwin's *The Fire Next Time*. And academic historians seldom write in a consciously tragic mode. Often only half aware that their writing reflects assumptions about the nature and philosophy of history, whether from a politically left or right perspective, historians of slavery, the Civil War, and Reconstruction still fashion sophisticated narratives of redemption, even as they greatly expand the limits of knowledge.[28] On some level, we all probably want to believe that the writing and learning of history can redeem the wrongs of the past. We all want to live in a narrative of progress, even as art and history remind us of how much suffering and self-delusion is required to even imagine it.

The idea of tragedy all but defies precise definition. It is contingent on time, place, and even perhaps on national culture, habits, and folkways. It can be exclusively an art form, invented by the Greek playwrights, its dimensions and methods the subject of endless debate down through the ages. But it can also be a view of life, of man's relationship to existence or to history, and therefore to such fundamental notions as fate, destiny, necessity, chance, Providence, and especially the mysteries of suffering and death and good versus evil. Indeed, our foreknowledge of death makes tragedy an obvious element of life itself, and prompts serious students of this outlook to conclude that only the naïve float through life without a sense of the tragic. But just as nature gave us memory, with all its terrors and tyrannies, it also gave us forgetting to ease the pain and potential sense of doom in the human condition.

Tragedy might be best understood, in the words of Raymond Williams, as a "structure of feeling," or as what Richard B. Sewall calls "mood, feeling, tone . . . an attitude toward life . . . a cast of thought." Aristotle famously argued that tragedy, through action and conflict, can bring a "purgation," or a "catharsis"—what the Enlightenment philosopher Algernon Sydney called "sweet violence." Such "pleasure" derived from suffering leads to an assumption about tragedy: that however destructive and bleak, however undeserved the suffering (such as in the Book of Job), the story must result in knowledge gained, in some form of learning and resolution from living through the pity, terror, fear, or madness.[29] Events of the twentieth century— the Great War, the Holocaust, the atomic bomb, ethnic cleansings, genocidal civil wars—and the terrorist attacks of September 11, 2001, have challenged to its limits this cathartic view of tragedy. But in literary terms, tragedy provides a very malleable form and is thus the source of much great drama and literature in which art and life are almost one.

It is this kind of unresolved, and sometimes unbearable, tension in defining tragedy that gives it such eternal resonance. And it is also why a sense of tragedy is so useful, even indispensable, to understanding history. The "tragic vision," writes Sewall, "pierces beneath the 'official view' of any culture to the dark realities that can never be hidden." A tragic sense of history rejects facile, "optimistic" conceptions of the past. It respects the power of the dark and evil side of human nature, as well as the capacities of the institutions humans create, to exploit and destroy in the name of ideology, nation, or religion. Early in *Moby-Dick*, Melville announces the tone and point of view of the book, as Ishmael declares: "the man who has more of joy than sorrow in him . . . cannot be true. . . . The truest of all men was the Man of Sorrows." A tragic view of history is not hopeless or merely "pessimistic," but rather what one might call informed, prepared, or chastened. A sense of tragedy can keep us suspicious of theories of revolutionary change or of stable progress.[30] The tragic mode of seeing and writing the past does not mean that the engine of history is to be found solely in the darkest recesses of human nature, in man's capacity for evil. Loosely used, a term like "human nature," indeed, can mean that responsibility for history can be generalized and spread around so diffusely that no person or people are ever deemed the source of radical evil. People are the engines of history, and sometimes very specific people and nations are explicitly to blame for crimes against humanity. The tragic mode, though, helps us to temper our rigid theories of history, conditions us for history's shocking surprises, and reminds us that each day when the sun rises again, in the human story, the night will come. A sense of tragedy makes real hope possible.

The idea of tragedy and the idea of progress are both essential for the achievement of knowledge from experience, but they are largely antithetical. Ishmael is awed and at times terrified by the maimed, all but demonically obsessed Captain Ahab, who chases his white whale for revenge. But *Moby-Dick,* unlike many classic works of tragedy, is not about the fall of a good and great man, or even about a flawed, hopelessly conflicted hero with impossible choices. "Melville," as F. O. Matthiessen wrote, "is not so concerned with individual sin as with titanic uncontrollable forces which seem to dwarf man altogether." It was these controlling "forces of tragedy" that concerned the four writers examined in this book—often explicitly in relation to the nature and significance of the Civil War and its legacies, but also on a broader philosophical level, as a way of comprehending the weight of the past in any given present.[31]

Each of these four writers surely had his heroes and villains, and his blindspots born of assumptions, ideology, or personal background. But what they offer, even as their historical and artistic conclusions diverge, is a way of understanding the Civil War both as something very American and as an event in a larger human drama. Most Americans are likely to approach the subject of the Civil War with a preferred narrative in mind. Those who sit with these four writers, long and seriously, will find their familiar story disrupted. Readers conditioned by the new wave of brilliant work on Emancipation as the central story of the war should read Catton's military narratives; they will learn not only how the war was fought, but what so many thousands of soldier boys died for, and they may wonder whether the sacrifice was worth it, short or long term. Those devoted to latter-day versions of Confederate nostalgia and vestiges of the Lost Cause should submit themselves to Baldwin's bitter chastisements of the racism at the heart of American self-righteousness, to his aggressive personification of the psychological and material legacies of slavery in African American life. For those whose Civil War is forever a just cause, ultimately for the greater good of a unified, more powerful, egalitarian America, let Wilson disorient your thinking with his withering critique of the Gilded Age and his admiring portraits of writers and diarists who remembered a real war, even as they fashioned the myths by which we still live. And above all, Warren, the true Melvillian, who hated piety and fanaticism on all sides, was the Southerner forever demonstrating in art and argument how the issue of slavery and race was the fundamental question at the heart of this war. Warren is a guide for any reader, however partisan, who remains open to exploring the genuinely tragic dimensions of this story, to asking why, as Warren said, the war "draws us as an oracle . . . of personal, as well as national, fate."[32] No one knows exactly where this American oracle is located, or the identity of the high priestess who speaks in its voice. Is it on Cemetery Ridge at Gettysburg, on Monument Avenue in Richmond, at the Lincoln Memorial, at the remains of slave cabins on a decaying plantation near Charleston, at any of the hauntingly beautiful Civil War cemeteries, or at Augustus Saint-Gaudens's magnificent Shaw Memorial in Boston? Each of us might have our personal choice. But we need help in seeing and knowing the tragedy embedded in all these remains and memorials. We might all begin with the common denominator of books.

In various genres, a tragic temperament informed the view of American history generally and the Civil War era in particular for Warren, Catton, Wilson, and Baldwin. Each came by a different path.

Their foil was not merely the perceived superficiality and commercialism of the Centennial, although each had much to say about that. The grain against which they wrote was the powerful post–World War II and Cold War American confidence that their past and present could always somehow be woven into a pleasing tale of consensus and the righteous progress of a problem-solving, redemptive people.

More than the other four, Warren was driven by the question of whether humans could be makers of their own fate, or whether history merely erupted, over and over, from a deep well of original sin and essential evil in human nature. Warren tried to weave his own use of tragedy into classical forms and metaphors; he saw history universally, and American history in particular, as a constant collision of fated contradictions. The Kentucky poet, however, never gave up seeking those dark lessons and redemptive entrails in historical outcomes: "evil," he beautifully said, is "the cost of good."

Catton wrote transcendently beautiful narrative about real people caught up in a tragic bloodbath, he believed, largely not of their own making. He crafted a military history, especially about the common soldiers, that drew his readers, in book after formulaic book, into the meaning of the war on its moral and enduring levels; he employed the term "tragedy" more than the other four writers, but often with little if any definition. In the end, his Civil War tragedy was not only redemptive and cathartic, but the wellspring of a greater, more powerful America, newly fashioned from the war's blood and sacrifice. Catton wrote a beguiling, enjoyable military history, but he never let his readers forget the killing and the enduring sense of loss in the land.

Wilson probably used the explicit language of tragedy the least among the four, but in his ferociously antiwar outlook in the midst of the Cold War, he came to believe that the Civil War was not worth its sacrifices, no matter how redeeming the national or sectional narratives have insisted on making its moral outcomes. Wilson's aim, even as he excitedly discovered one intriguing writer or memoirist after another, was to demonstrate the tragic qualities embedded in the myths and epics with which Americans, North and South, emerged from the war—myths that they used for a century to justify further war, exploitation, and the denigration of whatever ideals had once inspired the "causes" for which so many died. In the complexity of Wilson's epic literary history, he sounded the depths of those irresistible myths that have compelled Americans to make fierce claims on the past, even as they repeat its sins.

And finally, Baldwin represents as well as anyone in the 1950s and 1960s the voice of an African American counternarrative—an angry, volatile, but persistent critique of America's general inability, in his view, to acknowledge and act upon its history of slavery and racism. As an essayist and orator of great eloquence, controversy, and self-destructive fame, Baldwin demanded that white Americans in particular confront the raw horror at the heart of the Civil War of 1861–1865, as well as the inner civil war Baldwin fought within his own soul as a black American homosexual who desperately wanted to love his country and to be loved by it, but never quite achieved either goal. Each writer fed off contradictions, within the country and within himself; and each asked Americans to stare down and understand a protean tragedy they mostly preferred not to see.

This book is, therefore, many things at once: a look at the Civil War Centennial era, not primarily at the level of institutions or of popular culture, but through serious literature and historical narrative; a study of four prominent and prolific writers; a meditation on the nature of historical memory and the philosophy of history; a probing of the meaning of myth and tragedy in the American story; and a reflection, via four fecund sources, of the place of the Civil War in the ever-evolving master narrative of American history. In the end, whatever else it is, perhaps this discussion of four Americans in search of their country's history at a pivotal and deeply divided crossroads moment can help us begin to answer Ralph Ellison's 1965 proposition. Had the "last true note of tragedy" in America been "cast . . .

into the grave" when "the North buried Lincoln and the South buried Lee"?[33] Was that true at the Civil War Centennial? Is it still true at the Sesquicentennial? And if the Civil War and Emancipation stimulated these four kinds of meditations when those events turned 100 in American memory, how will our culture remember and explain them at 150?

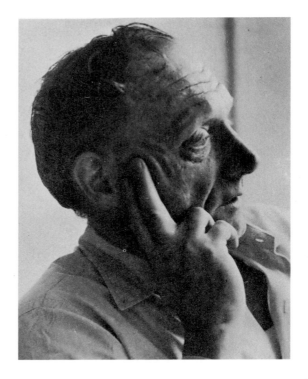

Robert Penn Warren, portrait by Sylvia Salmi, mid-1950s. Yale University Manuscripts and Archives.

· CHAPTER ONE ·

"Gods and Devils Aplenty"

Robert Penn Warren

History is not melodrama, even if it usually reads like that. It was real blood, not tomato catsup or the pale ectoplasm of statistics, that wet the ground at Bloody Angle and darkened the waters of Bloody Pond.

—Robert Penn Warren, *The Legacy of the Civil War*, 1961

ROBERT Penn Warren never stopped asking "what history was." Endlessly pondering the meaning and nature of the past was, to Warren, as natural as breathing. He first heard the music of poetry and storytelling as a small boy at his grandfather's feet, sitting on an unkempt lawn in front of a farmhouse in Christian County, Kentucky, in 1911. He likely did not know it was the fiftieth anniversary of the Civil War that year, but his grandfather Gabriel Thomas Penn, a Confederate veteran, did not let him forget it. Warren's grandfather lived on the isolated farmstead some thirty-five miles from the town of Guthrie, in southern Kentucky, where Robert Penn was born and grew up. In his youth, Warren's parents saw to it that the boy was surrounded with books, read aloud with him, and even paid him money for reading the Bible through in its entirety, despite the fact that they were not very religious.[1] But it was with his grandfather, on long summer days on the farm and in the woods, that Warren ingested and cultivated a child's wondrous sense of history.

Grandpa Penn was a lonely man (his wife had died many years earlier); he despised "progress" and most things "modern," but he was a masterful storyteller. He told his grandson that only two good things had come from modernity: "window screens and painless dentistry." Sitting in a wicker chair under a cedar tree, corncob pipe in his mouth, Warren's grandfather would regale the boy with stories of the Civil War. Six weeks after the firing on Fort Sumter in 1861, he had marched off in the 13th Tennessee Infantry; in April 1862, he had survived the bloody Battle of Shiloh, in southwest Tennessee; and before the winter of 1863, he had recruited eighty-five men to form Company H of the 15th Tennessee Cavalry, in which he served as captain under the legendary and notorious Confederate general Nathan Bedford Forrest. Grandpa Penn had also participated in the massacre of black Union troops at Fort Pillow in Tennessee in 1863, although he did not reveal many details to the youngster. He had been banished from Tennessee after the war, recollected Warren, because of his participation in the hanging of Union guerrilla troops. Crossing the Kentucky line had apparently provided a refuge for one Confederate veteran.[2]

Grandpa Penn loved to recite poetry and even to sing for the boy in a "cracked voice." Warren loved the annual renditions of "We'll Gather in the Canebrake and Hunt the Buffalo," or the sad song he was told the soldiers sang at Shiloh, "Hallie in the Valley." The old man's head "was full of poems," Warren remembered, such as "The Turk Lay in the Guarded Tent," by Fitz-Greene Halleck: "Strike—for the green graves of your sires: / God and your native Land!" Byron and Burns, served up in the grandfather's version of a "Scots tongue," were automatic, annual July treats. In this romantic, "backward-looking" world of "changelessness," said Warren, he found an "ever-present history" which he craved. But later in life he would resurrect it over and over for interviewers with a "kind of puzzlement," for he had "picked up," he said, "a vaguely soaked-in popular notion of the Civil War."[3]

Indeed he had. "I didn't get my impression of the Civil War from home," wrote Warren. "I got it from the air around me." And from the grandfather, who his aunts said was an "inveterate reader"—a phrase that Warren, with a wry chuckle, always remembered hearing as "Confederate reader." This puzzling but enthralling sense of the war came to him from Grandpa Penn in "bits and pieces, sometimes bloody, sometimes funny," the way most American Civil War enthusiasts still likely want to feel or comprehend that event. As a boy he recollected that the war was some mixture of the "wickedness of Yankees, the justice of the Southern cause (whatever it was; I don't know), the slave question, with Lincoln somehow a great man but misguided." His "sacred boyhood memory" thrived on the romance of military history, he told interviewer Richard B. Sale in 1969, and was always a matter of "supposing": "suppose that Albert Sydney Johnston hadn't been killed at Shiloh the first day . . . suppose that Jeb Stuart hadn't been on that city raid at Gettysburg." In boyhood, present and past had seemed utterly mixed, Warren said, particularly if the "tale told" came from "older people . . . big in the Great War of '61–'65."[4]

Forms of these earliest impressions never died in Warren's Civil War memory, both inherited and learned. They recur again and again throughout his many decades of writing. When his imagination wandered over the Southern landscape, as it did on a flight out of Memphis during his travels for the book *Segregation* in 1955, he looked down at the Tennessee River. "I wondered on which side Shiloh is," he wrote. "I had two grandfathers at Shiloh, that morning of April 6, 1862, young men with the other young men in gray uniforms stepping toward the lethal spring thickets of dogwood and redbud, to the sound of bird song." Then, as though lost in the memory of listening to his grandfather's stories, he simply quotes him unannounced: "One hundred and sixty men we took in the first morning, son. Muster the next night, and it was sixteen answered." With that backdrop, Warren moved on to the core of his book *Segregation:* interviews with diverse people about the nature and significance of racial segregation, almost one hundred years after the Civil War.[5]

In a cluster of seemingly contradictory notions, Warren steadfastly remembered his grandfather as a "Union man" who opposed secession, was against slavery, and knew it "couldn't last—even if I gathered from conversation that there must have been slaves in the family." But above all, Grandpa was a "good Confederate" who maintained that once war came, "you went with your people." Warren repeated many of these phrases and stories later in life, as though they had bled into his DNA. Steeped in what he called his "deep soaking" in Southern and military history, Warren would often end the retelling by declaring Grandpa Penn the "wonderful . . . idol" who had read history aloud to him. "There was nobody to talk to. . . . I got the benefit of his conversation. . . . He was a captain of cavalry under Forrest . . . and fought in many battles. He loved to relive the war with me: we'd lay it all out on the ground using stones and rifle shells."[6]

No wonder Warren came to love irony and hate ideology, to distrust idealism and abstraction, to probe ceaselessly, in his writing, the idea of original sin and the question of whether redemption from evil was possible. Grandpa was not all romance; he called the Civil War "a politician's war . . . just worked up by fools—Southern fire-eaters and Yankee abolitionists." Warren tried, throughout his work, to show how "irrational" history really was. During an interview in 1961, when he was asked yet again to explain how the Civil War was remembered in his youth, Warren fell momentarily into a haze of remembrance laced with remarkable honesty: "It was very much alive—not as an *issue*, but as a reality of life. It wasn't a matter of argument; it touched everybody's life. In this very static society, everyone you knew over a certain age had been in it . . . and it was just a part of the emotional furniture of life . . . just part of the faith, as it were, and the drama of it."[7] Anthropologists might take such language as a near-perfect description of how a deep mythology takes root in any community. Warren grew up knowing that the Civil War was the great, mysterious, romantic event—the self-affirming myth—that had somehow made the world around him.

In such reminiscences by Warren, we can begin to see how deeply Civil War memory had been embedded in the Southern and American imagination. And though he always waxed a bit misty about his grandfather's influence, Warren left no doubt that he understood the extent to which the South's memory of the Civil War was inevitably about the present. In his small hometown of Guthrie, he wrote, most people worried much less about which "color of the uniform your grandfather had worn," and much more about how "the Civil War seemed to have been fought for the right to lynch without legal interference."[8] All that "emotional furniture" (myth) might be about valor and devotion on the fields at Shiloh or Corinth, but it might also be about the violence it took to keep black men from getting white men's jobs.

As Warren and a sidekick explored the scraggy hillsides and backwoods around his grandfather's farm one summer, the youths imagined they were traversing some of the "dark and bloody ground" on which the Civil War had been contested. On one occasion they found bones, and on another a depression in the ground they imagined had been a soldier's grave. Later, in his series of "Kentucky Mountain Farm" poems, Warren imagined history buried in, as well as emerging from, the "rocks" of those fields and hills. In the ever-changing cycles of geology, of stone breaking down and reforming, Warren saw a metaphor for history: "The hills are weary, the lean men have passed; / The rocks are stricken, and the frost has torn / Away their ridged fundaments at last, / So that the fractured atoms now are borne." Then, in the poem "History among the Rocks," he imagined further long-ago scenes:

> Think how a body, naked and lean
> And white as the splintered sycamore, would go
> Tumbling and turning, hushed in the end,
> With hair afloat in waters that gently bend
> To ocean where the blind tides flow . . .
>
> In these autumn orchards once young men lay dead . . .
> Grey coats, blue coats. Young men on the mountainside
> Clambered, fought. Heels muddied the rocky spring.

Their reason is hard to guess, remembering
Blood on their black mustaches in moonlight.
Their reason is hard to guess and a long time past:
The apple falls, falling in the quiet night.[9]

How many Americans have walked through a battlefield park, or through even more remote areas of the border South, dreaming their way back into the Civil War past in just such a way as Warren seems to suggest in this poem? And how often are they moved and puzzled if they really imagine the dead in moonlight, not to mention the "reason" they fought? Warren seemed always to seek historical answers not so much in specific contexts or motivations or even people, but in the stuff of geological time, in the nature of the beast in mankind.

· · ·

Robert Penn Warren was a prodigy. He graduated from the Clarksville, Tennessee, high school (just across the border from Guthrie, Kentucky) at the age of sixteen, in 1921. His boyhood dream was to go to the U.S. Naval Academy in Annapolis. A congressman's letter of acceptance had already arrived, when—on a beautiful late-spring day, while he was lying on the grass in the family yard—his ten-year-old brother, Thomas, playfully threw a baseball-size piece of coal over a hedge. It hit Robert Penn squarely in the left eye. Warren steadily lost the sight in that eye, along with any hope of passing the physical exam for admission to the Naval Academy. The injury slowly, and almost disastrously, affected Warren's psychological well-being. His father, Robert Franklin Warren, was a small-town banker; and with the strong support of his parents, despite fears on the part of his mother, Mary, that Nashville might be a Southern "Babylon," Robert Penn entered Vanderbilt University. As early as 1923, while still a teenager, he joined the group of Southern writers known as the "Fugitives." With the tutelage and admiration of some of its members—Donald Davidson, Allen Tate, and John Crowe Ransom—

Warren rapidly saw many of his early poems published. "That boy is a wonder," Tate wrote about the eighteen-year-old as they invited him into this increasingly influential circle of white, post–New South poets who were determined to overthrow the backward thinking of the Lost Cause and transform modern poetry. Tate was Warren's undergraduate roommate and his closest friend. Warren owed much to the artistic atmosphere the Fugitive group provided him; he called it his "real university," which offered an "exhilarating . . . intellectual interchange with men twice my age." Its members were worldly and modern, and at the same time deeply Southern in their sensibilities. Above all, they devoted themselves to the aesthetics of poetry and ideas, at least for the four years that they published the well-received poetry journal *The Fugitive.* Warren majored in English, minored in philosophy, studied German and Greek, and wrote a good deal of poetry. Before graduating in 1925, *summa cum laude,* Warren had decided he would be a professional poet.[10]

At one point, Warren nearly did not survive those undergraduate years. In May 1924, he attempted suicide. Deeply depressed for most of a year, failing in his first love affair, and frightened that he was also going blind in his other eye, Warren was found unconscious in his Vanderbilt room with his head wrapped in (or next to) a chloroform-soaked towel. His recent poems, some of which were actually published in *The Fugitive,* had been bleak and sorrowful, and others had been heavily criticized or rejected. Whatever the combination of reasons, the nineteen-year-old had lost his hold on life and meaning; he was very young and, although he had caring mentors and teachers, he did not yet know what it meant to devote one's life to poetry. He felt maimed, half-blind, and ashamed. Later he remembered the episode in stark terms: "It was poetry or death for me then." After recuperating at home in Guthrie, Warren managed to complete his exams and reengage with life and learning. Ransom (who became a surrogate father) and Tate helped the young, confused romantic endure and graduate.[11]

In 1925, Warren's academic prowess earned him a scholarship to graduate school at the University of California, Berkeley. As a fish out of his normal waters, Warren did not find graduate work nearly as stimulating as the Fugitive seminars had been. In 1927 he transferred to Yale University, but did not, on this occasion, stay there long either. The following year, he won a Rhodes Scholarship and went to Oxford, where he began writing his first book. In 1929 he published *John Brown: The Making of a Martyr.* The book is long, overwrought, and largely a diatribe against the abolitionist beliefs and the radical methods and ideology that Brown represented. Warren considered Brown a terrorist, murderer, and liar, and the inventor to a great degree of his own legend. For its time, the book was well-researched and demonstrated that Warren could write powerful narrative. But his *John Brown* also signaled several enduring elements of his vision: his life-long absorption in the legacies of slavery and race in the South and the nation; his contempt for absolutes and for ideology; his deep interest in the drama of the Civil War as a mirror of any American present; his sense of how mythic figures are both irresistible and dangerous; his fascination with an irrepressible, tragic innocence in what he came to see as a peculiarly American brand of the human condition; a desire to understand the violence in the human heart; and the idea that stories (myths) and heroes (martyrs) are *made* by human beings regardless of the divine attributes we may invent for them. Brown, said Warren, "learned how to dramatize himself." Writing at a time when interest in John Brown flourished among artists and writers of many kinds, the twenty-five-year-old author generally scorned the abolitionists, especially those who participated so floridly in forging the martyrdom of the old warrior. "Because the Civil War was fought," Warren argued, "and because there was an Emancipation Proclamation," Brown became a figure not of reality, but of "commemoration" that "enshrined the fine things said by Emerson and all the rest."[12]

By the late 1920s the Fugitives had transformed into social critics and visionaries, indentifying themselves as "Agrarians." Led by Ransom, Davidson, and Tate, the Agrarians sought to defend the South against its critics—such as H. L. Mencken, who famously satirized its alleged cultural and economic backwardness—as well as to argue that the region's agricultural and pastoral values should be a bulwark against the ravages of modern, urban "industrialism." This intellectual movement included an exaltation of Southern and Confederate heroes; nostalgia for the Old South, its gentlemanly traditions of honor, its social and racial order; and an assertion of "spiritual" over "material" pursuits.[13] In 1930, the Agrarians published their famous collection of twelve essays, *I'll Take My Stand: The South and the Agrarian Tradition.*

At the invitation of his mentors, and while still in England, Warren wrote the essay "The Briar Patch," a meandering discussion of ruralism and the fate of "the Negro" in the South. Of Warren's massive literary output in several genres over more than half a century, "Briar Patch" may be the only work he lived to regret writing. It is clear he wrote it with ambivalence and an inability to say no to Ransom and Davidson. The piece is a lame defense of segregation. Davidson wrote to Warren, describing his assignment: "It's up to you Red to prove that Negroes are country folks . . . born and bred in the briar patch." Warren later admitted he was "just very uncomfortable with the piece," and it showed. The question of any evolving racial "equality" remained merely an "extraordinarily complicated one." The Reconstruction era had been a time of sordid exploitation of the South by greedy Northerners who poisoned white attitudes toward blacks. Booker T. Washington seemed the only legitimate black leader with the proper idea—vocational education and social segregation. "The Southern negro," Warren awkwardly asserted, should remain "a creature of the small town and farm"—places that properly fit his "temperament and capacity." Warren rejected outside (Northern) philanthropy for education or any other purpose, and left only this prescription for the South to develop a "productive negro community" and preserve peaceful relations between poor whites and blacks: "Let the negro sit beneath his own vine and fig tree."[14]

With time, Warren came to admit that "The Briar Patch" was a stilted and retrograde piece of writing; and he soon ceased to be anything resembling a passionate Agrarian. He returned to the United States, rejected a fellowship to study for the Ph.D. at Yale, took teaching jobs in English at Southern universities, and embraced a career as a writer. He taught first at Southwestern College in Memphis, then at Vanderbilt, and moved to Louisiana State University in 1934. In 1942 he moved north to the University of Minnesota as a full professor, and finally on to Yale in 1950, where he resided and taught for the rest of his career. Thus, from the early 1940s to the end of his life in 1989, Warren lived and worked at Northern universities. While he dwelled in Northern climes, the South, of course, remained the deep source of his artistic imagination. In the 1930s he began to publish fiction and poetry, and with Cleanth Brooks and others, he edited the *Southern Review* in Baton Rouge. In 1939, after two early novels were rejected, he published *Night Rider,* a long, philosophical tale about the violent Kentucky and Tennessee tobacco wars—between debt-ridden farmers and exploitative owners and buyers—of the first decade of the twentieth century, events the author had to a degree witnessed but also thoroughly researched. The novel's themes of escalating blood feud, mob violence, bitter racial and class division, and the descent of good but psychologically empty characters into evil anticipated much of Warren's later and more famous work.[15]

By the 1940s, Warren was by any definition making himself into a genuine "man of letters." In published poetry, in fiction both short and long, in nonfiction, and in literary criticism, he emerged as a writer with a remarkable range and an increasingly national reputation. In the late 1930s, with his friend, fellow Southerner, and future Yale colleague Cleanth Brooks, Warren coedited two books, *An Approach to Literature* and *Understanding Poetry,* burnishing his chops as a critic and a voice in the teaching of literature. Also in these years, Warren produced—first as a verse play, and then as a novel—his masterpiece, *All the King's Men*, a work many still consider the greatest American novel about politics. But *All the King's Men*, which won Warren the Pulitzer Prize for fiction (he later also won it for poetry in 1957), was, like so much of his work, a deep probing of the meaning of the past, especially the Civil War and its legacies, in the character of one Jack Burden, former historian, political operative, and lost soul in the toxic world of Southern politics.

Jack Burden is a fascinating, sometimes lovable, and increasingly disreputable character, one of the many fictional "drifters" Warren fashioned who are strivers against the tide of an overpowering and mechanical history and against the weight of evil in the human heart. Burden is repeatedly jolted by the reality that "history is blind," but learns that "man is not."[16] Warren's reader is tantalized by the sheer brilliance of the writing and the recreation of the mid-twentieth-century Southern landscape of weathered farmsteads, country stores, fast cars on highways, dank boarding houses, county fairs, dialects the author heard in his ear with perfect pitch, growing cities with Depression economies, and a politics driven by dreams of the small farmers and workers crushed under the weight of corrupt oligarchs. But the hero who would save this world from itself—Jack's boss, Governor Willie Stark, modeled in part on Huey Long of Louisiana—himself descends from the heights of populist and educated good intentions into the abyss and suffers a tragic and violent end, despite the best of motives. The boss does manage to forge some good out of bad, a veritable philosophy of life for Warren and his characters. If politics is the fine art of understanding and manipulating the hope and despair in human nature, no better book was ever crafted about that dark art.

Jack, whose last name symbolizes so much, is an aimless newspaper man who goes to work for the ambitious Stark. But we gradually learn that he is deeply burdened by the Ph.D. dissertation in American history that he never finished—a work based on the diaries and letters of his great-uncle, Cass Mastern, who had owned slaves and fought and died in the Civil War. In the course of accumulating his boxes of note cards, which he still keeps, Jack has learned of Cass's deep, tragic secret: his passionate love affair with his best friend's wife, Annabelle, a sin that left Cass with unbearable guilt, his best friend dead by suicide, and an honorable house slave named Phebe sold South away from her own husband by the wretched Annabelle because Phebe "knew" of the affair and suicide. Jack remembers first being enthralled by his research as an escape from his dull life, but then recoils from the dark past he finds. Rooted in long passages from Cass's dramatic journals, the great theme that pervades *All the King's Men* and so much of Warren's work thus emerges in layers of flashbacks and tragic turns between past and present. History, personal and collective, first shapes and then infests the present, making living itself a struggle to fight against fate at every turn. It is always the past, as Warren liked to put it, that "rebukes" the present, especially when proud humanity thinks it can live above or overcome it.[17] And the South's struggle to face its past of slavery and defeat in the Civil War had given him an endless trove of material in which to ply his trade.

With a sordid assignment from Stark to dig up dirt on a political rival, the good Judge Irwin, Jack begins to recollect his earlier research with haunting consequences. He is sent on his new research journey, emboldened, or so he wishes, with Stark's own philosophy of man's nature, which governs even the best of us: "Man is conceived in sin and born in corruption and he passeth from the stink of the didie to the stench of the shroud. There is always something." Jack admits to "hiding from the present," just as he "took refuge in the past" while he was a graduate student researcher. He had a mass of written material from Cass's journals and letters, in addition to one photograph of a young man wearing "the jacket of an infantryman in the Confederate Army," and with a "pair of dark, wide-set, deep eyes" that "stared out of a long, bony face." Jack has assiduously assembled the facts of

Cass's life and death; he is a good historian, drawn to the "enchantments of the past."[18] But the former research journey overwhelms his new one and all but ruins his own sense of self. Jack's enchantments unravel as he begins to all but relive Cass's prolonged nightmare; the book of the past, once opened, slowly takes over and debilitates the present.

Overwhelmed by guilt, Cass first goes in futile pursuit of Phebe's purchaser, hoping to buy the woman back and free her. Warren weaves past and present together in what becomes, for Jack, a frightening seamlessness. When Jack returns to Lexington, Kentucky, the place where much of this history took place, to do research, he visits the old brick slave pen and auction house—"Robards barracoon"—which is still standing. His great-uncle's journal records Cass's detailed descriptions of the auction of a young, light-skinned slave woman, with potential buyers inspecting and touching her nude body, and hangers-on providing jocular commentary. Cass gets into a knife fight with one of the men and is badly wounded. He moves to Mississippi, and for a few years, despite his psychological collapse, manages to prosper by growing cotton with slave labor. But he is unmanned by the "misery" of slaveholding, a new form of guilt, and as he frees his slaves "on a boat bound up river," he declares himself the "chief of sinners and a plague-spot on the body of the human world." Just as Annabelle could not "bear the eyes" of Phebe looking at her so knowingly, Cass speaks for what he believes are many slaveholders who "cannot bear their [slaves'] eyes upon them, and enter into evil and cruel acts of desperation."[19] The accusing "eyes" of slaves peering out of this real and living past are one of Warren's recurring metaphors in *All the King's Men.*

As the secession crisis and the Civil War arrive in 1861, Warren ingeniously develops Jack Burden's memory of Cass Mastern's willful enlistment in the Confederate army—as a private and not as the officer he could have been—into a stark symbol of a cause that in many ways was lost before it even began. Through his older brother,

Gilbert, Cass meets Jefferson Davis more than once, but most memorably as Davis boards a steamboat, the *Natchez,* to travel fatefully to Montgomery, Alabama, to become president of the Confederacy. Cass remarks on "how worn to emaciation" Davis appeared, "how thin the skin lay over the bone." The secession movement, according to Gilbert, was led by "fools," and the nascent Confederate nation doomed to failure or death. And it is death that Cass, in his self-destructive madness, persistently seeks. He refuses to fire his musket, believing he has already killed one man, and cannot bear to kill another. But he throws himself into the war, somehow surviving the horrors of combat, "as in a dream," at the battles of "Shiloh, Chickamauga, Knoxville, Chattanooga, and nameless skirmishes, and the bullet for which he waited did not find him." Warren deftly allows Cass the stern nobility of "the professional soldier" who endures and who admires his comrades, as well acknowledging as "a kind of glory" in some generals for their skill of command. Finally, "outside Atlanta, the bullet found him," and in a wretched Confederate hospital, Cass "rotted slowly to death."[20]

The journals abruptly ended. Returning to Jack Burden's graduate student apartment, with Cass's papers all over his desk, we see a historian paralyzed inside by his inability to confront and write the story he has uncovered. Jack quits his dissertation; the past has become something he has skillfully dredged up but now recoils from with fear and avoidance. In Cass's mortally wounded self, Jack discovers too much of his own barren soul, and Warren found a way of viewing the South, the Civil War, and humanity itself. At the heart of this great allegory about the human condition, Warren offers a theory of history as the reason for Jack's renunciation:

> Cass Mastern . . . learned that the world is all of one piece. He learned that the world is like an enormous spider web and if you touch it, however lightly, at any point, the vibration ripples to the remotest perimeter and the drowsy spider feels the tingle and is drowsy no more but springs out to fling the gossamer coils about you who have

touched the web and then inject the black, numbing poison under your hide. It does not matter whether or not you meant to brush the web of things. Your happy foot or your gay wing may have brushed it ever so lightly, but what happens always happens and there is the spider, bearded black and with his great faceted eyes glittering like mirrors in the sun, or like God's eye, and the fangs dripping.[21]

This was Warren at the height of his art, and the novelist as philosopher of history.

Warren's mastery of the history of the Civil War period is what makes it possible for this tale to work so effectively on all the levels the author intended. Warren's invention of Jack Burden, who in turn discovers and studies Cass Mastern's tragic self-destruction by slavery and the Civil War, provides an intricate and enduring metaphor of the nation's struggle to assess the history that Cass lived and that Jack could not bear to write. All human beings are wayfarers on a journey, and so are peoples and nations. They have countless moral choices to make along the way, and once those choices are made, and consequences sewn into the fabric of the story, it is best, this mighty book suggests, not to erase, avoid, or lie about the self-knowledge gained along the journey. But alas, frail humanity desperately needs its denials, it pleasing narratives, its self-justifying stories that make the past serve the present. In American culture, despite the efforts of some artists and historians, we tend to demand a redemptive history, often without knowing that we have erased the tragedy.

Warren believed, and created characters who learned, that one gained a sense of integrity, dignity, even wisdom from knowing and experiencing tragedy. Judge Irwin commits suicide when the corruption in his past is revealed, but Warren portrays this as essentially an act of honor. As one Warren critic has written, only through "confrontation with fate," even if we lose the high-stakes struggle, do we really understand what it is to be human. "For only those who are mortal can possibly be brave," writes John Burt about the impact of *All the King's Men,* "and only those who suffer limitation can be generous." In the end, Warren does at least have Jack attain some self-knowledge, and a useful, conscious sense of tragedy. Finishing his dirty deed, uncovering the scandal in Judge Irwin's past as we readers also learn Irwin is Jack's father, and serving Willie Stark as ordered, a chastened Jack has learned at least what "historical researchers believe." "For nothing is lost," Warren concludes inside Jack's numbed head, "nothing is ever lost. There is always the clue, the cancelled check, the smear of lipstick . . . , the condom on the park path, the twitch in the old wound . . . , the taint in the blood stream. And all times are one time, and all those dead in the past never lived before our definition gives them life, and out of the shadow their eyes implore us."[22] Warren captured in his art one of the deepest truths in American memory: there are no dead like the Civil War dead, and the slaves who buried them.

. . .

As the Centennial neared, Warren demonstrated his mastery of the Civil War period and reworked the idea of history's burdens in yet another remarkable novel, a much shorter work, *Wilderness: A Tale of the Civil War,* published in 1961. Critics, by and large, have not always been kind to *Wilderness,* but it is a finely crafted story and evidence of the impact Warren hoped to have on serious readers during the Centennial. It puts on display the author's careful knowledge of the war, captured in an allegory about the quest of humans for self-knowledge and freedom in the fullest sense. It is also Warren's way of taking up most of the themes that drove his historical and artistic imagination: the nature of history, myth, innocence, idealism, guilt, determinism, original sin, good entangled with evil, and, laced throughout, the draw of the Civil War as America's most pivotal and symbolic event.

Based on classical mythology, especially on Ulysses in the *Odyssey,* the lead character is a young German Jewish immigrant named Adam Rosenzweig, who emigrates from Bavaria to New York in July

1863. Adam the wandering Jew becomes, in the Civil War, an American Everyman. He is burdened with a club foot, but, inspired by his father's heroism in the 1848 Revolution in Germany, he comes to America to volunteer in its Civil War and fight "für die Freiheit" ("for freedom"). Shortly after disembarking, he hears the noise of a crowd and sees a great tumult that he mistakes for a celebration: he has landed squarely in the midst of the New York City draft riots. One of the first things he sees is a black man hanging from a lamppost, a lynching victim, naked, mutilated, covered with dried blood—"the first black man he had ever seen."[23] He sees others dying in the streets and hiding or drowning in cellars, and is himself saved from the mobs by a black man and former slave named Mose Talbutt. The shocked and confused immigrant nevertheless tries to enlist in the Union army, but is rejected because of his deformed foot and the odd boot he must wear on it. Instead, he hitches a ride in the sutler's wagon of a Southerner named Jedeen Hawksworth, and his servant man, Mose. The book becomes the tale of the young man's long journey toward and ultimately into the war, but only through a series of experiences in the Pennsylvania and Virginia countryside that Warren executes with artistic skill. The war is always the context, the epic event moving by its own inexorable and destructive logic just offstage, while small human dramas play out onstage with large symbolic stakes.

Some critics in 1961 found *Wilderness* too cynical or too philosophical, or its plot too thin. Others may have wished that Warren had written a more explicit war novel, a Blue-Gray melodrama to feed the tastes and fit the season of Civil War nostalgia. But Warren pandered to no such expectations. Some critics have greatly admired the book, describing it as being "like a poem committed to images . . . like a play, willing to foreshorten everything but dramatic truth." Warren's hero, Adam, has his idealism repeatedly crushed, his faith dissipated, and he must learn to lie and kill in order to find any meaning in his quest. In sparing but careful ways, Warren weaves his moral tale into the chronologically and geographically accurate details of the war in 1863–1864, thus giving the book its narrative verve and its aesthetic beauty. A big sutler's wagon, symbol of crassness, commerce, and materialism in the midst of a "holy" war for competing ideals; the thoroughly cantankerous, morally ambiguous, Southern-born owner and operator Hawksworth; his assistants, the (initially) pitifully idealistic Adam and the stoical, road-tested, former slave–survivor, Mose, eager to see and get into the war—these make a compelling team of observers, as well as agents, of man's fate. At the helm of the wagon rides Hawksworth, looking like a "centaur," his bottom half animal-like, "adapted to the dreary grind of life and the brute work of the world," and his upper half adorned in "frock coat" and "waist coat," a "gold chain" and "high beaver hat . . . moving like a smokestack of a steamboat across the green land of Pennsylvania, a steamboat drifting with an idle current, the fires dead."[24] The story is a small piece of a very big war, but a vantage point from which Warren tells us virtually everything the conflict was about. He does so not by philosophizing and preaching, but—as Mark Twain did with Huck and Jim on the famous raft—through the actions and language of the characters. *Wilderness* is a neglected and splendid example of history rendered in art. But in 1961 it was a harsh, bitter history that most Americans preferred not to countenance.

On Adam's journey from innocence to the tree of knowledge, he learns a great deal about the American problem of slavery and race, and about how closely good and evil are intertwined. Here we see Warren's own particular point of view on where righteousness might be found in this war—namely, almost nowhere, except in outcomes that man, if he learned deeply enough, only marginally controlled. An anguished Adam watches as a black soldier bleeds to death on a field hospital table after saving the life of his white officer, while that officer stands by complaining that he cannot bear the indignity of having survived because of the heroism of a Negro. "The black son-of-a-bitch is going to die to spite me," the officer keeps wailing. Adam watches in astonishment as the officer sits on a stool, telling all within earshot that he "had never asked any nig to save his life." Adam seems to choke on the amorality at the heart of the war; he goes into the woods, kneels, and tries to pray, but cannot form the words in his head. The most racist character in the story is a Union soldier, Simms Perdew, who has received a medal of honor for bravery in battle, but who gets drunk and brutally abuses black camp hands by forcing them into a game of entertainment: after tying their hands, Perdew dunks their heads into tubs of flour as they try to retrieve dollar bills from the flour with their mouths, all to the glee and amusement of Yankee soldiers. The scene is reminiscent of the "battle royal" in Ralph Ellison's *Invisible Man*. In this case, rather than a blind and bloody collective boxing match for money and the perverse entertainment of white men, black men are humiliated by the chance to earn a little lucre at the risk of suffocation. When Perdew wearies of his fun, one of the blacks rolls out of a tub, his hands are untied, and he sits up, presenting an unforgettable image: "The fellow sat up and wiped his face, swiping off the flour, clumsily . . . his teeth were clenched . . . With his right hand the fellow took the thing from between his teeth [a greenback] . . . held it up, still puffing and wheezing. Beneath the streaks of flour the face was grinning. It was a wan, sickly, distorted, flour-streaked grin, but a grin."[25]

In one scene or character after another, evil and good are thrown into tortured juxtaposition. In an episode loaded with compelling metaphors, Mose murders Jed after the sutler humiliates his "nigger" one too many times, repeatedly calling him a "worthless black son-of-bitch." Jed, it turns out, once testified in a court proceeding in the South to save Mose from an unjust conviction and likely hanging; but as Adam slowly learns, Jed did not do this for any heroic reason. And Mose, as well, may have deserted from the Union army and has been branded on the leg for his alleged crime. When the dispirited Mose finally comes undone and in the middle of the night kills Jed in his tent, Adam discovers the next morning that the black man has fled, taking not only Jed's "money belt" but also the "alphabet cards" with which Adam had been teaching the former slave to read. Adam stands over the dead body at dawn, hears the "first bugle," and "felt an unmanning constriction in his chest. Something too complicated, too terrible, for him to give a name to was in him, was in the world." The night before, Mose had told Adam just before falling asleep that he had wanted to be that black man on the field hospital table, "bleed-nen" from a soldier's wounds, and not from a "wuppen."[26]

By himself, Adam takes the sutler's wagon and finally catches up with the armies on the move, in May 1864, toward Grant's epic clash with Lee in the Battle of the Wilderness in Virginia. Adam hears the battle raging, and moving from one section of the dense forest to another; he hears the screams of the wounded trapped in the burning woods. In a "glade" where he parks his wagon, a small band of Confederate skirmishers, crazed with hunger and battle fatigue, storm into his encampment. In an "instant outside time and place," Adam finds himself in combat with men who have become savages. One of them tears the boot off Adam's club foot, but the young immigrant finally grabs a musket, the first he has ever fired, and shoots one of the "rebels." Adam marvels at his deed: "I have killed a man . . . that is why I crossed the ocean and came all the miles. To do that." The novel ends enigmatically, with Adam first peering into the dead man's eyes, convincing himself that it "was the face of a man who, clearly, might as well never have lived," but then wondering "what his own face would be like in death." Hobbling and kneeling barefoot in the "ferns," he stares back at the dead man, lying propped over a dead horse, and repeatedly tells himself: "what I have done . . . I did for freedom . . . I did nothing I did not have to do." Adam feels an ener-gy, a "dawning sense of awe" he has never experienced, as though he has discovered some kind of truth in killing. He begins to steal the boots from the dead Confederate, only to realize that it is a Federal boot, and hence that the footwear of dead men are merely passed on to the next potential victim of the killing. With Adam constantly reassuring himself that he has done "only what he had had to do," he listens to the "cries" of the wounded in the forest fires and imagines their plight, but no longer with innocence: "the steam sap in the vernal wood . . . exploding festively like firecrackers, and wounded men, those who were able, would drag, pull, claw, hunch, hump, roll themselves, inch by inch, over the ground in a lethargic parody of flight until the moment of surrender when the summarizing scream of protest would be uttered, but heard by no ear."[27]

We do not know whether the glade will protect Adam from the fires, but he does seem to have reached some form of anguished, mature self-knowledge. We do know that Warren's Civil War is, in this instance, less about anyone's righteous cause than about man's incessant pushing back at inevitability and fate. "Do you know what history is?" Adam's one Jewish relative back in New York had asked him. "It is the agony people have to go through so that things will turn out as they would have turned out anyway." Or in words that Adam keeps hearing in his head, and that Warren uses to chastise the moralistic nostalgia of the Centennial: "God is tired of taking the blame. He is going to let History take the blame for a while."[28]

· · ·

Warren's work, his very outlook on the world, and his approach to history were imbued with a sense of tragedy. In a way, Warren may be said to have embraced tragedy not only as a mode or timbre for writing, but as a conception of the human condition. Tragedy was more than a theme for him: it was a natural lode of limitless ore from which to fashion art, and thereby for him to understand life and man's reason for being. For Warren, genuine tragedy had little to do with the sunny side versus the dark side of life and history. He simply assumed that the darkness, the instinct for natural, fated evil beyond ultimate human control, drove history, whether the history of an individual or that of a nation. In this tragic worldview, we can best comprehend Warren's conception of the Civil War's place in American history and memory. And only in an effort to find a genuine sense of tragedy through which to understand the Civil War can we ever peel away its beguiling, mesmerizing sentimentality. Although Warren never stopped declaring his respect for soldierly virtues, he ultimately wanted the Civil War viewed not through the heroism of the Blue and the Gray, but through a lens fading in and out of dark, in mood if not in sight. But in the darkness would still emerge meanings and stories that could instruct and illuminate minds conditioned by pity, loss, and a clear-eyed sense of America as a place riddled with as much tragedy as almost anywhere else. The sheer seriousness of such massive fratricidal sacrifice for existential causes, Warren believed, deserved an artistic and historical response that matched its gravitas.

Warren's remembrance and use of the Civil War were very personal, located in experience and regional identity, in the tales in his head he could never unload, in his Southern border state–war zone origins. But the meaning of that event was part of a much larger view of art and history, his broader meditation on the idea of people as creatures with pasts, partly knowable and partly not, pasts we cannot dispose of even as we concoct one illusionary and idealistic device after another in order to believe that we can. No one can "break the bank of history," Warren wrote. Machiavelli, Darwin, and Freud had all tried, but even in their new and brilliantly conceived modern world, "the bank of the future remains unbroken." Especially for Americans, who wish to live in the future, unburdened by the past, "some explosively recalcitrant fact gets left out of the fine scheme, and this fact, like an unexploded grenade in a rubbish heap, is likely to cause trouble."[29] Many of those grenades, believed the old Kentucky poet, had been strewn over the American landscape—literally and metaphorically—by the Civil War. Gettysburg, Andersonville, and a thousand old plantation houses and slave quarters were still minefields into which Americans were bound to stumble. Warren insisted that history was both dreadful and inspiring.

For this reason, in his own pantheon of writers, he tended to praise Herman Melville and Nathaniel Hawthorne and scorn Ralph Waldo

Emerson. Warren declared his vote by borrowing from Henry James: "Emerson, as a sort of spiritual sun-worshiper, could have attached but a moderate value to Hawthorne's cat-like faculty of seeing in the dark." It was easy, Warren maintained, to love Emerson's "sweet nature" and "noble prose"; but it was in the darker, tragic spirit of a Hawthorne that one found America's truer soul and more honest past. As a literary critic, he would return to a writer like Katherine Anne Porter, whose short stories pursued tragic, fated characters through a "tissue of contradiction" and an "intricate tissue of paradox."[30] Those were the same tissues from which Warren, with various degrees of success, molded his own art.

Theodore Dreiser, the author of *An American Tragedy*, inspired an abiding respect in Warren. "Dreiser is an old passion," he told an interviewer in 1977. "Humanly he was a monster," but Dreiser's work, Warren contended, searched for "root tragedy," which he defined as "tragedy concerned, as tragedy must be, with the nature of destiny . . . grounded in the essential human situation." "Man's lot is always the same," Warren argued, using Dreiser as his cover. He is a "mechanism with consciousness," and "his tragedy lies in the doubleness of his nature." Humans are doomed or entrapped in a double bind: they seek a clear ideal, a self-justification, the good society, but so often find themselves violating the very ideals they wished to live by and crushing themselves in violent destruction. In an essay entitled "The Sense of the Past," Warren mused that amid all ideal pursuits and modern America's endless desire for material happiness, "there is one more evil to conquer—that of human nature." It was a tragic "tissue of contradiction" running through American history that far too often went unlearned or unacknowledged. Warren believed the country ought to know but could not fully face the fact that it had buried its innocence in the blood of the 1860s. The past could never be escaped: "History is what you can't / Resign from."[31]

And Warren frequently admitted he had "always been crazy

about" Melville. From his perch in western Massachusetts and by 1865 in New York City, Herman Melville had charted his reactions to the shuddering impact of the Civil War in dozens of poems he eventually collected in *Battle Pieces*. Indeed, the war seems to have turned Melville, author of many novels by then, to poetry. He claimed that the fall of Richmond in 1865 inspired him to dive into the meaning of the war, into its results, and especially into the shattering of so much innocence and youth on so many ghastly battlefields. It was not so much Melville's style or technique that fascinated Warren, but his imagination, his "concern with the fundamental ironical dualities of existence: will against necessity, action against ideas, youth against age, the changelessness of man's heart against the concept of moral progress . . . the bad doer against the good deed . . . ignorance against fate." These were the same wrenching opposites that Warren probed so deeply in his own poetry and prose. If Melville did not "master the craft of verse," Warren wrote with knowing sympathy, he thought the author of *Moby-Dick* had pursued the most elusive meanings of the Civil War with insight.[32] And Warren hitched on to Melville's poetic visions as a way of understanding his own sense of how the Civil War was an enlightening if disturbing window into human nature itself. Grasping Warren on the Civil War requires seeing him, to a degree, through Melville.

Melville had not been a soldier (he was forty-two in 1861), and a certain feeling of remoteness from the fray characterizes many of his war poems, most of which were written after the war was over. But the best of them delve into the meaning of sacrifice, into the agony of loss and its withering, endless legacy. And though he was a staunch Unionist, he speaks of the nobility and bloodlust on both sides. The poems challenge the idea of cause and ideology—subjects Warren himself often blistered with sarcasm even as he betrayed certain enduring loyalties. Warren wrote an extensive introduction to the volume of Melville's poems that he edited in 1967—an essay deemed by Melville's best modern biographer, Andrew Delbanco, a "brilliant assessment" and one of the most original essays about the novelist-poet "ever written."[33]

Despite, or perhaps because of, Melville's struggles with verse, Warren could not resist him, especially in *Battle Pieces*. After early success with his sea stories and the profound achievement of *Moby-Dick* in 1851, Melville had fallen on hard times as a writer by 1861, when news arrived in his hometown (Pittsfield, Massachusetts) of the firing on Fort Sumter. Physically ill, floundering in self-pity, and broke financially and artistically, Melville was undergoing, Warren perceived, a "rejuvenation and the tapping of old, nigh-forgotten energies" from the surge of the war crisis. The war poems offered "releases" and "compensations" for a near "death" of his "self" that could now be "sublimated in the national tragedy, and his own distress, in contrast, could be shrunk to a manageable scale." Warren boldly "hazarded" that Melville had an "inner . . . *civil* war" between his deep skepticism and a search for religious understanding, between those eternal antagonists "individual and ideology."[34] These were, of course, some of Warren's own long-standing personal and artistic preoccupations. Warren was forever trying to purge the *sentiment* for the Civil War planted in his soul by his grandfather, and to supplant it with a sense of tragedy. He seemed to find a welcome companion in Melville.

"The Civil War made Melville a poet," Warren argued. "It gave him the right subject . . . a big, athletic, over-mastering subject . . . bloodily certified by actuality." But this was not merely some male-gendered need for violence and contest, at sea or on land. What Melville needed in order to create art was "action . . . perfectly balanced by the centripetal pull toward . . . unresolvable mystery or tormenting ambiguity." And the Civil War, wrote Warren with a certain gleam in his own eye, "offered Gods and devils aplenty." What Warren found in Melville was an authentically tragic vision of the war and of humankind itself. Warren believed with every fiber of his being that the only ultimate meaning in history was the "tragic complexity of man's fate, the painful limit of man's rational vision," the fact that evil was not only "inevitable" but indeed the "cost of good."[35] Melville helped Warren find comfort in his own desire to explode the melodrama and sentimentality at the heart of Civil War memory, and at the same time inspired him to keep probing its sublime dramas. *Evil as the cost of good*—and the eternal quest to comprehend both sides of that transaction in history and life—may have been the overarching theme of Warren's literary career.

A recurring theme in Melville's war poems is the way the innocence and lives of youth are squandered when young people are enlisted as the "champions and enthusiasts of the state." The phrase comes from "March into Virginia," a poem that Warren greatly admired:

> Youth must its ignorant impulse lend—
> Age finds place in the rear.
> All wars are boyish, and are fought by boys . . .
> In Bacchic glee they file toward Fate,
> Moloch's uninitiate . . .
> But some who this blithe mood present,
> As on in lightsome files they fare,
> Shall die experienced ere three days are spent—
> Perish, enlightened by the vollied glare.

Warren loved Melville's sense of irony, as the nineteenth-century poet described his young, blithe soldiers marching off to "no berrying party," "no picnic party," but "gayly" to their deaths. The romantic boy-soldiers, like the romantic youthful nation, had to die in droves to find adulthood. Innocent individuals and innocent nation both find enlightenment only in the blinding and deafening cacophony of a million gunshots. That was the sort of history filled with fated contradiction that Warren seemed to crave. He called it "Melville's old obsessive theme": the tragic engagement with the world, whether a person was chasing the great, mysterious white whale or finding manhood and destiny on the ghastly fields of Manassas or Shiloh.

Every man must find his own "end of illusion," Warren observed in awed respect.[36]

By reading *Battle Pieces,* Warren worked out his own vision of the meaning of the Civil War. In "On the Slain Collegians," Melville mixed the two themes of death of innocence and scorn for ideology. This was an intellectual's poem about students, young learners drawn irresistibly into war's clutches and its ultimate doom. In this timeless poem we can read about the deaths of young soldiers in any war and feel its terrible truth. Its message is both ancient and modern; it could have come from a poet of the Great War, circa 1916, or from a Greek bard in the Peloponnesian War:

> Youth is the time when hearts are large,
> And stirring wars
> Appeal to the spirit which appeals in turn
> To the blade it draws.
> If woman incite, and duty show . . .
> Or whether it be truth's sacred cause,
> Who can aloof remain
> That shares youth's ardor, uncooled by the snow
> Of wisdom or sordid gain?

Out of the "liberal arts" and "culture," Melville continued, boys rose up and

> Went from the North and came from the South,
> With golden mottoes in the mouth,
> To lie down midway on a bloody bed . . .
> They knew the joy, but leaped the grief,
> Like plants that flower ere comes the leaf—
> Which storms lay low in kindly doom,
> And kill them in their flush of bloom.

Where "ardor" met "sacred cause" and "spirit" collided with "golden mottoes," Melville found his story. Who or what was doing the killing here? Yankees or Confederates? Proslavery or antislavery advocates? The killing was born in man's deadly, unstoppable nature, and all sense of cause or justification dissolved:

> Warred one for Right and one for Wrong?
> So be it, but they both were young—
> Each grape to his cluster clung,
> All their elegies are sung.[37]

Perhaps it was simply this elegiac mode in Melville that inspired Warren so. It reached for the depths of "the human," as Warren so often said of his favorite writers. And after all, he was forever trying to explain away his combination of affection for and worry about those days, remembering the way his grandfather designed Civil War campaign lines and battle strategies on the ground with sticks and shells.

Warren, like Melville, loved the "polarities" in human nature and experience, and nothing quite like war exposed the "most painful polarity of all . . . that between all values and the blank fact of annihilation." Melville's slain collegians had learned "gentleness" and "grace," even "nurture sweet," but they were now dead, their beauty crushed in so many unmarked, shallow graves. Warren's heroes though, like Melville's, were usually those who survived, and gained knowledge of the "tragedy of the human plight" without forfeiting the "ability to act." When all was said and done, there was still history to be traced, a future to be lived, action to be taken at Petersburg in 1865 or Selma in 1965. And art to make. What concerned Warren was the insatiable human capacity to mold experience into "legend," thereby draining it so that all meaning was "bleached out." Then, wrote Warren, "we are left to meditate on merely the gestures and stances—the Passion—of the old participants: the passion with which they play their roles." In this language Warren captured the formulaic, mythic elements that keep Civil War memory alive in the imagination of so many enthusiasts, in America and abroad. Many readers and reenactors *love* the Civil War, so long as the actors play their expected roles.

Warren and Melville insisted that passion alone was never enough for understanding the "ultimately tragic" character of the Civil War or any other great story. Both would lose their battles to subvert passion and legend with a sense of the tragic, but not for lack of trying. When responding to those who would merely celebrate or revel in the past or take refuge in its picturesque pleasures, especially about military action, Warren would hurl a few lines from Melville's "Commemorative of a Naval Victory" at them:

> But seldom the laurel wreath is seen
>> Unmixed with pensive pansies dark;
> There's a light and a shadow on every man
>> Who at last attains his lifted mark.[38]

Warren's conception of tragedy vacillated between the fated, bleak, no-exit kind of human darkness where man and history are essentially driven by evil, and the kind that demanded redemption or resolution through struggle and catastrophe. In the end it was this second mode of tragedy, a demand that suffering produce redemptive knowledge, that led Warren, primarily via prose rather than poetry, to his understanding of the Civil War. He had, after all, adored Melville's *Battle Pieces* because the poems were "analytic" as well as "dramatic." His search for a kind of "grandeur" in tragedy frames his major meditations on Civil War memory during the Centennial years, in fiction as well as nonfiction.[39]

. . .

The Legacy of the Civil War, published in 1961, came out at the beginning of the Centennial. As the critic Leonard Casper observed, the novel *Wilderness* was Warren's "fictional counterpart" to *Legacy,* and the two works could be profitably read in tandem.[40] If *Wilderness* was a poem in the form of an allegorical novel, *Legacy* was a prose poem as history. Published in its first form in *Life* magazine, *Legacy* merits a close reading today; parts of it hold up remarkably well in the face of modern historical scholarship, and parts do not. The book instructs and provokes on intellectual and imaginative levels all at once. It is an essay essentially about the power of myth at the heart of national historical memory. Much of it is idiosyncratically Warren's personal taste and point of view. But as America experiences the Sesquicentennial of the Civil War, there is no better place to begin than Warren's *Legacy.*

The book offers one of the most explicit examples of Warren's famous contention that poetry and history are not only compatible, but indispensable partners in the search for an understanding of the past. In the foreword to *Brother to Dragons: A Tale in Verse and Voices* (1953), his first of three epic historical poems, which included footnotes to his sources, Warren mused about mixing poetry with historical research and attention to fact. A poem, he declared, "could be totally accurate as history and still not worth a dime as a poem." But he demanded that poetry be "more than fantasy" and that it "say something . . . about the human condition." He left this oft-quoted passage through which we might comprehend his task in *Legacy:* "Historical sense and poetic sense should not, in the end, be contradictory, for if poetry is the little myth we make, history is the big myth we live, and in our living, constantly remake."[41] That statement is a serviceable definition of the nature of historical memory. And Warren loved to wrestle with the big myths, sometimes exploding their pieties and sometimes reinforcing them.

In *Legacy* Warren wrote, in effect, a prose poem about the big myths we live about our Civil War. Informed modern readers of this text will see that it is deeply informed by Warren's never-ending quest to pose the question: Are we makers of our own fate, or is it all made for us in our nature? Or as he put it: "Can we, in fact, learn only that we are victims of nature and of history? Or can we learn that we can make, or at least have a hand in the making of, our future?"[42] It was his way of raising the perennial question about the Civil War's inevitability, with regard to both its causes and its scale of blood and destruction.

Warren began his Centennial meditation with big claims about the place of the Civil War in American consciousness. Boldly, he called the war "the great single event of our history . . . our only felt history, history lived in the national imagination." Until the 1860s, the nation's founding and growth had been only a "daydream of easy and automatic victories, a vulgar delusion of manifest destiny, a conviction of being a people divinely chosen to live on milk and honey at small expense." Warren's "nation" here was the exclusive, mainstream, "white" population and not blacks or Indians, whom he would represent in other writing as unpersuaded by that vulgar delusion. These were a poet's broad strokes, indeed, but he made his point: only with the Civil War did Americans earn an "awareness of the cost of having a history."[43]

Warren framed his meditation on the Civil War squarely within the Cold War context of the early 1960s. The Civil War, he maintained, was in "our blood stream," deeply pertinent to "our personal present." The conflict with the Soviet Union, which put "national existence" at stake, demanded that Americans "learn . . . from that great crisis of our national past." He wondered if the Cold War was a struggle of such moral difference that war with the Soviets might be inevitable. "If so," he mused perversely, "when do we start shooting?" In the crises over Berlin and the nuclear arms race with the Russians, Warren saw the same great question posed by the Civil War: Could people shape their fate, or was it determined by forces in history beyond their "making"? Was the vexing and disastrous struggle over slavery in America a template for understanding the ideological contest between Soviet communism and the Western democracies? Was a disastrous outcome predictable this time as well, in the irreconcilable terms of debate over how to create a society? Did the nuclear fear and brinksmanship of 1961 evoke 1861 again for Americans? "And so the Civil War draws us as an oracle," Warren mused, "darkly unriddled and portentous, of personal, as well as national, fate."[44]

But what kind of oracle had it—has it—been? In *Legacy* Warren wrote an aesthetic treatise with historical judgments, supplied with numerous authoritative passages from his favorite historians to back him up. But his primary concern was memory, or, as he put it in a letter to Cleanth Brooks in the summer of 1960, to "distinguish between historical importance" of the war and its "fundamental appeal to the American imagination." This question of the *appeal* of the war to our enduring national and collective imagination is where Warren is richly relevant as a guide to our own time. His answers from 1961 are not necessarily our answers of 2011, but they ought to be surprisingly familiar to serious students of the war and its legacies. Writing to Jerry Korn, his editor at *Life,* Warren described his most "nagging" conceptual dilemma. All those "attractions" and "motives" for the war—those of 1861 or 1961—were hardly "worthy" he admitted. He captured his own and our enduring fascination as though it were a guilty pleasure: "Because the war made us great we like to look at it—as the dog likes to look at the icebox door."[45] Warren cautioned people to be self-critical as they fed at the trough of Civil War nostalgia.

Warren stated confidently that most Americans at least understand, in some vague sense, that the Civil War was "a fountainhead of our power and prestige among the nations." He may have been overconfident about American historical consciousness, but no one can deny that the "event stands there larger than life." He grandiosely declares the war "massively symbolic in its inexhaustible and sibylline significance." Foremost in its appeal to Warren are the war's epic qualities and "powerfully mythic" figures, such as Abraham Lincoln and Robert E. Lee, or Sam Davis, the teenage Confederate hero executed as a spy, or Robert Gould Shaw, the Harvard boy who commanded the black 54th Massachusetts Regiment and died with his troops at Fort Wagner in 1863. "That was our Homeric period," Warren announced, "and the figures loom up only a little less than gods." In those words and images, one can find a direct inspiration for filmmaker Ken Burns's sensibility—even his structure and argument—in his famous 1990 public-television documentary series on the Civil

War. We should never underestimate the "Homeric" appeal of the Civil War to generations of modern Americans, as well as to people of other nations, who have faced war, destruction, or simply industrial and urban alienation. How dearly some of us pampered moderns have yearned for those contests in which men seemed to draw their weapons on honorable enemies in causes seemingly nobler and clearer than our own. How often, generation after generation, young men who have never read Homer yearn to experience something Homeric. How authentically real but tragic those yearnings have been in the age of modern warfare. And so Warren gave his nod to these "lineaments and passions of men" before digging deeper.[46]

An oracular event had to offer more than passion. Virtually all of Warren's gods are fallen gods, except perhaps Lee, whom he apparently could only adore. At least their causes and meanings are part of a fallen man's struggle with himself, his own internal self-destructive battle with good and evil. Such struggles made the Civil War more appealing to the imagination than the American Revolution because, for Warren, the Revolution was "too simple," too "comfortable" a contest of "good against bad." He admitted this judgment was "somewhat unhistorical," but he was operating in the realm of imagination and mythic power, not interpretive nuance. The war of 1861–1865 was a *civil* war of great "inner drama," the "prototype of all war," throwing men against one another with primal motives born of "old ambivalences of love and hate . . . all the old guilts, the blood brothers of our childhood." One might call this, although Warren did not, a biblical rather than a Homeric conflict. The stuff of Cain and Abel, of fratricidal bloodlust, made the Civil War a "great mirror," Warren suggested, "in which the individual may see imaged his own deep conflicts, not only the conflicts of political loyalties, but those more profoundly personal." Warren was irresistibly drawn to the paradox of national or blood brothers raging against and slaughtering one another for the best definition of their country's future. When men acted on hatreds and stared down evil in society or themselves, they became especially interesting to Warren. Herein were the "agonies and contradictions" caused by slavery and racism as a shared fate; in them "we find the echo of our own lives, and that fact draws our imaginations."[47] Obliquely, at least, Warren saw in the Civil War a mirror to reflect the civil rights struggle of his own time.

Hence, Warren saw the Civil War as a source of prophetic—"sibylline"—self-understanding; hence, too, his insistence that one of the biggest attractions of the war was the "question of will and inevitability." He freely admitted that such questions as free will and historical determinism were better left to the "metaphysician," and he quoted a constellation of historians such as James Randall, Arthur Schlesinger, Jr., Charles Beard, Pieter Geyl, David Donald, and Kenneth Stampp to establish the point.[48] But as if scratching a persistent itch, Warren would not leave the question of the war's inevitability alone. It had a beguiling endurance that allowed Southerners, Northerners, and historians of different generations and persuasions to either avoid confronting guilt for the war or to spread it around in all directions—and Warren did a good deal of that himself.

At stake, of course, was responsibility for the war, and Warren preferred to leave no one blameless. "Inevitability theory," as he termed the idea, could allow Yankees to "re-allocate all guilt to the South." In this vision, the war had been "morally" irrepressible, and the North was therefore "the bright surgical instrument in the hand of God, or History." Ex-Confederates and their allies in Northern publishing, on the other hand, could blame fanatical abolitionists and politicians on both sides for a needless or avoidable war and "feel a little less lonely" with their "guilt about slavery." Warren harbored his own contempt for abolitionists, but the only "fruitful" way to consider inevitability, he contended, was to recognize that "there can never be a yes-or-no answer." As a writer, he thrived on the lifeblood of ambiguity, and chastised historians and lay readers alike for seeking the "obscene gratifications of history," the comfort of claiming utter certitude in their interpretations. In the end, he maintained, historians were mere "human beings," but they were also craftsmen of human nature of a sort, "bound to pick the scab of our fate."[49] Warren could be a bit abstract sometimes when he wrote about "fate." Yet here he called on historians to be fearless in seeking the fullest, or darkest, meanings of the past, whatever the consequences.

But if the historians failed at this task, Warren called for poets to carry on the work—they surely would not shy away. The problem, of course, is that having the scabs plucked from their fates is not generally what even serious readers of history desire, especially about those events in which they may find their personal or national identity. Warren knew Americans loved the pathos in Civil War memory; he declared his own deep attraction to the warm and endearing story in which ex-Confederates served as pallbearers at Ulysses Grant's funeral, and he admired far too seriously the irony that Confederates themselves were willing to recruit blacks into their army toward the end of the war. At the same time, he wanted no one to get off with any "moral narcissism" about the causes or consequences of the war.[50] In the long struggle over Civil War memory, both sides had developed comfortable havens of self-righteousness, morally narcissistic arguments for which Warren coined lasting labels. In so doing, he spoke to the culture of both 1961 and 2011.

After musing on the human, physical, and economic "costs" of the Civil War, Warren arrived at his more familiar terrain: the psychological costs. Historians are not always comfortable with notions of a collective psyche, but poets can be. The war's results gave Southerners, according Warren, a "Great Alibi," and Northerners the "Treasury of Virtue." These symbolic paradigms—versions of collective memory—are worth examining over time and against the context of the Sesquicentennial. For Warren, these catchy labels were shorthand for his almost ecumenical sense of who and what were responsible for the Civil War, as well as the "thousand ways" the conflict still infused the "temper" of American society during the Cold War and the Civil Rights Movement.[51]

The "Great Alibi" was Warren's name for the Lost Cause tradition, at least the way it had become a set of excuses for every grievance and resentment that animated white Southerners. The Confederacy had lost the war solely because of the North's "superior numbers and resources," as Lee put it in his farewell address to his troops after surrendering at Appomattox. Southerners had never really fought for slavery, but rather had been defending home, hearth, independence, and their sovereign rights. The South had been occupied and exploited by greedy and dangerous radicals during Reconstruction, a regime of corruption and misguided racial revolution that Southerners had risen heroically to defeat politically, and violently only when necessary. The Great Alibi took root in the idea that loss is so often more noble and even beguilingly more interesting than victory, especially when the victor possesses the cold power of industrial might. Above all, the Lost Cause had served as an enduring story by which white Southerners had managed to convince not only themselves, but many Northerners as well, that they alone could manage and control race relations and the fate of African Americans.[52]

Like cheap ready-made clothing at the dime store, the Great Alibi provided a cover for anything resembling backwardness or bad behavior in the South. "Pellagra, hookworm, and illiteracy," Warren growled, might become "badges of distinction." "Laziness" might be judged an "aesthetic sense," "resentful misery" a "high sense of honor," and "ignorance becomes divine inspiration." Warren clearly enjoyed these chastisements of his fellow Southerners, as he wrote from his summer retreat in rural Vermont. In Lost Cause legends, he contended, the white Southerner "turns defeat into victory, defects into virtues." Warren saved his harshest satire for Southern racists. With the Great Alibi, he said, "any common lyncher becomes a defender of the Southern tradition, and any rabble-rouser the gallant leader of a thin gray line of heroes." So deep is the well of the Great Alibi for Southerners, Warren argued, that the "race problem" grew simply as the "doom defined by history," a natural, unchangeable system not of their own making. In this system, Southerners were "guiltless," mere "innocent victims" of the forces of history they could not control. They could explain their intransigence to any racial change as though willingly trapped in the "City of the Soul that the historical Confederacy became."[53] Few ever captured in more stinging and poignant words the mythic and tragic qualities of the Lost Cause tradition. Warren knew it well; he had been raised in it, and he had spent a long literary career purging it from his soul.

But the white mobs in the South resisting racial integration at every turn were not reading Warren's *Legacy*; they were living it. So were moderate whites who did not join the White Citizens' Councils or the Ku Klux Klan but still staunchly sought to preserve segregation. Warren insisted that the Confederate flags of the mobs in Little Rock, Tuscaloosa, and Oxford be strictly separated from those folded at Appomattox. "Does the man who, in the relative safety of mob anonymity, stands howling vituperation at a little Negro girl being conducted into a school building, feel himself at one with those gaunt, barefoot, whiskery scarecrows who fought it out, breast to breast, to the death, at the Bloody Angle at Spotsylvania, in May 1864? Can the man howling in the mob imagine General R. E. Lee, CSA, shaking hands with Orval Faubus, Governor of Arkansas?" Here, Warren defended the members of what he believed was an authentic nobility in the Confederate war effort, whatever their cause. He was defending his grandfather, the veteran who had taught him to care so much about this story, from the cowardly racists of 1961 who would hold back the hands of time. Just how great the separation is between the Confederate flags folded in 1865 and those waved in 1913, 1961, or 2011 is an enduring debate in our popular and political culture. And Warren made his own little retreat into personal nostalgia on that question. But on matters of race, he wanted his fellow white Southerners to look inside themselves and in effect see their own "original sin"—to know that when they screamed against black civil rights, they screamed against "some voice deep" in themselves. The Great

Alibi, said Warren, "rusts away the will to confront" that which most mattered in the South: the long, grinding struggle to create genuine racial equality in a society where whites and blacks were so intermingled by history and by blood.[54]

Northerners, too, found enormous comfort rusting away in a "Treasury of Virtue," a set of pat arguments justifying their self-definition as noble victors. Aiming now at Yankee hearts, Warren argued that if Southerners could feel trapped by history, Northerners felt "redeemed" by it. By virtue of winning the war and saving the Union for the good of all, allowing a great nation to find its world destiny, Northerners thought they possessed a "plenary indulgence, for all sins past, present, and future, freely given by the hand of history." How true this rings if one has met the occasional New Englander or New Yorker who has never been south of Philadelphia and wonders aloud if civilization, culture, non-redneck whites, and a decent restaurant can be found in Dixie. Not only are such questions asked in William Faulkner novels; they are still mouthed in New England colleges and Midwestern suburbs at the beginning of the twenty-first century. Northern righteousness derived from the war may not be as "comic or vicious" as Southern myths and biases, Warren said, but it could be "equally corrosive."[55]

The Treasury of Virtue allowed Northerners a wide range of forgetting at their pleasure. Warren pokes deep into a well of what he considers Northern hypocrisy. They forgot the limits of the racial vision of Lincoln's Republican Party; they forgot that in 1861 the president himself would have accepted a constitutional amendment giving slavery permanency in the South, and that the Emancipation Proclamation, "forced by circumstances," had serious legal limits. Warren flirted with at least some old Lost Cause denunciations of Lincoln. But he was surely right as his litany of Northern forgetfulness continued: Northerners sabotaged the Fourteenth and Fifteenth Amendments nearly as much as Southerners, General William T. Sherman was as racist at the core as almost any Confederate officer, and hundreds of thousands of common Union soldiers did not look fondly on liberating slaves. The Treasury of Virtue provided such a wealth of glory that generations of Northern youth were educated to see the war through the iconic image of a "boy in blue striking off, with one hand, iron shackles from a grizzle-headed Uncle Tom weeping in gratitude, and with the other passing out McGuffey's First Reader to a roly-poly pickaninny laughing in hope." Effectively, Warren takes the knife to Yankee pride: "When one is happy in forgetfulness, facts get forgotten."[56] Yet it must remembered that such an admonishment applies southward as much as northward. Indeed, he tilted the scale a little too far; the images of faithful slaves and happy darkies in American popular culture were creations largely of Southern pens, although consumed happily, as Warren says, by Northern imaginations.

So ubiquitous are some of these myths and images of the Civil War's meaning, Warren contends, they do not need to be published history. Myth works on a different level: it resides in our imaginations, floats in the air we breathe, makes folk music of the stories we inherit at home. For the Northerner, the Treasury of Virtue, writes Warren in phrasing that could apply equally to the Great Alibi, "lies open on a lectern in some arcane recess of his being, ready for his devotional perusal."[57] Is this not the nature of Civil War memory in America for thousands if not millions? Our stories and understandings await us, ready-made, lying on the teacher's desk, exhibited at battlefield sites, and written in many a triumphal, redemptive book— battle cries of freedom for us to take up and sing when we need them.

· · ·

Intellectually and temperamentally, Warren hated absolutes; hence his disdain for abolitionists. Whether creating characters in fiction, finding a piece of truth in a line of poetry, or interpreting history with an artist's flare, Warren gravitated toward the ironic, the tragic, the inner struggles of flawed realists against idealists. Thus, he could despise a John Brown and admire an Oliver Wendell Holmes, Jr., joyfully ride the wind into darkness anywhere with Herman Melville, and dismiss Henry David Thoreau as a "big old meatball of a fake— with a genius for prose style." This can open Warren to the accusation that he simply held everyone and no one responsible for the Civil War, spreading around the blame so evenly that he seems, at times, to attribute all the bloodletting simply to "human nature," as he once argued in defense of his claims in *Legacy*.[58]

Warren's catchy, if sometimes vague, labels for the two rationales that drove North and South into war were "higher-lawism" and "legalism." "Higher law" encompassed Warren's contempt for piety of all kinds, especially that of abolitionists, whom he saw as self-righteous activists who stood "outside of society," "repudiated . . . institutions," and were willing to "reform everything but themselves." The abolitionists, Warren believed, simply cast too many stones and ruined any hope of "reasonable" compromise on the great slavery question. Here, Warren seems to have swallowed whole the analysis in the 1950s by historians David Donald and Stanley Elkins, who had judged abolitionists and Transcendentalists (as though these terms meant the same thing) to be radical individualists, impractical, anxious elites peddling abstractions and condemning, as he contemptuously quotes Thoreau, "dirty institutions." In *Legacy*, Warren spent many pages railing against the dangers of radical abolitionists, accusing them of "longing for the apocalyptic moment," urging the nation toward violence and blood.[59]

Anyone reading *Legacy* in 1961 might easily have concluded that were it not for the abolitionists, the war could have been avoided in 1861, a position that still held an essentially mainstream place in Civil War scholarship at that moment. Scholars' sympathies for and interpretations of abolitionists would change drastically, for the better, over the next decade and beyond. Warren took from the abolitionists with one hand and gave back—to some extent—with the other. He could snarl about their "vainglorious dreams" and their "apocalyptic *frisson*," and then acknowledge their cause as "just" and their

labors as "noble." Warren never claimed the war was truly prevent-
able, yet he used *Legacy* to argue that "personal absolutism" might
appear more heroic, more memorable, in its epic moments of ambition and principle, but that historical outcomes are often better and
less bloody when men can "lower the rhetorical temperature."[60]

Southerners in 1861, however, were no paragons of sweet reason either, in Warren's eyes, and their obstinate "legalism" appeared
almost as dangerous. With organic conservatism and rigid resistance
to change, defenders of slavery and the South's constitutional sovereignty created a "closed society," in siege-like contempt for the "concept of life itself." Slavery, Warren believed, constricted the Southern
mind in defense of a system on the wrong side of history. This lover
of paradox now found his stock in trade. "If in the North," he wrote,
"the critic had repudiated society, in the South society repudiated
the critic; and the stage was set for trouble." By his awkward term
"legalism," he meant the Southern leadership's steadfast adherence
to states' rights doctrine, as well as to its vaunted code of honor, its
"bravado, arrogance . . . and reckless or ignorant disregard for consequences."[61]

To a degree, Warren's story in *Legacy* is an ancient one: when reason dies, men are left with undaunted bloodlust. But he is quick to
say that he did not believe the war was merely "caused by the extremists on both sides"—a claim not altogether credible, even as Warren
sees the birth of a great American idea in all that blood and misguided idealism. If there is a hero in *Legacy,* it is less a person than an
idea: the philosophical worldview or the method of thinking known
as pragmatism. For Warren, pragmatism meant—as it did for William James, one of his heroes—a habit of mind, a belief that no idea or
institution is ever completely fixed, that the only thing utterly determined is change. The pragmatists urged a passionate commitment to
the open mind, to the testing of all truths and principles no matter
how firmly held. This notion of truth as unfixed made possible the
liberating idea that Warren called the "experimental imagination."

The Civil War was won by this adaptable habit of mind, or, more specifically, by "Grant's systematically self-nurtured gift for problem-solving" and Lincoln's deft ability (Warren is here quoting Sidney Hook) "to be principled without being fanatical, and flexible without being opportunistic."[62] It is hard to see the carnage at Fredericksburg, the senseless slaughter at Cold Harbor, or the disease and starvation at Andersonville Prison as pragmatic or experimental outcomes. But beyond all the death that surpassed explanation, in interpretive terms, Warren found in pragmatism an enduring way of comprehending the political, constitutional, and ideological consequences of the war. As he searched for meanings, he found them; his Civil War, though harrowing, was not merely a disillusioning bloodbath.

Hence, the seeker of irony and paradox had his antidote and his deepest "legacy" with which to thwart those "absolutes." Warren was clearly influenced by James's writings on religion, psychology, and pragmatism. Warren wrestled with James's definition of truth, even as he tried to adopt it. As James famously asked in "What Pragmatism Means," what happens when competing truths "clash"? "The greatest enemy of any one of our truths may be the rest of our truths," he wrote. "Truths have once and for all this desperate instinct of self-preservation and the desire to extinguish whatever contradicts them. My belief in the Absolute, based on the good it does me, must run the gauntlet of all my other beliefs." Now, if human beings and nations could truly, calmly live by this philosophy, reason might yet tame bloodlust. Warren did not suggest that such pragmatic thinking should or could have saved the country from secession and Bull Run. But he was convinced that the war, in its horrifying scale and transformative results, forged a "climate" in which pragmatism grew into a national practice.[63]

This is another of the intriguing ironies about Warren: his rather dark view of human nature and history marched in step with a profound admiration for great pragmatists and problem solvers like James or Lincoln. But it makes sense, since both of those men possessed a similar and life-affirming sense of tragedy. Warren was such a devotee of James's writings that in the introduction to the 1953 edition of *All the King's Men*, while fending off the recurring question of whether his famous character Willie Stark had been based on Huey Long, Warren said: "Long was but one of the figures that stood in the shadows of imagination behind Willie Stark. Another one of that company was the scholarly and benign figure of William James."[64]

To Warren's mind, the Civil War's collision of extreme passions, not to mention the personal experience of combat and wounds, had produced a towering legal figure: Justice Oliver Wendell Holmes, Jr., who rejected rigid ideology and pressed for a constitutionalism born of experiment, "the felt necessities of the time." Writing from the context of the Cold War and an election year (1960) in which he voted for John F. Kennedy, Warren believed the Civil War had bequeathed America a two-party system resistant to ironclad ideology and "over-politicization." "Somewhere in their bones," Warren argued, "most Americans learned their lesson" from the election of 1860: do not let the logic of fanatics prevail, or the political culture could be torn asunder. With the burden of Cold War consensus weighing on early 1960s America, and given Warren's own distaste for ideologues, it is easy to see how he could believe Americans had some sort of "compact" against political extremes. He drove home the point with a Warrenesque metaphor: "The wildebeast on the extreme left of the Democratic tent looks more like the wildebeast on the extreme left of the Republican tent than like the hypocritically drowsy lion facing him from the extreme right of his own show."[65]

In the long, sometimes turbulent history of electoral politics in America, from Appomattox to Birmingham, there is some truth to Warren's assertion that "the Civil War confirmed our preference" for nonideological politics.[66] But there are many holes in this theory and in the timeline. It is one conclusion in *Legacy* that cannot be sustained in our own deeply polarized, partisan political culture of the early twenty-first century. Today we wage a near holy war of rhetoric over big-versus-small government, over the place of religion in law and society, and especially over countless racial, gender, and class legacies of the very era in which Warren wrote his meditation. The wildebeasts at the extremes of the Republican and Democratic parties imagine they are living in a different country from that of their counterparts. In our twenty-four-hour media culture, political extremists on the right, in particular, have managed to cultivate an often ill-informed fervor that no pragmatic vision—born of a longer historical sensibility that Warren might admire—can thwart. And we have far more guns today than Americans did in 1861.

To judge from what he wrote in *Legacy*, Warren would be surprised at the political demagoguery of our time, at the right-wing populism of a Sarah Palin or a Glenn Beck, who have taken the idea of pious higher-lawism to an unprecedented level. If the Civil War taught us the dangers of ideologically divisive politics, we seem to have unlearned that lesson. Instead of searching for modes of consensus or a social contract still vaguely tied to the tragedies of 1860 or 1929 or 1968, we are political tribes yelling and blogging right past each other in technological anarchy. In important ways, the conservative movement that took root in the Barry Goldwater campaign, spawned at the very time Warren wrote *Legacy*, has shown us a good deal of what does and does not survive from Warren's conception of the Civil War's long aftermath.

. . .

Warren's *Legacy* was terse, philosophical narrative, written in prose both slashing and abstract. His audience—or target—was the broadest possible reading public, as well as those mysterious things we might call national memory and conscience. The book garnered many positive reviews and notices, especially from historians, who seemed pleased that such a book (which they could not write) had been written at all amid the banal wasteland of Centennial popular publications and events. Warren's friend C. Vann Woodward praised the book's governing ideas, especially "the Civil War as the origins of Pragmatism." Sharing a point of view reflecting their mutual roots in the South, Woodward "thought quite happy" the "Reb-Yank antitheses . . . the Great Alibi and the Treasury of Virtue." He urged Warren to make even more out of his border-state angle of vision, calling Kentucky "Lincoln-Warren country between revelation-happy Yank and deduction-bitten Reb, Alsace-Lorraine of pragmatism between the crusaders." Woodward really captured his friend's point of view, but seemed even more pleased than Warren to see the war's guilt and blame spread around evenly. The historian agreed with the poet that the "puzzle of inevitability" was best left to the "metaphysician," but he was equally convinced it had everything to do with why the war "stirred the American imagination." Woodward wondered why Warren had avoided popular questions such as why immigrants became Civil War enthusiasts, and why roundtables and reenactments had proliferated like a "cult." But he thought the book "magnificent for understatement."[67]

Some serious reviewers raved about *Legacy,* calling it "deeply dug and beautifully executed" (*New Yorker* writer Richard Tobin) or gushing that it was "a perfect gem of a book" (Richard Harwell, a literary historian of the Confederacy). Others, like Alfred Kazin, moaned in disappointment that Warren had written such a sparing book on such a large subject. From Warren, Kazin seems to have wanted the great nonfiction masterwork that only this Southerner-moved-North could write. After all, wrote Kazin, "in a sense all of Warren's work could be called *The Legacy of the Civil War.*" Kazin believed that both Warren and Faulkner were snarled in a "quarrel with themselves" about human nature, rather than about the specifics of Southern guilt. The critic landed a telling punch: "Sometimes the only way out of a circle of defeat, disillusionment, and guilt is a certain mordancy about human nature in general, an impatient cry that one should not have expected too much of people anyway."[68] Readers of great Southern writers can forever weigh that insight; the South has given us much to ponder on the question of whether sin is truly our own as individuals or an attribute of our species.

Unsurprisingly, since *Legacy* appeared to search for middle ground in the national memory trove, Warren got hammered from the right and from the left. In the *National Review,* Richard Weaver complained that the book had too many "passages sounding like Mrs. Roosevelt," making "decrees of a central government" in a persistent "crusade against the South." Warren was attacked in coded language by a conservative for supporting civil rights for blacks in one case, but then he was chastised by Truman Nelson in the *National Guardian* as an "apologist" for the white South and for too much "psychologizing" and "romantic ambiguity" about pragmatism. Nelson stung Warren when he said he had finished the book "wondering when people are going to realize that this nation's 'legacy' of the Civil War is still in chicanery and will not be collected until all of its citizens can go to common schools and vote a common ballot." And in the *New Republic,* Peter d'A. Jones read *Legacy* as a segregationist appeal that the Centennial should be an "experience from which the Negro American is apparently excluded."[69]

Jones's accusation prompted a heated reply from Warren to the magazine. He condemned the reviewer's suggestion of "guilt by association" between Warren and the White Citizens' Councils of Mississippi. Even more forcefully, Warren declared three principles for which he stood: that all Americans should have complete rights of citizenship; that a "man's worth should be judged by his qualities of manhood"; and that any state official who does not punish those who commit violence against an individual's rights should be "impeached." He then went further, declaring Martin Luther King, Jr., a "great man" and the sit-ins a strategy that "will win." Warren even went so far as to renounce his racial views of "1929" (meaning his "Briar Patch" essay in *I'll Take My Stand*). "In my youth, I was wrong—and even now I sometimes do not feel myself entirely above error."[70] It was neither the first nor the last time a reader misread Warren on race or judged him only by his pre-1930 writings. And it was hardly the last time Warren would defend himself. Interestingly, it took an impatient, ideologically motivated, pro–civil rights critic to inspire Warren to express his own deepest understandings of how fully alive the long-term legacies of the Civil War really were in 1961.

Warren wrote *Legacy* fast, in the summer of 1960; one wishes he had attempted a longer nonfiction analysis of Civil War memory, as Kazin desired. Or perhaps not, since in longer, ponderous prose we might not have as much ambiguity to quarrel with in Warren's conception of the war's meaning. The anchor in *Legacy* that keeps the book steadied—if one reads closely, which most reviewers did not at the time—is the idea of tragedy. And Melville was his lookout high up on the mast, as Warren tried to explain the enduring meanings of the war to the world of the early 1960s. The war had left, said Warren, a "tragic aura"; the tone of his phrase is much like that of Melville's "Supplement" at the end of *Battle Pieces*. Warren fondly quoted Melville's ending: "Let us pray that the terrible historic tragedy of our time may not have been enacted without instructing our whole beloved country through pity and terror." Warren posed the question: "Have we been 'instructed' by that catharsis of pity and terror?" "Sadly," he said, "we must answer no."[71] In 1961, that "no" was not widely popular in the public imagination about the Civil War. Without doubt, it was Warren's riff on the civil rights revolution as a crisis in motion—a current event, fraught with terrifying violence and unknown outcomes, linked inextricably to the blood of the 1860s. And we should continue to ask: How does that "no" sit with us today? Melville's common prayer that Americans would be lastingly, morally instructed by the blood of the 1860s might be described as the most meaningful such plea in the nation's collective memory.

Warren had posed his question and found his mood: the tragic. It is a mood that some found out of place in 1961 and that, for some Americans, is always out of place in the land of hope and new beginnings. He knew he had to qualify his use of the language of tragedy for American readers, accustomed to a triumphal history, especially after World War II, and in a society riven with racial strife and memories that had never been reconciled. "The word *tragedy* is often used loosely," he admitted. But now he wished to "use it in its deepest significance: the image in action of the deepest questions of man's fate and man's attitude toward his fate. For the Civil War is massively that. It is the story of a crime of monstrous inhumanity, into which almost innocently men stumbled; of consequences which could not be trammeled up, and of men who entangled themselves more and more vindictively and desperately until the powers of reason were twisted . . . and virtues perverted." The "crime" was the exponential scale of the war itself, with a "climax drenched in blood but with a nobility gleaming ironically, and redeemingly, through the murk."[72] Indeed, here was that grand "subject" that Melville and Warren, among others, had found for their imagination and their art. Framed in this Melvillian sense of redemptive tragedy, Warren punctured some enduring sentimental aspects of Civil War memory, while also recycling a few others. In the borderland of his mind and imagination, he hoped in the end not to settle a score, but to make the enthusiast think and the partisan to feel something about the other side. For Warren, redemption may have simply meant, in Melville's terms, the ongoing *instruction* of a half-attentive, sentimental American public. Whether he could write a little book that would make the racists blink and look at themselves—well, countless others have tried and failed at that dream.

• • •

Warren loved ambiguity, the things in-between. By temperament and experience, he was, perhaps a bit like Lincoln, an ironist and a border-state pragmatist. He was always in-between himself— between South and North, between history and fiction, between the age of segregation in which he grew up and the age of civil rights in which he matured. Truth had never been clean or obvious to Warren. Yes, he could dislike abolitionists and lampoon a Thoreau or a John

Brown and gush over a Holmes or a Hawthorne. By 1964–1965, he would also, as we shall see, interview and write about dozens of black civil rights leaders and thinkers with a hard-won sympathy and seriousness. But truth—especially about something as vast and transformative as the Civil War's ultimate meanings, or for that matter the essence of good and evil in the human heart—was just too messy and elusive, too easy to confine in easy judgments. Piety was the inner impulse that Americans needed to curb, if not destroy. As Warren aged, it was in his poetry that he kept trying to name and even define truth. But truth was a subject for the ever-squinting eye and fertile imagination, not an intact treasure to be mined and actually found. In a poem called "Truth," Warren almost got there:

> Truth is what you cannot tell.
> Truth is for the grave . . .
> Truth is the downy feather
> You blow from your lips to shine in sunlight.
> Truth is the trick that History,
> Over and over again, plays on us.
> Its shape is unclear in shadow or brightness,
> And its utterance the whisper we strive to catch . . .
> Truth is the curse laid upon us in the Garden . . .
> And is the sun-stung dust-devil that swirls
> On the lee side of God when He drowses.[73]

God never completely slept while determining History's lessons, but neither did the Devil. For Warren, the Civil War was the country's bottomless lode that could be mined for truths and lessons, for the good of the Republic and for the poet of human nature.

Bruce Catton, at his home in Benzonia, Michigan, mid-1970s. American Heritage Center, University of Wyoming.

· CHAPTER TWO ·

A Formula for Enjoying the War

Bruce Catton

There is no sense . . . in being bemused by the backward glance.
The world we have lost might be a nice place to visit but we would
not want to live there.

—Bruce Catton, *Waiting for the Morning Train*, 1972

L IKE Robert Penn Warren, Bruce Catton "soaked up Civil War
history" in his youth at the turn of the twentieth century. For
the man who would become the most prolific and popular historian
of the war, that soaking occurred way up north in Michigan, in the
"cut-over lumber country" almost three hundred miles northwest of
Detroit. Into this "friendly, changeless world," the boy named Charles
Bruce Catton was born in 1899, in the little town of Petoskey. Soon
afterward, the family moved a bit farther south to Benzonia, near
beautiful Crystal Lake. His father, George R. Catton, was the devout-
ly Christian principal of Benzonia Academy, a local private school.
"Benzonia," wrote Catton in his autobiography, "was a good place
to wait for the morning train." Surrounded by books, readers, and
educators, but especially under the spell of some elderly Union army
veterans who spent time waiting for the "morning limited" in the
company of impressionable young boys, Catton cultivated a lasting
and romantic imagination for the Civil War. The veterans "made it
[the war] a living thing," Catton recollected privately in 1954, "which,
in my youthful imagination, had somehow happened . . . just over the
next hill and just five or ten years ago. It was very real and terribly
important, and probably I never got over it."[1]

Indeed, he never got over it. And he made sure, in the Centennial years of the 1950s and 1960s, that his millions of readers never got over it either. Catton almost always wrote about the Civil War with a sense of the epic, and of romance and an appeal to the nostalgic, as well as his own brand of realism. In an autobiographical remembrance in 1972, he acknowledged that he had been raised in a world of small-town innocence, where people actually believed "the big wrongs were all being righted." "My boyhood," he wrote, "was a slice of the town [Benzonia], with its quaint fundamentals greatly magnified." Even "on the eve of the terrible century of mass slaughter . . . of concentration camps and bombing raids, of cities gone to ruin and race relations grown desperate and poisonous, of the general collapse of all accepted values and the unendurable tension of the age of nuclear fission . . . , it was possible, even inevitable, for many people to be optimistic. The world was about to take off its mask, and our worst nightmares did not warn us what we were going to see."[2] No matter what he saw, the boy from Benzonia wrote about America's greatest historical nightmare with lyricism and optimism.

Catton and his childhood friends shared a passion for playing "the Civil War game" that was second only to their love for baseball. In a twelve-acre park in the center of Benzonia, the boys would pretend to be Union army soldiers. They "never lost," he remembered; and sometimes, with "authentic Civil War veterans" looking on, "Johnny Reb died by the . . . battalion before our unerring musketry." But it was the festivities and cemetery rituals for Memorial Day—then called Decoration Day—that left the most indelible impressions on the young boy's memory. With every returning spring and with lilacs blooming in everyone's yard, each family would march behind the veterans to the cemetery and drop their blossoms on or near the homemade monument to the war dead; the old soldiers could not afford to buy an official, factory-produced one. Catton said that, for the rest of his life, he could never see or smell lilacs in bloom without remembering the old men "in blue uniforms with brass buttons and black campaign hats." The future historian of the Army of the Potomac and other

Yankee battalions remembered some of these men by name. There was Elihu Linkletter, "who had lost his left arm in the Wilderness," and John Van Deman, who once told the wide-eyed young Catton he had "been wounded in some battle in West Virginia." Lyman Judson had served in General Philip Sheridan's cavalry, "his horse being shot out from under him." And in 1916, Cassius Judson, who had served in the Atlanta campaign with General William T. Sherman, "went down to Manistee [Michigan] to see *Birth of a Nation*," D. W. Griffith's epic film about white supremacists. Upon returning, Judson answered the teenager's questions about the battle scenes: "Well, it wasn't much like the real thing."[3]

Catton remembered these gray-bearded veterans as "men set apart" by a mystical experience, but also as "pillars . . . of the community" and the "embodiment" of all the values of the small-town America that he would admit was slowly dying: Christian steadiness, patriotism, the "nation's greatness and high destiny," and especially a rock-hard belief in "progress" and the "future." Writing at the time of the Watergate scandal in the 1970s, and, more important, during the depths of America's bloody debacle in Vietnam, Catton saw these Civil War veterans as his lilac-scented wellspring of inspiration. They had actually tramped the fields of those places with "terrible names out of the history books—Gettysburg, Shiloh, Stone's River, Cold Harbor." One of them had even journeyed all the way from Michigan to the fiftieth-anniversary Blue-Gray reunion at Gettysburg in 1913. When someone forgot to send a buggy to pick him up after his long train-ride home, the old man had walked the five miles from the depot to his house outside of town.[4] Catton would have been thirteen, perhaps sitting around the train station or in the town park, when he took in that piece of local lore.

These heroes from E. P. Case Post No. 372, of the Grand Army of the Republic (GAR), were one living source of a Michigan boy's historical imagination and dreams of escape from the stultifying backwater in which he came of age. At least, this was the situation prior to 1916. That year, the local GAR post sponsored a performance by a traveling duet: the "Drummer Boy of the Rappahannock" and his storytelling sidekick. The drummer, a "professional Civil War veteran" who roamed the Midwestern states entertaining audiences for a living, possessed a "set line of patter, memorized and carefully rehearsed." The routine included bad jokes that only the veterans seemed to enjoy, and the playing of "Taps" as well as other military standards on a drum. Their finale was a rousing beating of the drums to represent the sounds of a battle, from a full charge of infantry, to a routed enemy, "down finally to scattered sniping by rear-guard parties—then silence." The awful "racket," Catton remembered, filled the auditorium. But this whole event disturbed the young Catton. "Instead of looking heroic . . . , giants from the magical mist of an age of greatness," he wrote, "they [the veterans] suddenly looked pathetic."[5]

What troubled Catton most was that the elderly drummer boy introduced his performance as the sounds not of 1864 battles but of the present-day struggles on the "Western Front in France." Benzonia was "isolated," Catton remarked, but its citizens "read the daily papers" about World War I. This was 1916, and "Verdun," he said, had no place in the nostalgic gatherings of old Civil War soldiers and their youthful acolytes. For Catton, this disturbing episode was the "pinprick that exploded the toy balloon." Pity now diminished the veterans in his eyes, and that vaunted sense of "permanence" and "progress" which was the lifeblood in his small universe of Civil War lore was "subject to revision."[6] Amid the Cold War culture of the 1950s, and through a penchant for grassroots research and an extraordinary gift for narrative prose, Catton would try to reclaim, even reinvent, that "magical mist" of the Civil War era that he had temporarily lost in 1916. No amount of foolishness and pathos can quite kill the scent of lilacs in May, or the jingling of medals dangling from the breast of an old soldier—especially when the war he represents never quite seems to end and even bigger wars crowd in for comparison.

. . .

When Catton graduated from Benzonia Academy he went off to Oberlin College in Ohio, a school famous for its deep abolitionist roots. He majored in English but left school in his second year, joined the Navy, and served during the final year of World War I. Catton never saw combat and briefly returned to college, only to drop out after his junior year. In time, he publicly embraced the role of celebrated writer as college dropout, even at the school he had abandoned, which gave him an honorary degree in 1956. At twenty-one, he became a journalist, and would always describe himself professionally as a "newspaperman." Catton wrote for papers in Cleveland, Boston, and eventually Washington, D.C., where he emerged by 1939 as a nationally syndicated columnist and analyst for the National Enterprise Association (NEA), a syndicate of the Scripps-Howard newspaper empire. In his early years writing for the *Cleveland Plain Dealer* and the *Boston American,* he moved beyond mere reporting and wrote book reviews, Sunday features, and editorials.[7] Catton learned how to make a deadline and write reader-friendly stories with vivid characters and pungent metaphors.

As early as 1938, Catton was hired by the federal government as a public information officer, initially for the U.S. Maritime Commission. As World War II unfolded, Catton worked as a professional public relations man for the Franklin D. Roosevelt administration, especially on the pivotal and controversial issue of industrial war production. In the spring of 1941, Catton was hired by Robert W. Horton, a fellow Scripps-Howard reporter, as a key member of a growing staff of journalists who would promote FDR's efforts to forge an alliance between government and business in order to produce matériel for the war in Europe. A staunch New Dealer with left-leaning sympathies, Horton built a team of more than fifty reporters and writers to run the information campaign for defense production. Horton ran the effort like a newsroom, issuing hundreds of news releases with minimal spin and a determination to tell the public the truth, as he saw it, about the Nazi threat to the United States and the need for American engagement. The "Division of Information" functioned as an autonomous White House operation, with offices in the newly constructed Social Security Building. By all accounts Catton was one of Horton's "stars," writing countless press releases and giving public talks to local and state press associations. Catton was a very good propagandist, and he believed in the cause. By the fall of 1941, a few weeks before Pearl Harbor, Horton designated Catton the personal press officer for Donald M. Nelson, the presidential "production czar" heading the Office for Emergency Management, which was soon renamed the War Production Board (WPB).[8] Catton served in that position through 1944, and this rich insider experience became the basis for his first book, *The War Lords of Washington*.

The volume was published by Harcourt Brace in 1948, while Catton was still a federal employee. It featured a jaunty, scene-setting narrative style (complete with dialogue) that the author would soon make famous in his Civil War books. By war's end, Catton dearly wanted to become a full-time writer and escape government service. In *War Lords,* he told a story that had a lasting impact on the country's eternal debate over what President Dwight D. Eisenhower would later call the "military-industrial complex." After nearly three years working closely with Donald Nelson at the WPB, serving as his spokesman and speechwriter, Catton was able to tell a gripping cautionary tale of the war-within-the-war between big business and the New Dealers, who not only struggled to win World War II with massive production, but idealistically hoped to reform American democracy by creating more autonomy and power for workers and the "people" in industrial relations. Catton observed what he deemed a "world revolution" not only in the fascist threat to global democracy, but in the potential transformation of the relationship of government to the economy and to common citizens, once victory was won in 1945. But his story chronicles the reform's failure, caused by a "paralyzing fear of change" among the scions of business and industry who "sat in the driver's seat," often as "dollar-a-year men" inside the government. That fear of change, Catton contended, "kept our war from being a people's war."[9]

"Between a business big shot planning a public relations campaign," Catton wrote, "and a government bureaucrat meditating the announcement of a new action program, there is a profound similarity." The trouble was, of course, that they were using similar methods but intended different outcomes. At times, Catton could be frustratingly vague about just what he meant by a "people's war" and what forms the new "democracy" ought to take. But as director of information at WPB, he closely witnessed what he called the "Battle of Washington" and its many warring parties: labor versus management, military brass versus civilian bureaucrats, ultraconservative industrialists versus visionaries like Nelson and even Henry Wallace, former vice president during FDR's third term and commerce secretary in the fourth (Catton worked closely with Wallace as WPB information director). Catton saw himself as a veteran of a "cold bloodless war— a conflict of theories, of ideas, of programs, of orders." He seemed to conclude that, at the end of the day, the war production effort of World War II had sold out the American working class rather than buttressing and empowering it. In 1948, the views he had expressed in *War Lords* landed him in the dock at a Republican-majority congressional hearing, where he vehemently defended the role of the federal information officer: such an official was "not a public relations man," but a "channel" of unvarnished knowledge to the public.[10] Catton the PR man was defending good PR against what he clearly saw as bad PR. This was perhaps useful training and practice for someone who would write solidly researched, increasingly popular histories of America's most divisive event.

Congress may also have sought testimony from Catton because of his biting commentary on how Americans at the beginning of the Cold War had become irrationally "nervous" about "communism." In *War Lords,* he denounced communism as "alien to the dream we have dreamed . . . a threat and a menace." America, he believed, must "limit it, check it, beat it down." And there would be a "showdown" sometime soon with "this present danger." But, he concluded, Americans could not defeat communism with "words" and "dollars" alone; they first had to overcome their "fear of change" at home, win "minds and hearts" in the United States, and broaden their own democracy. Like a populist muckraker, Catton argued that the American fat cats protecting their profits had won out over the common folk, and had weakened democracy as a "revolutionary force" against the communist threat. "We retreated from democracy because democracy means change," Catton argued, "if it means anything worth the life of one drafted sharecropper."[11]

War Lords was picked up by a left-leaning book club, the Book Find Club, in late 1948. That volume, and the political, intellectual, and bureaucratic experience from which it sprang, convinced Catton to try to make a career as a full-time writer. The reviews were good, some calling Catton's writing especially "dramatic" and "provocative," and his story "sad" and "bitter" but "redeemed from cynicism by the author's sense of tragedy and abiding faith in the people." From his eight years' experience deep in the abyss of government propaganda and war production, Catton had certainly learned a great deal about power as a force in shaping history. He also seemed to sharpen, perhaps deepen, his concern for the common man's place in the unfolding of history. As a chronicler of the Civil War, Catton would on occasion be compared to Leo Tolstoy, whose epic novel *War and Peace* was set during the Napoleonic wars. Whether such praise was merited or not, as Catton now turned back to his true love—America's Armageddon of the 1860s, rather than the war of the 1940s—the journalist from Benzonia would have agreed with Tolstoy's formulation: "What is the cause of historical events? Power." And though he would in time become a biographer of Ulysses S. Grant and write tellingly about individual leaders, Catton started his career as a historian agreeing, in all likelihood, with Tolstoy's ringing challenge: "A king is the slave of history. History—that is, the unconscious, common, swarm life of mankind—uses every moment of the life of kings as an instrument for its own ends."[12]

As Catton prepared for his effort to rehabilitate the Northern armies in the Civil War, especially the Army of the Potomac, he collected and read dozens of regimental histories and thousands of pages of the *Official Record of the War of the Rebellion*. He also reached back to his original inspirations and decided he would write the collective story that those Union veterans in his hometown had symbolized. Catton drew upon the overwhelming, chastening experience of World War II that he witnessed indirectly from Washington offices, and threw himself—for the rest of his life—back into days of yore, where he could rekindle old passions and faiths even as he was writing about war as an inevitable, horrible, transformative, tragic, but fascinating beast he had come to love and hate. With time, he would make his readers feel the same ambivalence.[13]

• • •

At the beginning of the 1950s Catton began a very long and successful publishing relationship with Doubleday. *Mr. Lincoln's Army* (1951), *Glory Road* (1952), and *A Stillness at Appomattox* (1954) appeared in rapid succession and, practically overnight, made Catton the most popular and celebrated writer about the Civil War. *Stillness* garnered him the Pulitzer Prize and the National Book Award, massive sales, and a regular place in the Book-of-the-Month Club. Residing in Washington and making daily use of the Library of Congress, Catton found time to write a short biography, *Ulysses S. Grant and the American Military Tradition*, in the famous series published by Little, Brown and edited by Oscar Handlin, a professor of history at Harvard. Handlin wanted writers who could make the biographies in the series "accessible to the common reader," and after reading *Mr. Lincoln's Army*, he asked Catton to capture Grant as "a symbol of the strength and weaknesses of the American common man" and the "dynamic aspect of life in the middle west." Catton, the Midwesterner who had not really wanted to write biography, devoted the final third of his book to Grant's presidential years and, following in the footsteps of the late Lloyd Lewis, helped to launch the modern revival of Grant studies. Handlin wanted Catton in his stable of biographers, but in his detailed editing of the Grant manuscript, he noted that the ending was "too triumphal." This was not the last time someone would characterize Catton's work in such a way, and yet, by the mid-1950s, Catton had become a unique publishing phenomenon in the field of history. How did he do it? What was the "Catton touch," the "Catton secret"?[14]

The "Catton touch" was in the storytelling, and in the author's uncanny ability to plant his flag in the North while writing about the war as a grand, national experience in the ultimate spirit of reconciliation. But his magic, knowingly or not, may have begun where Catton himself began. He decided to write the history of what seemed to be the neglected Northerner, the common Yankee soldier in the most famous and oft-maligned army, the Army of the Potomac—initially losers, but ultimately the big winners. Catton set out to find everybody's loss and then everybody's victory, in his reconciliationist narrative. That he did so through the lens of the Northern enlisted man is an extraordinary achievement of both literary and marketing skill. The South's story of heroic defeat in a noble cause, the Lost Cause tradition, laced with simultaneous denials and embraces of white supremacy, had cried out for a popular counterpart. This was especially the case in the midst of the Cold War and as the Civil Rights Movement took hold in the divided and turbulent South. In the Army of the Potomac, the old veterans whom Catton had known and in whose fading glow he had basked as a youth, Catton found his story. It was the piece of history he most wanted to research and write; but he quickly learned that as the Centennial of the Civil War approached, he had tapped into an expanding public appetite for military honor and glory in the wake of World War II.

As Catton set up a contrast between the beguiling romance and the destructive reality of war in the opening chapter of *Mr. Lincoln's Army*, he drifted back to personal memory. "In the end," he rhapsodized, the Army of the Potomac would become the stuff of "legend, with a great name that still clangs when you touch it. The orations, the brass bands and the faded flags of innumerable Decoration Day observances, waiting for it in the years ahead, would at last create a haze of romance, deepening spring by spring until the regiments . . . became unreal—colored lithograph figures out of a picture book war, with dignified graybeards bemused by their own fogged memories of a great day when all the world was young and all the comrades were valiant." In such long sentences, Catton seduced readers who needed, perhaps demanded, their reality coated with a little romance. It was the 1950s: the economy was booming for the middle class; America had just won the biggest war ever fought; families with automobiles were "seeing the USA in a Chevrolet" as they traveled to historic battlefields; and millions of readers, largely male, and conditioned by their own military experience, were eager for great war stories.[15] Like the works of Francis Parkman in America and Thomas Macaulay in England before him, Catton's works became a kind of national Siren-call into the past, to the scenes of a distant but deeply resonant war.

The three volumes of Catton's original Civil War trilogy could be read as stand-alone books, but they were also connected thematically and chronologically. Few of Catton's readers ever read one without moving on to the next. *Mr. Lincoln's Army* placed its main focus on General George B. McClellan, who built and commanded the Army of the Potomac from August 1861 through the Battle of Antietam in September 1862. Still, the driving force of the narrative was the story of young men from all over the North, whose voices and experiences Catton recovered from regimental histories and collections of letters sent to him by dozens of ordinary citizens. Those common soldiers were heroic, even in defeat, as they were so often badly led by fumbling generals.

The second book, *Glory Road*, is the riveting, bloody story of how

the Civil War became an all-out affair, fought either to sustain an older order or to create a new, redefined country, a struggle from which
neither side could ever "call retreat." *Glory Road* takes the story from
the wintry slaughter at Fredericksburg, Virginia, in December 1862
into the year of Emancipation, through the Battle of Gettysburg in
July 1863, and finally to a subtle, moving conclusion as Abraham Lincoln is about to deliver an address (unquoted, since every reader is
assumed to know it) at a cemetery on that battlefield in November of
the same year. Edward Everett, who on that day spoke for two hours
before Lincoln, is still droning on about Pericles and how the Greeks
commemorated their dead, as Catton describes the scene:

> There were many thousands of people at this ceremony, and among
> them were certain wounded veterans who had come back to see all
> of this, and a knot of these wandered away from the crowd at the
> speakers' stand and strolled down along Cemetery Ridge, pausing
> when they reached a little clump of trees, and there they looked off
> toward the west and talked quietly about what they had seen and
> done there.
>
> In front of them was the wide gentle valley of the shadow of death,
> brimming now in the autumn light . . . and the voice went on, and
> the governors looked dignified, and the veterans by the trees looked
> about them and saw again the fury and the smoke and the killing.
>
> This was the valley of the dry bones, waiting for the word, which
> might or might not come in rhythmic prose. . . . The bones had lain
> there in the sun and the rain, and now they were carefully arranged
> state by state under the new sod.
>
> They were bones of men who had exulted in their youth, and
> some of them had been unstained heroes while others had been
> scamps who pillaged and robbed and ran away when they could,
> and they had died here. . . . Back of these men were innumerable
> long dusty roads reaching to the main streets of a thousand youthful
> towns and villages where there had been bright flags overhead and
> people on the board sidewalks cheering and crying and waving a last
> good-by. . . .

Perhaps there was a meaning to all of it somewhere. Perhaps everything that the nation was and meant to be had come to a focus here, beyond the graves. . . . Perhaps the whole of it somehow was greater than the sum of its tragic parts, and perhaps here on this wind-swept hill the thing could be said at last, so that the dry bones of the country's dreams could take on flesh.

The orator finished, and after the applause had died away the tall man in the black frock coat got to his feet, with two little sheets of paper in his hand, and he looked out over the valley and began to speak.[16]

And in *A Stillness at Appomattox,* to this day probably his most widely read work, Catton narrates the war from the point of view of what was now Grant's army, from February 1864 until the surrender of April 1865, rendered hauntingly and beautifully by Catton in some of his most remarkable prose. Even a modern cynic, appalled by war and its horrors in the twentieth century, could hardly help being seduced by the opening chapter of *Stillness,* which portrays a gala ball held for the officers of the Second Corps of the Army of the Potomac on Washington's birthday, in winter quarters in northern Virginia. Impending doom hangs over the occasion, which is deceptively bright with the fancy dresses of the women, the polished brass and boots of the men, and everyone's awkward attempts to maintain an air of "gaiety." Handsome men in blue had "swords neatly hooked up to their belts" and "wore spurs." "Escorts and guests seemed to make a particular effort to be gay," Catton wrote, "as if perhaps the music and the laughter and the stylized embrace of the dance might help everybody to put out of mind the knowledge that in the campaign which would begin in the spring a considerable percentage of these officers would unquestionably be killed." The dancers "quoted Byron to themselves," Catton continued, "and borrowed . . . the tag ends of implausible poetry describing a bloodless, bookish war. It was born of a romantic dream and it was aimed at glory, and glory was out of date, a gauzy wisp of rose-colored filament trailing from a lost world."[17] Elegiac, and reaching for tragedy: How better to set the scene for the bloodiest campaign of the war than with the sights and sounds of a military ball on the eve of the slaughter? Readers now had to stay with Catton on that road, to see just how much and how irredeemably the notion of "glory" was out of date.

By any measure, *Stillness* is a work of great war literature. If by the 1950s the United States still awaited its Tolstoy of Civil War fiction, it no longer had to wait for one in narrative history. Catton wrote with a matchless sense of both realism and redemptive tragedy. And he found some perfect metaphors for the kind of historical turning point represented in the blood of 1864. Catton described two armies engaged in a confused madness of daily slaughter, moaning and stumbling into the siege of Petersburg by late summer:

> Since May 4 everything that had happened had been part of one con-
> tinuous battle, a battle three months long, with advance and retreat
> and triumph and disaster all taking place together, so that words like
> *victory* and *defeat* had lost their meaning. All that had gone before
> was no more than prelude. The nation itself had been heated to an
> unimaginable pitch by three years of war and now it had been put on
> the anvil and the hammer was remorselessly coming down, stroke
> after clanging stroke, beating a glowing metal into a different shape.

Whether true victory or defeat was even possible Catton left to the rest of the story, but he had a way of projecting those deepest meanings in soft sentences that allowed both sides among his readers to feel a sense of ownership in the outcome of that remorseless hammering on the anvil: "The war had taken on a new magnitude ... but it was moving inexorably toward its end, and when it ended many things would end with it, in the South and in the North as well. Some of these were things that ought to end because they shackled men to the past, and some of them were fit to be laid away in the shadowland of dreams that are remembered forever. ... After that there would be a new beginning."[18]

. . .

Catton's first three books together were a huge commercial success, and stimulated some remarkable fan mail. Such letters reveal a good deal about how and why Catton succeeded in forging such a lasting audience in the Centennial era, as well as about the nature of mainstream, predominantly white Civil War memory in the 1950s. Some readers said they would never forget where they were when they read the ending of *Stillness,* or the description in *Glory Road* of the Iron Brigade marching into its last fight at Gettysburg with its flags waving and the men singing "The Girl I Left Behind Me." Some admitted reading passages out loud to anyone who would listen. Catton's connection with his readers began with his powerful prose, his sense of drama, the storytelling that so many of his fans found to be utter "pleasure" or "thrilling" or "sheer joy." Catton made reading history "exciting" as well as edifying. "Lord God how you can write!" was a typical line in a fan letter. Some would write and say they read "only a few pages at a time so that the book [*Glory Road*] will last longer." In 1955, an old colleague from government service wrote to Catton and swore he had taken all three of the "Army of the Potomac" books to Cuba on a vacation, but instead of seeking "sun, glitter and gaiety," he had lain "in bed for three days . . . to re-read them!" Still, the same correspondent admitted that he "often wondered, just what is the Bruce Catton touch . . . ?"[19]

Catton combined what certainly appeared to be the authority of research (which improved and deepened with time) with a sense of drama that drove this disciplined and prolific writer to produce five books in six years—and then to repeat the same feat in the 1960s. He had a genius for conveying a sense of turning points within the war's shifting stages, as well as in American history as a whole. One example from the Centennial series, in *Terrible Swift Sword,* illustrates Catton's virtuosity—the sheer boldness and captivating audacity of his writing. In the late summer of 1862, the purpose of the war was fundamentally changing as Lee's army was invading northward.

Here we see Catton rewriting Julia Ward Howe's "Battle Hymn of the Republic":

> There was nobility in the idea that there ought to be a peace without victory; yet in August 1862 America's tragedy was that it was caught between the madness of going on with the war and the human impossibility of stopping it. . . . Neither Mr. Lincoln nor Mr. Davis was going to assume anything of the kind. Each man was fighting for a dreadful simplicity. Neither one could describe a solution acceptable to him without describing something wholly unacceptable to the other; neither man could accept anything less than complete victory without admitting complete defeat. Both sides had heard the trumpet that could never call retreat. The peacemakers could not be heard until the terrible swift sword had been sheathed; but the scabbard had been thrown away, and now the Confederacy was carrying the war into the enemy's country.

It is rare that a historian can capture the past with both accuracy and the skills of a dramatist. Jay Monaghan, the official historian of the State of Illinois and no mere pleasure-reader, admired Catton's writing for its "color and accuracy, sentiment without sentimentality." The work was "solid history but as entertaining as a good play, each chapter a new set." And that "final curtain" at Appomattox made readers feel as though they were there "on that momentous April day."[20] Catton greatly relished his fan mail; he had found his stride, and legions of readers who, like Shakespeare devotees seeking the next interpretation of *Hamlet,* impatiently awaited a new book from Catton as the Centennial arrived.

Catton engaged the emotions of his readers as well as their minds. He appealed to their sense of awe, of horror and beauty, of human venality as well as heroism, and even of mystery. The "Catton touch" made many readers weep, and they needed to tell the author about their reaction. The editor-in-chief at Doubleday, Ken McCormick, said Catton's books moved him "to tears many, many times." A World

War II infantry veteran from California found in *Stillness* a kind of "magic"; it made him "literally emotional" about "those trapped Confederates at Appomattox." And in 1956, when Catton published his fourth Civil War book, *This Hallowed Ground* (a work that covered the entire war from the North's perspective), among the many gushing responses was one from a Pennsylvanian who could digest the "inconsolably tragic slaughter" in the book only with "tear-packed sorrow." Catton did not write merely to convey tear-jerking pathos; but he did understand sentiment, and he viewed the Civil War as America's great collective emotional trauma from which it had never fully recovered. In 1957, he responded to the editor of a book society in London who was promoting *Hallowed Ground.* She asked Catton to help a British audience comprehend the depth of American interest in the Civil War. He declared that the Civil War was an integral part of "the emotional subconscious of most Americans. . . . It was the biggest experience this nation ever had, and the average American's response to it is something instinctive, bred in the bone and growing out of a very complex network of national memories and ideals."[21] The complexity of that national memory intrigued Catton endlessly, but as a writer he searched for a certain inspiring common denominator in all of those bones, and he captured it in the music of words.

Catton admitted that he had first tried to use his fascination for the Civil War to write novels, but had failed at it. He loved to portray the Civil War at its deepest levels of cause and consequence as and viewed it as essentially an unfathomable *mystery,* its profoundest meanings perhaps just beyond human comprehension, like the ultimate significance of life or religion. He wrote about the war as though it contained some sort of holy grail for understanding America, as well as for illuminating the human condition. He frequently referred to the war's lasting impact as "mystical," rarely explaining just what that meant in relation to American life. None other than the famous mystery writer Ellery Queen—whose real name was Manfred B.

Lee—wrote to Catton, gushing over the "uncanny evocation" in the historian's prose and the "exquisite unbearability" with which he could write about the "slaughter" on all those "tragic landscapes." Lee seemed enthralled with Catton's power to describe the horror and the macabre attraction of battlefields. And in his own speeches and defenses of his writing, Catton loved to suggest a bit of mystery at the heart of history. "The Civil War," he said in a public address in Kansas in 1957, with "its lights and shadows, its rights and wrongs," ought never to be merely a "swords-and-roses affair to be remembered with loving care." "Underneath," he portrayed the war as a kind of treasure chest containing "the far-off indecipherable cause of it all, the thing that gave it its fearful meaning." That elusive meaning might be found, he mused, in "a few very simple questions: How does the family of sinful man get along with itself? Are all men brothers, or are there grades and classes in the human race? Did we mean it when, in the Declaration of Independence, we said that all men are created equal, or did we have certain crippling reservations?"[22] Simple questions? Catton loved to get close but not too close to those moral ambiguities; and he certainly treated the war with loving care. In the end, he simply invited his readers along on an intellectual and spiritual journey through the Civil War, the story that became the love of his life.

Many traditional academic historians as well as famous writers admired and befriended Catton during his years of success, especially after 1954, when, at the urging of Columbia University historian Allan Nevins, Catton took the job as editor of the newly reconstituted *American Heritage* magazine in New York. Somehow, Catton coped with the demands of the position—the daily grind of soliciting articles, conceiving ideas, and editing the glitzy, popular hardcover magazine about a furtive and triumphant American history—while finding the time to write his own books. Catton also contributed a book review to nearly every issue of *American Heritage*, which soared in readership numbers and brought its editor many kudos. One avid reader of both the magazine and the books wrote to Catton in 1957, declaring that the author connected with his audience like "no one else . . . since Stephen Crane," and that his gift for ending a story was "much like that of Dickens." Nine years Catton's senior, Nevins became a close friend and avid supporter of his nonacademic fellow author; both men were writing multivolume histories of the Civil War aimed at posterity as well as the markets of the Centennial. Nevins's eight-volume classic, *Ordeal of the Union,* poured forth from 1947 to 1971, and the two authors read each other's manuscripts and reviewed each other's books.[23] Nevins ended his career as a resident historian at the Huntington Library in San Marino, California; and although he tried to recruit his friend to join him, Catton remained in New York, with an apartment on the Upper East Side and as a regular among the martini-drinking lunch crowd at the Algonquin Hotel.

Catton craved the respect of his academic and literary peers. Benjamin Thomas, the major Lincoln biographer, thought the secret in "Bruce's technique" was his ability to make the reader "feel the army's heart-throb." Responding to Catton's second Grant book, *Grant Moves South,* in 1960, T. Harry Williams of Louisiana State University meant nothing backhanded when he offered: "I've always admired your talent for evocation. But here you handle stuff that don't 'evoke,' and this is something that particularly appeals to academic people." Catton and David Donald, the rising academic star of Lincoln and Civil War history, exchanged several letters of mutual admiration; Donald warmly reviewed Catton's work in the *New York Times* and invited him to academic conferences. The great literary historian and American Studies scholar at Michigan State, Russell B. Nye, wrote in 1959, enthralled by Catton's work and telling at length the story of his own grandfather, a Civil War veteran, at whose feet Nye had gained his own sense of awe about the past, including "the parade on Decoration Day, the dust and drums." And two notes from Carl Sandburg were among Catton's keepsakes. In 1955, the poet described hearing many friends cherishing *Stillness,* especially the famous television journalist Edward R. Morrow, "their tone of voice and lighted face testifying it is that rare thing, a much loved book." More poetic yet, Sandburg wrote a year later savoring *Hallowed Ground:* "so readable, so companionable, so well-rooted a book." "The book cost," Sandburg observed; "you wrote it in high tension. You were not afraid to have sentences carry music and color. . . . Saludos!"[24] No wonder Catton thought he had found his groove. He felt at times burned out by his intensive writing deadlines, but he planned to stay with the project. Nothing breeds success like success.

Although they admired and even envied him, some historians viewed Catton as a talented popularizer. Not as a gentleman amateur; his research in original sources was far too rich for that scornful epithet. Catton rejected the label "popular" historian, preferring to be accepted as a *writer* whose beat happened to be history. What the subject of history needed, said Catton, was not the "popularizer who invents dialog," not a "breathless, isn't it exciting approach which is keyed strictly to the marketplace." The field, he maintained, needed "craftsmen rather than charlatans." In his National Book Award acceptance speech in 1954, Catton tried to pass himself off as a simple journalist applying his trade on a broader canvas. "A newspaperman is a historian without knowing it," he declared. "He does what the historian does . . . he tries to find out exactly what happened and . . . to tell about it so that people who were not there may know what was going on."[25] He was a craftsman, and a very artful one. With the help of Doubleday, the erstwhile public relations man kept a keen eye on the marketplace.

In 1955, building on the success of the first trilogy and planning a second one to coincide with the Centennial, Catton began an extraordinary collaborative relationship with his research assistant, the historian E. B. Long. Born Everette Beach Long in Whitehall, Wisconsin, in 1919, and generally known as "Pete," he was twenty years younger than Catton and likewise a journalist (he'd spent eight years with the Associated Press). Long had attended Miami University (in Ohio) and Northwestern, but, like Catton, possessed no graduate training in history. Long and Catton were introduced by Ralph Newman, a founding member of the Chicago Civil War Roundtable and the owner of the Abraham Lincoln Book Shop on West Chicago Avenue. In all likelihood, there has never been a more productive and successful writer-researcher team, at least among historians. Long worked primarily from his home in Chicago, aided by his wife and collaborator, Barbara Long. Catton lived in New York, where he edited *American Heritage* and used all of his available time for writing. Doubleday paid Long directly and full-time for at least the first five years of the arrangement (1955–1960), and then, it appears, half-time until 1965, when Long went to work for Nevins as a researcher on a similar basis. Long's title was Director of Research for the Centennial History project.[26]

By any measure, E. B. Long made Bruce Catton possible. Driven by a mathematical as well as interpretive obsession with detail (he tried to provide his boss with material on all sides of a question), Long chased and "gnawed," as he once put it, for the facts about every conceivable aspect of the Civil War, including its political and economic history as well as the main threads of the military chronicle. Long journeyed all over the country to dozens of archives, historical societies, and historic sites. His travel and research itineraries are wearying merely to read. No back road seemed to have been left untraveled, no battlefield or pertinent crossroads untramped, no manuscript collection unexamined. Catton read voraciously and also did original research, but his job was to pull the poetry from the mountains of information. Masses of half-page paper note cards, typed top-to-bottom and margin-to-margin, flowed into Catton's office, accompanied ·often by monthly reports describing the scope of the research. Long's voluminous notes and reports were the sort of stuff one would think only a mass-production efficiency expert could love.[27]

But Catton did love them. Attached to each inch-thick pile of note cards on any given subject is a small index card, on which Catton himself would scrawl a list of a dozen or so of "Pete's conclusions" or "Pete's highlights," with specific page numbers in the notes.[28] From memoirs, diaries, soldiers' letters, government manuscripts, the *Official Record of the War of the Rebellion*, and countless newspapers, Long fed Catton the raw materials and somehow Catton Incorporated kept up with its production schedule. The new models all made it into the showrooms on time—*The Coming Fury* in 1961, *Terrible Swift Sword* in 1963, and *Never Call Retreat* in 1965, the three books covering the period from the political conventions of 1860 and the ensuing secession crisis to the end of the war, the surrenders, and the initial plans for Reconstruction.

Catton and Long both understood quite astutely the language and methods of marketing. In 1960, responding to a graduate student in Florida who had taken Catton's "contribution to American literature" as her research topic and obsequiously sought the author's sense of his own "influence," Catton demurred: "I have no idea." The one thing he knew was that historical writing must be "appealing," and that historians should not "attempt to get the exact and complete truth out of a set of distant facts" at the expense of "the ultimate consumer—the person who is . . . reading what he writes." Early in his relationship with Doubleday, Catton wrote extensive book proposals to his editors in which he stressed his reader appeal. In thumping language, he told Doubleday's managing editor, Walter Bradbury, that *Glory Road* would show how the war was all about "the People themselves, in their capacity as Boys in Blue." The story of the divided nation flowed through the "men in the ranks," he said, and in the end he wanted to tell a story of "just devotion, an eternal blazing flaming mystery." And in *Stillness*, he planned "a story of the army itself, told in terms of the 1864 GI Joe who had to do the fighting." Whatever it took, he said, he would "get the shine and shimmer and color of that oddly romantic army."[29]

Similarly, Long knew that his job was to do research in the archives and trenches, but also to "promote the Centennial" to the larger public. His remarkably detailed monthly reports are nothing compared to his astonishing annual year-end updates and summaries, including careful descriptions of the nature and origins of the project, details of the methods used and hours logged by Long and his wife, access information for file cabinets and safe-deposit boxes, and always a full accounting of exact numbers of all "assets" (items of research) in the operation. Long's reports would have made the supervisors of inventory at General Motors very proud. When Doubleday's publicists produced marketing material for the Centennial series, they trumpeted Long's research prowess nearly as much as Catton's literary reputation; both were part of the same smoothly packaged "syndication," replete with Long's millions of words and thousands of miles traveled, and Catton's formidable sales statistics. Even before the storied collaboration with Catton and Doubleday had ended, Long estimated that he had produced 9.1 million words and 24,000 pages of research from 3,500 sources, for what became Catton's three-volume Centennial history.[30]

As Catton's fame grew, some distinguished historians took note of both his historical acumen and his commercial appeal. In a review of *Two Roads to Sumter*—a book about Abraham Lincoln and Jefferson Davis and the coming of the war, spun off by Catton and his son, William, in 1963—Avery Craven, a dean of Southern historians, wryly remarked: "In spite of the romance and glamour with which Bruce Catton has so richly endowed the Civil War, he now finds it to have been the nation's greatest tragedy. A people predominantly moderate . . . became victims of their times." Implying that Catton did not fully grasp genuine tragedy, Craven suggested that the Cattons' thesis—that both presidents were essentially well-meaning "moderates" trapped by radical historical change—was "just too pat to fit the complexity of the situation." Such complexity, Craven said, "would have spoiled the formula."[31]

The Catton "touch" had become a formula requiring several elements: America's tradition of moderation being ruined by fanaticism, glory enough to go around on both sides, dramatic turns of events on battlefields causing endless suffering for the ordinary soldiers of both armies, a "tragic" bloodletting from which the nation emerged better and stronger, its ideals given a "new beginning." And always, the beautiful, sometimes transcendent if muscular prose. Paul Angle, a prominent Lincoln scholar in Illinois, admired the "inimitable touch" of Catton's language, but admitted that sometimes his "inexplicit words threw a haze over substance." People noticed, though, how the formula had worked so well. Roy Nichols, distinguished historian at the University of Pennsylvania, found Catton's *Hallowed Ground* "reminiscent of . . . Tolstoi in War and Peace"; he admired Catton's ability to make an army such a living thing, as well as his "gift for portraiture." But he simply could not abide the full thrust of Catton's "romanticism." "Catton's inspired writing," argued Nichols, "points out a danger by showing so clearly why so many thousands enjoy this war a hundred years afterwards." Catton had lulled his readers into becoming a vast club of descendants, relishing their grandfathers' "noble task completed after great sacrifice." As the Centennial arrived, Nichols challenged, "should we not do more than vicariously enjoy the war?"[32]

A formula for *enjoying* the war: although Catton himself denied this accusation in numerous forums, legions of devotees who came of age reading his books or who discovered them in their mature years experienced a vicarious, if ennobling *pleasure*—sometimes guilty and often not—in learning about the war. They came to "love" the Civil War in an age when war, with its unfathomable destructiveness, was no longer lovable. Catton offered them young heroes fighting for what they considered right, and willing to sacrifice their lives for something larger than themselves—a story with particular resonance in the Cold War era of inhumane, push-button weapons of mass destruction. His appeal and success in conveying the human face of war were so great that to some commentators his name became a verb. The frequent *New York Times* book reviewer Charles Poore snidely remarked in 1962 that the appeal of Civil War Centennial books may have flattened a bit. "Although many new books about the Gray and the Blue appear, few, these days, achieve brucecattonizing appraisal."[33]

Catton's name, whether he wished this or not, did indeed emerge as a label, a brand that seemed to represent all things popular about the Civil War. In reviews of Catton's Centennial series in the *New York Times*, Orville Prescott only half admired the author as a "literary phenomenon" like no other, calling him the "high priest of the Civil War cult" who possessed a "gift for the specific and concrete" but also for weaving touching "vignettes amid carnage." Charles Poore reserved space to satirize Catton when he needed him, inventing conversations at fictitious gala book award events where Catton would match wits with John Updike, Truman Capote, James Baldwin, or William F. Buckley and his "Yale guests." In a long poem celebrating the year in books in 1960, Poore sighed: "Bruce Catton's Civil War is doing fine. / No matter how you braid them / There are more novels than you ever saw / On rebels and the villains that betrayed them." No matter who the writers were, or in which genre, it had become Bruce Catton's war. And Henry Patrick, a reviewer for the *Wall Street Journal*, captured something important in what appears to be a compliment, when one considers the racial and sectional conflict in 1961. Catton, wrote Patrick, "writes with sympathy and authority. His manner is that of a family elder discussing a quarrel between two favorite grandsons, each of whom seems to have much on his side." The distinguished Yale historian John Morton Blum recalled a conversation with Alfred Knopf circa 1965, when the famous publisher offered this telling comment on the popular historian: "Bruce Catton is the last survivor of both sides."[34]

Some of this criticism, though inevitable, was only partially fair. Lampooned for formulaic popularity, Catton constantly tried to claim that the charge was unfair and to defend his seriousness. In a little book entitled *America Goes to War* (1958), which he fashioned from research for the Centennial series, he warned that the Civil War was becoming a "museum piece . . . set off by heroic attitudes, a strange and somehow attractive never-never land in which our unaccountable ancestors chose to live for four picturesque years." On the one hand, he could say that "there is no particular harm . . . for us to look at it that way," and then adamantly insist that his readers "forget the swords-and-roses aspect, . . . the gloss of romance," and seriously treat the war as "something to be studied, to be prayed over, and at last to be lived up to." Yet despite all his protests and dogged research, his name remained attached to many expressions of Civil War Centennial fatigue. Another *New York Times* reviewer lamented in 1961 that for Christmas-gift seekers eager to "indulge the Civil War buffs . . . there is, of course, Bruce Catton—year in, year out, there is always Bruce Catton somewhere in the book stalls."[35]

One week Catton might want to banish the mystery, pathos, and sentimentalism he evoked, and the next he might stir their intoxicating brew. Among his speeches in manuscript is one defining the characteristics of a Civil War "buff," whom he described as one who must read a good number of books on the war, join a local "roundtable," get in a car and visit the battlefields, study campaign maps, and otherwise torment his spouse and family with his incurable obsession. Catton wanted buffs to be serious about the war's importance and legacy, but he did not hesitate to feed their addiction when necessary. He was very much in his element when he spoke to Civil War roundtables and other worshipful public groups, especially when his subject was the "boys in Blue" (the Union armies and their common soldiers) or the overall meaning of the war, which allowed him to declare American history generally a "unique" passage for humankind, and the Civil War in particular a glorious "mystery: a flaming, heaven-sent mystery, a strange business which comes out of men grappling bare-handed with fate, a complex and inexplicable affair in which ordinary human beings do, finally, confront destiny."[36] Why bother to try to explain the unexplainable?

Catton, it seems, loved to play with notions of "destiny" and "fate" and triumphal "progress." In an address in Schenectady, New York, in 1956, with nary a hint of irony, he tried to speak for the whole happy land. "We," he boldly announced, "have always had the feeling that life in America began to the sound of trumpets. Somewhere behind us we feel there was a golden dawn."[37] One wonders if Catton's adoring white audiences at these gatherings, some of whom were veterans of the World Wars, understood just what he may have meant by such rhetoric. Some mixture of a little bit of intellect, nationalism, and spirituality went a long way in Cold War America. The doctrine of progress, bone marrow to American civil religion, needed history, especially the Civil War, on its side now that the Russians had the A-bomb too. And no one likely asked the mother of the murdered boy Emmett Till, or the Little Rock Nine, or the weary, sore-footed women who held together the Montgomery Bus Boycott whether they felt part of Catton's "heaven-sent mystery" or his Civil War–induced, all-encompassing "we."

.   .   .

Despite the commercial phenomenon that Catton and Doubleday created, his work tapped into more than mere romance. His fan mail demonstrates that most of his readers did not consider themselves mere pawns in a literary commodity exchange. His books put readers in emotional touch with their fathers and mothers, grandfathers and grandmothers, uncles and great-uncles who had fought in or otherwise endured the war. Intended or not, this filial connection was part of the Catton "touch." A woman from North Carolina wrote to Catton after reading *Hallowed Ground*, admiring his "not unduly partisan account of what occurred on the Yankee side." She was almost apologetic about "Lost Cause . . . sentimentality and even venom in uncivilized minds." But she warned Catton that on race relations, "don't expect the millennium soon," and informed him that her Confederate grandfather had been "killed at Petersburg only a few short months before Appomattox." Catton's readers were by no means all male. After reading *Stillness,* an Ohio woman reported that she had never taken "such a personal interest" in a book, in the war's "beautiful suffering"; her "mother's cousin" had ridden in "Sheridan's cavalry," and she herself was "falling in love" with the victorious general who had conquered the Shenandoah Valley late in the war. From Florida came a missive from a "thrilled" reader who had "relived the Civil War" continually after talking to his "eight grand uncles . . . five Northern, three Southern," who had fought in the conflict. Another Floridian, a "true Civil War fan," thanked Catton for helping him at last to know the grandfather he had never met, "6th Wisconsin, Iron Brigade." And a deeply moved Massachusetts man wrote that he had just read *Stillness* with the diary of his great-grandfather (32nd Massachusetts Infantry) by his side; he even thought one of Catton's scenes came from the diary, and quoted it for the author.[38]

Catton had harnessed a good portion of those millions of Americans who still knew the Civil War as intimate family history, who had absorbed its lore from parents and grandparents. He gave them a new language for retelling an old story, revisiting documents and photographs, and singing the old songs again. Homer T. Bone, a judge on the U.S. Court of Appeals in San Francisco, found *Stillness* "thrilling but sad." Bone had "lived among" many Union veterans in his youth, especially his father, who as a member of the 7th Indiana Regiment had been captured, imprisoned, and exchanged, and had fought in the Army of the Potomac until the end of the war. And his mother had lost her first husband and two brothers, all killed in action. If your own father had felt the "stillness" at Appomattox and your mother's two brothers had not survived to feel it, Bruce Catton was telling your own family's history.

And then there was Clarence Foster of Southampton, New York, who thanked Catton for giving him "the feeling of actual participation." Even more, he informed the author that an "incident" he had narrated—"of a Union cavalryman dining with a colored family at Lebanon," credited to the "Reminiscences" of one Alonzo Foster—

was the work of his own father. As Foster read Catton, he surrounded himself with personal mementos: "Dad's . . . cap, with two bullet holes thru it, the canteen which his comrade Harry Sharp took from his own shoulder and hung around Dad's neck when he was wounded, the belt he wore and the bullet which was taken from his hand at the field hospital." And before closing, Foster referred to Catton's use of the idea of "Byronic" language exchanged at that officers' ball in the opening scenes of *Stillness.* His father had also left him a volume of Byron's poems, confiscated from a "negro cabin" (slaves had taken it from their evacuated master, according to the father), near Williamsburg, Virginia, during the Peninsula campaign in May 1862.[39] Catton had struck a mother lode of more than mere nostalgia. In the 1950s and 1960s, millions of Americans still felt intimately and elementally connected to the blood and sacrifice, the place names and stories, of the 1860s. In narrative that often sings as it informs, Catton became their personal troubadour.

But he was no mere entertainer. Appointed by President Dwight Eisenhower in 1957, Catton was one of the original members of the unwieldy and ultimately controversial Civil War Centennial Commission. Among a large assortment of congressmen, senators, and businessmen, Catton joined only three other historians, Allan Nevins, Bell Wiley, and John A. Krout. The commission—initially under the leadership of superpatriots and racists like Ulysses S. Grant III, pro-Confederates like Karl S. Betts, and a Virginia congressman, William Tuck—ran aground over and over with its planning for an intersectional celebration, complete with battle reenactments and minimal attention to the story of Emancipation and its legacy. With time, Nevins, Catton, Wiley, and a younger Southern historian named James I. Robertson played ever more important roles, especially as spokesmen and public speakers, in the effort to impart a more national and inclusive tone to the commemoration. All, however, despite good intentions, were white, and that fact continued to disappoint African Americans, who wanted a place for their story in the Centennial.

Catton ultimately refused to countenance commemorative activities that used the Civil War to thwart the Civil Rights Movement and sustain segregation. He did so, by and large, as a racial moderate who continually tried to use his writing and lecturing to forge a sense of the war with glory enough on both sides and long-term racial progress for the entire country.[40] Catton insisted that Civil War memory should unite the country, and he considered such unity to be a major function, indeed a mission, of his work.

As the Yankee historian and household brand name for Civil War enthusiasm, Catton performed a North-South balancing act that often came with mixed messages. He seems to have kept some readers guessing as to his partisanship. "I still can't determine," wrote a South Carolinian approvingly, "whether your heart is Yankee, Rebel, or border state Marylander!" A Georgian who descended from a slaveholding family that was solidly Confederate, and who was a former colleague from the newspaper days, said he had read no writer "half as fair" as Catton in showing the "abuses and excesses on both sides." Clifford Dowdey, the Richmond-based Southern novelist-historian, who wrote popularly as a partisan Lost Cause counterpart to Catton, carried on an extended correspondence with his Yankee friend, complete with humorous intersectional rivalry and banter, as well as musings about baseball and football. But Dowdey did admit that Catton had won over some white Virginia diehards, staunch supporters of the Confederate States of America. "You would be gratified in this CSA citadel," he said, "to know of the deep response to your work from devout neo-Confederates who would never before read a line by a non-Southerner." Only half pulling Catton's leg, Dowdey admitted he "did not aspire" to his friend's "objectivity," but informed him: "yours was the first time I was ever moved by the enemy's feelings at Sharpsburg."[41] Much of Catton's success stems from the fact that he ultimately represented the Civil War as an intersectional, mutual tragedy with plenty of heroes on both sides and no real true human villains, only the mysterious evils embedded in the forces of history or human nature itself. This was the stuff of epic, America's own *Iliad*—a moving, bracing, if bloody rebaptism of a better America now struggling to sustain its superpower leadership and survival in the Cold War. Catton seemed powerfully motivated by the idea that America needed a redemptive history of its most divisive event that would ultimately reconcile and unite it.

Catton's magic knew no geographical boundaries. A great story is a great story. While writing book after book from a Union point of view, and at least at first from largely Northern sources, Catton crafted a beguiling narrative of common-soldier valor with equal glory on both sides. He always stressed that the war had left 600,000 dead Americans, not just more than 300,000 dead Yanks. When answering fan letters that questioned his loyalties, he frequently included sincere statements about trying "to see both sides." In a typical response from 1955, he declared himself a "Northerner, but it does seem to me that I can be just as proud of Southerners, as brave and devoted Americans, as the Federals." Catton thought the "Federal side was right," he concluded, "but I don't feel any need to let my own blood pressure rise over it at this late date."[42] "Catton's war"—part of the formula—was a national, Cold War–era, reconciliationist spirit, breathed into his legions of readers via the sheer beauty and mystical power of the storytelling.

Catton did not see the war as merely a raucous, manly outing that had taken place in an earlier, uncomplicated time. He believed it was *about something* profound and enduring. In his one book-length treatment of Civil War causation, *The Coming Fury* (1961), Catton drew upon an older scholarly interpretation, arguing that the Union had dissolved and the war had ensued because "politics lost its flexibility," and "emotional . . . stiff-necked and obstinate" politicians had lost all ability to compromise. He flirted with the old "needless war" interpretation, first fashioned by "revisionist" historians in the 1930s and 1940s who blamed a "blundering generation" driven by blind ideological and sectional partisanship. In a Cattonesque sentence, he nodded to this viewpoint without fully endorsing it: "The story of 1860 is the story of a great nation, marching to the wild music of bands, with flaring torches and with banners and with enthusiastic shouts, moving down a steep place into the sea."[43]

But Catton had also read the post–World War II historians and adopted much of their sense of the Civil War as an "irrepressible conflict." He declared over and over that the deep roots of the war lay in the "argument over slavery," which was usually couched in an almost ubiquitous and sometimes frustratingly vague use of the term "tragedy." Without doubt, Catton saw slavery as the war's central cause—in the long and short term. Southern leaders of secession, he argued, resolved that the "institution which Southern society lived by" (slavery) must be preserved at all costs. Yet, oddly, he still maintained that the secessionists' "motives," the "fated" reasons "why" they bolted from the Union, "remain riddles to this day." Here was his confounding sense of mystery again, muddling an otherwise careful interpretation of a profound historical question. Catton and Robert Penn Warren were working in the same vein of fate, tragedy, and the nature of history. But the Michigander did not quite probe to the same depths as the Kentuckian. Human motives are always "mixed," Catton said. Hence, his contradictory conclusiveness in *The Coming Fury:* "None of the many separate decisions which brought war to America in 1861 is wholly explicable."[44] If one repeats often enough that the Civil War was not entirely "explicable," then it becomes so, and no one or no thing in particular is ever responsible. Fate is a great and powerful literary device; but sometimes it can mean everything and nothing at all, and it can be the perfect slippery substance of healing by denial. Declaratively, Catton instructed his readers that slavery was *the cause* of the war; and in the next breath he let them lamely look away from that confounding "riddle," so that they could more vividly feel as well as understand their national epic.

When it came to confronting the power of the Lost Cause tradition, thriving and lethal in the midst of the Civil Rights Movement, Catton almost took on the role of national literary reconciler-in-chief. Reviewers often criticized this element of Catton's work, especially in *The Coming Fury*, even as they unwittingly revealed their envy of the author's ability to "ring up sales on cash registers." "No villains walk the stage in *Coming Fury*," wrote Rembert Patrick. "Fire-eater and rabid Republican, Southern moderate and restrained Northerner wear heroic faces. Villainous slavery lurks in the background, but that bygone institution cannot hurt the sales of a Civil War epic." Patrick did not quite capture Catton's own personal way of acknowledging slavery at the center of the war's causes and consequences. *The Coming Fury* contains a forthright, even moving discussion of the horrors of the Atlantic slave trade—a portrait in which Catton folds blacks into the universal category of "immigrants" along with every other ethnic group. They did not come as "volunteers," and their voyages were "worse—fearfully, unspeakably worse"—than those of other groups. Their slavery was "comparatively benign," but "still slavery." These strokes seem to come right out of old "plantation school" histories, but they also anticipated the later work of such scholars of the black experience as Nathan Huggins and Peter Wood, who considered African transplantation into the Americas through an "immigrant" paradigm.[45]

In planning for the Centennial trilogy as early as 1955, Catton instructed E. B. Long to assemble "just about everything we can get on the underlying slavery and race prejudice issues." His private letters to Long reveal not only a research plan, but an overall point of view about American race relations. "I want to present this whole slavery issue as basically part of the racist problem," he informed his researcher, "and to show how it was related to the general Ku Klux spirit. . . . I am not altogether clear on how this ought to be done, but . . . we need to have a pretty thorough grounding in the widespread feeling of prejudice and racial superiority in America around 1860."[46]

He was already a master of narrative military history; now, within his limits, Catton strove to be a scholar of race as he persistently tried to link past and present.

In a speech on a college campus in Kansas in 1957, Catton expressed his conception of race and slavery in Civil War history about as explicitly as he could. Seeking what the war "really meant," he declared all possible causes—agrarianism versus industrialism, aristocratic tradition versus equalitarianism, tariffs, states' rights—subordinate to the all-encompassing "race problem." "We lived, to be blunt about it," asserted Catton, "in the 1860s, by a philosophy which unhappily has not yet disappeared—the philosophy of pure racism." Catton captured in firm strokes how the war for Southern independence on one side, and preservation of the Union on the other, evolved quickly into a thoroughly practical effort by the North to destroy slavery as a means of conquering the Confederacy and winning the war. The necessities of total war made the racist Union soldier aware that "he had allies—black folk," who helped him to win, on and off battlefields. And this grand, unintended result of the destruction of slavery was the result not of "any lofty pronouncements," but of the sheer "fog of war" and the power of events. Forthrightly, Catton considered Emancipation's legacies to be the "profound . . . unfinished business" of the war—and "we have not done too well at the job since then." In a point of view that fits neatly with almost all modern, liberal visions of the conflict's meaning to this very day, Catton gave to this "tragedy" the status of a Good War, which left a lofty "heritage" that "did at least commit us to the attempt to solve the race problem." And he did not lay racism merely at the feet of modern Southerners; "if Little Rock appalls us, so does Levittown," and other points north, he said, where too many people still "think the word 'Negro' is properly spelled with two 'g's."[47]

But in the long run, Catton's approach to race and slavery seemed to result from an odd mixture of serious engagement, selective reading and research, and a sense that such questions were preliminaries to the main event: the epic military narrative of countless ordinary, primarily white soldiers swept up in a death struggle they only half understood. In a speech to Oberlin alumni in December 1956, Catton argued that the war, therefore the country, "destroyed slavery almost entirely as a by-product of its effort to do something else . . . despite the gospel Oberlin had been preaching." In the end, Catton told those Cold War liberals from his alma mater, "slavery was destroyed simply because it was in the way." Catton's discussion of slavery—in books and speeches—gives some attention to blacks generally, but virtually none to black Civil War leaders. He appears to have hardly known about Frederick Douglass, and though he knew full well of the participation of black troops, they are not humanized in the same manner or to the same extent as the men of the Army of the Potomac. After acknowledging that the Civil War simply would not have happened but for the presence of blacks and their enslavement, Catton could conclude: "Since he was not allowed to talk, the Negro did not complain much . . . but the business was disturbing to other people because it was obvious that slavery was morally wrong and everyone knew that things morally wrong could not endure." *The Negro did not complain? Everyone knew?* Dudley T. Cornish, a historian at Kansas State College, and the author of the 1956 book *The Sable Arm: Negro Troops in the Civil War, 1861–1865,* wrote to Catton and challenged him to take more notice of the role of black soldiers in the war, both in his books and in *American Heritage* articles. Cornish criticized Catton for his comment in the magazine that, on the topic of the Civil War, "very few facts of any real consequences still remain to be dug up." Catton wrote back, admitting he had neglected black troops, a subject he deemed "quite new." This apparent ignorance of the antebellum slave narratives was actually a perfect representation of mainstream America's broad ignorance of the African American experience generally. Frederick Douglass's now famous 1845 *Narrative* came back into print after nearly a century only in 1960, the very year Catton finished writing *The Coming Fury.*[48]

. . .

The Civil War had found its place, and its popular voice in Catton, in the midst of Cold War consensus. To the overwhelming majority of Americans at the beginning of the Centennial, if American history contained black people, they were still largely voiceless and invisible, despite the roar of contemporary events across the South from Greensboro to Birmingham. One might say a kind of fault line lay underneath the epic Civil War portrayed in Catton's books and in popular culture by the early 1960s—a fracture waiting to produce quakes and tremors with demystifying impact. It was all a matter of forcing people to dial their ears to a different frequency. By will and by inertia, and under the numbing influence of a powerful and lingering Lost Cause tradition, most readers of Civil War books could not yet hear the new sounds from their past.

Catton and the Centennial commemorations he became associated with had fierce critics on the left, and especially among blacks. Attacks on the commercial excesses of the Centennial often targeted Catton. In the *Nation,* in 1960, Dan Wakefield lampooned the amounts of money spent by state and federal commissions, as well as magazines and television, in "planning Blue-Gray extravaganzas" for entertainment as the Civil Rights Movement ripped the fabric of American society. Record companies intended to "assault our ear drums from hi-fi and jukebox," mused Wakefield, "with everything from 'Just Before the Battle, Mother' to rock'n'roll variations on the Rebel yell." "Soon," he predicted, there would be "a meeting at the summit between [popular bandleader] Mitch Miller and Bruce Catton." After chastising the national Commission for ignoring Emancipation in their planning, Wakefield ridiculed a piece Catton had published in *Life* magazine, "End of the Gallant Rebs," in which he gushed about the prowess of Confederate soldiers, especially their "savage, inspired ferocity . . . almost unstoppable when . . . making an attack," and their "dogged endurance . . . on the defensive." Such language, Wakefield said, sounded like "a pre-game story of the Syracuse football team on the eve of the Cotton Bowl." And in Catton's hands, concluded Wakefield, the "Civil War, if we aren't careful, may replace night baseball by 1965."[49]

Occasionally, Catton's books received blistering reviews by those unwilling to abide any sentimentalizing of the Civil War. Catton, wrote Anthony West in a *New Yorker* critique of *Hallowed Ground*, "does not care much for precision of thought or language"; he "likes to fatten the bare record of events with drama and intensity." With long quotations from some of Catton's vague if beautiful flourishes of language, West accused the author of forcing "mystical value . . . and a purpose to give meaning and dignity to everything in the war." In *Hallowed Ground*, Catton writes of members of the Fifth Corps of the Army of the Potomac who celebrated their realization that the war was over by lighting candles, putting them in the barrels of their rifles, and marching through their camp at night. Catton cannot resist such pathos, and lurches for its meanings: "But for the moment the lights still twinkled, infinitely fragile, flames that bent to the weight of their own advance, as insubstantial as the dream of a better world in the hearts of men; and they moved to the far off sound of music and laughter. The final end would not be darkness. Somewhere, far beyond the night, there would be a brighter and stronger light." In disgust, West wondered "what in thunder this brighter light is supposed to be," other than a "shoddy rhetorical device." Whatever Catton's popularity, and perhaps because of it, West portrayed Catton as a writer who could not "outgrow" his own "sentimentality," and who had converted the slaughter of thousands of Americans into a lucrative "consoling legend."[50]

Most of Catton's legions of fans had probably never read such a withering critique, although as a New York intellectual himself, Catton surely had. He likely did not see the columns about himself in African American newspapers. An editorial in the *Baltimore Afro-American* in 1958 took issue with a speech Catton had delivered in which he paid tribute to "Lee" and the "ragged Confederates" who had never "asked for anyone's forgiveness" and only sought "understanding" of their cause. "We don't think there was ever any misunderstanding," declared the black editor, "about what the Confederates were trying to do. . . . They tried by the force of arms to keep a large segment of people in human bondage so they could exist in luxury off the fruits of their labor." Accusing Catton of "maudlin sentimentality," the Baltimore journalist portrayed him as "hypnotized by his own writings." "The world fully understands the architects of the Confederacy," concluded the *Afro-American*'s editor, as well as "their descendants who are trying to hold back the clock with their massive resistance schemes." Catton hated such associations, but his public utterances honoring the Lost Cause in the name of national cohesion landed him justifiably in that company. His name was used as well by the black poet Sam Cornish to define a part of America's racial pain through parody:

> My white father my white old man stares over the color line at me
> All of his children are gathered here come today
> Their brown and auburn faces their olive skin and green eyes
> Their hustling jungle laughter have no shame and smile
> At the whites gathered here they think of Bruce Catton
> And see the sabers glare I think of my Irish grandfather's fiery
> white hair.[51]

Catton never seemed to grasp that in the wake of *Brown v. Board of Education of Topeka* (1954), which banned the segregation of public schools, and in the cauldron of the civil rights struggle, most African Americans had little tolerance for the "mystic power" of the Civil War to fashion sectional and racial peace.

· · ·

Catton tried his own hand at poetry during the Centennial. In December 1960, *American Heritage* published "Names of the War," a long prose poem in which Catton tried to imagine how nondescript place names all over America, where "nothing ever happened . . . except . . .

springtime plowing . . . corn-huskings and barn-raisings," had been remade by soldiers' "postmarks on the letters" into new "names that would echo in American life forever afterward." The poem was partly an homage to the Civil War buff's interior landscape. But it was also a moving testament to the withering, haunting grief of war when the real bodies and names of young men could be associated by their loved ones only with places they wished to forget, "names that meant fear and heartache and undying loneliness." "Sharpsburg and Spotsylvania . . . Chickamauga and Gaines Mill . . . Gettysburg, Corinth, Manassas" were, wrote Catton, "quiet names of doom, stamped on soiled envelopes, going across all of America, weaving a crimson thread into the nation's memory."[52] For anyone familiar with the war's history, the names of Civil War battle sites do still resonate with Catton's sense of epic tragedy. And in prose or poetry, Catton's writing demonstrates how acutely he understood the fundamental connection between place and historical memory.

By the 1960s, Catton was in a sense trapped by his fame. Appointed to various literary societies and distinguished writers' clubs, and invited to special occasions at the White House by presidents Lyndon Johnson and Richard Nixon, Catton became a celebrity as he maintained a staggering output of writing and lecturing. In 1954 he became enmeshed in planning a CBS television documentary series on the Civil War; at the same time, he was writing weekly columns for the *Los Angeles Times,* mostly short dramatic vignettes about military history or the westward movement, but also sometimes an homage to a poet like Stephen Vincent Benet, whom Catton adored. His journalistic writings, as opposed to his books of narrative history, often seemed to have quite different purposes and divergent tones. The newspaper columns were laced with the American doctrine of "progress," maintaining that American history uniquely "has always been a moving *toward* something." To call Catton a voice of American exceptionalism in the midst of the Cold War is an understatement. In the *Los Angeles Times* columns, as well as in *American Heritage,* consumers could also order their very own Bruce Catton–designed "'See America' Travel Plan," complete with Bruce's thirty favorite "places of American history" to visit on family vacations.[53] Simultaneously, Catton wanted Americans to engage and learn from the civil rights revolution occurring in their midst, while he and his publishers provided one way after another to escape the disorder of that revolution into the more orderly, absorbing displacement of Civil War history.

Catton conducted an extensive interview with President Eisenhower, whose retirement home was at Gettysburg; and President Gerald Ford, who hailed from Catton's home state of Michigan, honored him with the Presidential Medal of Freedom. In 1957, Harvard University gave the college dropout an honorary degree with the citation: "The spell of his words brings to life half-forgotten moments of our nation's agony and heritage." In January 1965, along with Allan Nevins, Catton was one of only two historians among fifty artists given special invitations to Lyndon Johnson's inauguration. And a year later, President Johnson chose a passage from Catton's most recent book, *Never Call Retreat,* to read to a group of twenty congressional leaders. The president chose the moment when Abraham Lincoln decided to make his own personal decision about war strategy against all manner of contradictory counsel and criticism—and Johnson did so as a way of declaring his own path of escalation in the Vietnam War.[54]

As Catton's prose was being read by presidents at the White House, to buttress policy or perhaps merely for moral and emotional strength in crises, his royalties and paperback book club deals made him a brand-name author for Doubleday. In 1960, Catton even found time to write some 60,000 words of narrative for *American Heritage*'s extraordinary, bestselling *Picture History of the Civil War,* a work with an initial print run of 300,000 copies, splendid artwork and original maps, and, most striking of all, special photographs taken at battlefield sites on the date and at the hour each battle occurred. "Being there" had taken on new meanings in the Kodak age of heritage tourism. Prior to Ken Burns's 1990 television documentary on the Civil War, no other source combining well-crafted narrative with visuals had ever lured as many Americans into the web of fascination with the war as the 630-page *Picture History.* Catton had already been the key figure in an unprecedented publishing phenomenon. By the eve of the Centennial, before the new trilogy had even appeared, Catton's first four Civil War books had sold, in nine years, a total of 214,000 copies, and that figure did not even include his first two Grant books and a very popular work for young readers, *Banners at Shenandoah.*[55] Catton was the face and voice of Civil War history, and his sales were soon to increase many times over.

As Catton aged, a certain quaintness crept into his many interviews and relationships. He carved his own collection of wooden Civil War soldiers, and in a 1955 *Life* magazine profile he could be seen earnestly hovering over a diorama displaying them. In the late 1950s, a distinguished team of authors—a "Who's Who" of American historians that included John Morton Blum, Arthur M. Schlesinger, Jr., C. Vann Woodward, Edmund Morgan, and Kenneth Stampp—courted Catton to write the chapters on the Civil War and Reconstruction era for their American history textbook, *The National Experience,* to be published by Harcourt, Brace. According to Blum, that courtship (which proved unsuccessful) required frequent martini-fueled lunches with Catton at the Algonquin Hotel in New York. As Blum tells it, Catton would greet him by spilling out a pocketful of musket balls he had recently retrieved from some recent Civil War battlefield visit.[56] The successful college-dropout author cherished the friendships and recognition of the famous academic historians, but he had already outdistanced them all in royalties and did not need the textbook job.

Catton often commented on the fact that his years of writing about the war made him feel like a member of those Union armies. When Bill Moyers asked him in a television interview if he ever "felt like" he was "living much of [his] life in the last century," Catton replied: "I get mixed up occasionally, yes. I've caught myself speaking of myself as a veteran of the Civil War. You know, I remember what it was like on such and such a campaign." When Moyers inquired about what side Catton had fought on, he answered: "Usually the Union side. Although I occasionally get over on the other."[57] The historian had expressed more than mere humor; he had spent almost twenty-five years as a Yankee providing the narrative poetry to reconcile both sides.

Given his popularity as a kind of reconciler-in-chief during the Centennial, it is remarkable how warmly Catton embraced the Lost Cause and what he approvingly referred to as the "Confederate Legend." To the end, Catton would give with one hand and take with the other, his method often depending on his audience. He would write to one Southern woman correspondent, saying that he could "sympathize very deeply" with Confederate traditions and memories, and then write to another woman in California that everyone must abandon the "white-pillared mansion legend" of American history. In a speech to the New Jersey Historical Society in May 1961, Catton angrily condemned recent attacks on black civil rights activists in Alabama. "Neanderthal types with flecks of foam on their lips who meet buses with lengths of gas pipes in their fists," he charged, "bring shame on the name of America. We might as well stop trying to find a comfortable middle ground half way between the ideas of Abraham Lincoln and Adolf Hitler. There simply isn't any such place." In a speech at Berea, Kentucky, in March 1965, as the Centennial mercifully waned, Catton delivered a full-throated (for him) expression of how issues of race were thrown into bold relief by the poignancy of Civil War anniversaries in the midst of the Civil Rights Movement. He linked Sherman's U.S. Army of 1865 marching through Georgia and South Carolina with the current deployment of U.S. troops to protect the participants on the famous Selma-to-Montgomery march of 1965. The Civil War wrought a "revolution," declared Catton; "it destroyed slavery and made the Negro a free person," and the nation was "still grappling with the change."[58] Then, for his eastern Kentucky audience, Catton narrated in gripping detail the surrender at Appomattox, providing elegiac drama, martial heroism, and honor for the defeated in just the right mixture to keep the Confederate legend flourishing.

That same year, 1965, in an essay entitled "The End of the Centennial," Catton threw his arms around the Lost Cause. As he reflected on the exhausting and turbulent Centennial period, he marveled that any nation could commemorate a *civil* war so openly and thoroughly at all. "We rallied around both flags at once," he wrote approvingly. Then, in language that seems astonishing today, Catton said: "The memory of our Civil War has not been a divisive force in this country. On the contrary, it has been a source of unity—something that ties us together and gives us a new depth of mutual understanding." For helping to forge all this "unity," Catton gave much credit to Grant and Lee and the nature of the surrender at Appomattox. They helped to give birth to the "Confederate legend," Catton rhapsodized, which had "grown . . . until now it is a possession of the entire country." He called the deep threads of the Lost Cause "a mighty omnipresent force in the land"—rooted in Lee as Christian hero in defeat and in the "incredibly gallant, heroic long-suffering mortal" Confederate soldier, "who triumphed over . . . everything except the force of superior numbers." Could Civil War memory drip with more pathos than this? "In all seriousness," concluded Catton, "this legend of the Lost Cause has been an asset to the entire country"; and in the end, it "saved us."[59]

One might be aghast that Catton could reach such a conclusion in 1965, the year after the murders during "Freedom Summer" in Mississippi, and the turbulent but historic passage of the 1964 Civil Rights Act. These were startling sentiments from a writer who repeatedly declared his sympathy with the aims of the Civil Rights Movement. Catton's understanding of the Lost Cause, though, was not rooted in research; it was rooted in a rather barren but fully mainstream understanding of African American history and the history of race relations. His Lost Cause was the one that Southern partisans had so often peddled publicly—a benign cluster of myths about waging a noble crusade, upholding tradition against rapacious modernity, defending womanhood and home, and maintaining the ideal of soldiers' undying valor in holy defeat. What Catton did not grasp was just how much the Lost Cause "legends" had become an aggressive racial ideology in the late nineteenth and early twentieth centuries, fueling the virulent white supremacy at the base of the legal and social structure of Jim Crow America.[60]

As late as 1974, in his interview with Moyers, Catton unblinkingly celebrated how the Lost Cause had been "enshrined in Northern memory as well." "Here's the point," he told Moyers. "The undischarged emotions, the tremendous emotional tension that was left in the South . . . discharged itself through that legend—that what might otherwise have been enduring bitterness, and hatred, and violence, went off that way." Catton frequently waxed eloquent about the Confederate Lost Cause as a positive force, either unaware of or denying the thousands of lynchings, riots, and other horrors in America's violent racial history. This irony embedded in Catton's misunderstandings of the Lost Cause is a telling measure of mainstream thought about Civil War memory in the 1960s, as well as an indication of the crooked paths we have traversed to reach new understandings fifty years later. At the end of the 1965 essay about the demise of the Centennial, Catton did assert that Americans "ought to start listening to the Negro." After all, he said, "the Negro was what the war was about, somehow." In such Cattonesque words, the only things left for all to contemplate as the Centennial faded were "memories of a great and tragic experience."[61]

Catton's warmth for the Lost Cause, and his fuzzy vagueness in the use of the idea of "tragedy," provoked some bitter criticisms. In 1972, one correspondent wrote admiringly about Catton's memoir, *Waiting for the Morning Train*, with one exception: "I strongly disagree with the thesis that the Civil War brought together the USA. Nuts. It did just the opposite." The embrace of Confederate legends earned Catton the label "highly prejudiced" from a black columnist in the *New York Amsterdam News*. Another black paper, the *New Norfolk Journal and Guide*, conducted an editorial debate about whether Catton's writings had paid enough attention to the role of black troops in the Civil War. And in 1966, a British reviewer of *Never Call Retreat*, the concluding book in the Centennial trilogy, acknowledged Catton's "brilliant narrative," but complained that his sense of tragedy and his assertion that the Emancipation Proclamation had greatly expanded the "horizon" of American freedom "all the way out to infinity" (Catton's words) was simply "too vague, too unanchored to be much use to the reader."[62]

When Catton employed the term "tragedy," which he often did as though it were mood music for openings, and the obligatory tone for endings to all books and speeches, it was not that he did not understand its literary meanings. In a speech at the Citadel in Charleston, South Carolina, for the official beginning of the Centennial in 1961, Catton labeled the Civil War "the great enduring tragedy in all our American experience." But he wanted the Citadel cadets and his public audience to think classically. "Contemplating it [tragedy]," said Catton, "does not leave one with a feeling that life is futile and meaningless. No man arises from *Hamlet*, or *King Lear*, with a depression of spirit. Instead, it is precisely through great tragedy that we get . . . our realization that there is in the human spirit something that is unconquerable, indomitable, deathless." Similarly, in other settings throughout the Centennial years, he loved to combine the "Hamlets and Lears, the Lincolns and Lees, these buck privates in blue and grey," to show that the Civil War could be for America what perhaps it was for the boy from Benzonia, that the story which "purges the emotions . . . shows us man contending with fate," and "that there is something in man that triumphs even in the hour of loss and defeat."[63] But there were also times when Catton threw the word "tragedy" around like popcorn at the county fair, and his version of this great American story, written so often with transcendent beauty, required—one might say *tragically*—an almost blind embrace of a mystic version of the cause his inspiring old Michigan veterans had fought to destroy.

When Catton wrote the dark endings of his memoir in 1972, and reflected on the troubled and violent fate of mankind, perhaps he was entirely aware after all of the full character of the story he had told and sold so well. Remembering his innocent youth one last time, the seventy-three-year-old accused himself of "regarding the past so fondly we are unable to get it in proper focus, and we see virtues that were not there." And then he gave his own brand of Americanized tragedy a devastating blow: "It is easy to take the tragic view (which I proudly supposed that I was doing), as long as you do not know what tragedy really means. Pessimism has a fine tart flavor when you know that everything is going to come out all right."[64] After such success, was the poet and the former PR man admitting he had enjoyed the war too much?

In the wake of the violence of the 1960s, the urban riots and assassinations, and the American tragedy unfolding in Vietnam as well as back home, perhaps Catton recalled with ambivalence some of the writing he had done in the passion and optimism of the Centennial era. He might have remembered his brief epilogue in *American Heritage*'s *Picture History*, "A Sound of Distant Drums," printed on one two-column page next to a painting of a Union veterans parade from 1890. With nostalgia in high tide, and at the end of the most evocative visual recreation of the Civil War ever produced, Catton summed up the war's "haunting memory." It was understandably about the valor and loss of so many young soldiers and about the societies and worlds from which they came that could never be retrieved. Here was Catton in full flower. In the war, the country had lost the "dreams that had brought fire and a great wind down on a land that meant to be happy and easygoing . . . the whole network of habits and hopes and attitudes of mind it [the war] had ground into fragments—these were remembered with proud devotion." But what dreams and what habits? In a 325-word epilogue that never mentioned slavery or emancipation—that never even implied their presence in Civil War remembrance—Catton referred to "decaying plantation buildings" as "shrines simply because they somehow spoke for the dream that had died, the vitality of the dream gaining in strength as the physical embodiment of it drifted off into ruin." What the country above all must "never forget," Catton urged in his ending, "was the simple memory of personal valor." Catton had not always kept it so simple, and his work should still be read today. But after so often leaving his readers choked up with mystic emotion about "the fallen" yet little wiser about the war's meaning and consequences, perhaps the Catton in the memoir of 1972 felt a strange kind of survivor's guilt. The Yankee who became the "last survivor of both sides" went home to Benzonia, and spent his last years in the north woods of Michigan.[65]

Edmund Wilson, 1951, as he began to write and publish essays on Civil War literature. Corbis Images.

CHAPTER THREE

"Lincoln and Lee and All That"

Edmund Wilson

In connection with the Civil War . . . it is astonishing to what extent the
romantic popular legend has been substituted for the so much more
interesting and easily accessible reality.

—Edmund Wilson, *Patriotic Gore,* 1962

E DMUND Wilson came relatively late to the history of the Civil
War. He did not soak it up in childhood amid his well-to-do
family in Red Bank, New Jersey, at the turn of the twentieth century.
It would take two World Wars, one of which he participated in and
the other of which he opposed, a Cold War he loathed and for which
he refused to pay his taxes, and nearly fifty years before he would
seriously read and write about the war that shaped his father's generation. But as a shy only child, born in 1895, he did grow up loving
books and soaking in literature, which became for him a necessity as
important as breathing. Wilson also grew up with an enduring fascination for the nature and meaning of history, especially as it forged
the factual and creative fount of literature. Wilson's father, Edmund
Senior, born in 1863, was a successful, if neurotic and hypochondria-
cal, lawyer who maintained a criminal as well as corporate practice.
The senior Wilson was prone to depression and stern Presbyterian
rebukes of his son's habits, but the future author of the classic and
controversial *Patriotic Gore: Studies in the Literature of the American
Civil War* (1962) derived a great deal from this troubled but influential relationship. Unlike Warren's grandfather, who reminisced about
riding in Forrest's cavalry, or Catton's old Union veterans parading on
Memorial Day, Wilson's father provided a stalwart, civic example of

the post–Civil War Republican party—a good railroad lawyer, strong on business and the tariff, patriotic and devoted to the republic that had prevailed in the 1860s against the rebel South, and fascinated with self-development literature. Wilson's father, scion of the professional class, a one-term attorney general of New Jersey who moved and out of sanitariums with mental breakdowns, nevertheless taught his son to strive for success, hate mediocrity, and love Abraham Lincoln.[1]

In his youth, Wilson tried hard to believe that he was the polar opposite of his father; he avoided reading about Lincoln, and was sometimes genuinely fearful of the man who retreated for long hours behind a felt-covered office door, inaccessible to his lonely son. Wilson often sought refuge in the protections and mutual loneliness of his mother, Helen Mather Kimball Wilson, who suffered from deafness, read little, and wished futilely that her son would embrace athletics.[2] But before the father died, in 1923, the young writer came to see for the first time how much the elder Wilson had planted a deep fascination for ideas in his mind.

Wilson's privileged education did the same. From 1909 to 1912, he attended the Hill School in Pottstown, Pennsylvania. At this Congregational and evangelical prep school, Wilson seemed to lose his Protestantism but thrive on the Protestant ethic. From excellent teachers, he learned Greek and read Homer in the original; he published his first stories at fourteen, discovered H. L. Mencken's satire, and read George Bernard Shaw's dramas about human reason. Most of all he simply became a "literary boy," immersed in literature, so much so that he would imitate certain writers in letters to friends. Wilson fondly remembered being drilled in grammar by Mr. John Lester, who taught him his first disciplined lessons in style through the "Great Trinity: Lucidity, Force, and Ease." Despite all the evangelical preachers trotted in to instruct the boys in personal morality and Christian faith, it was the humanistic tradition that Wilson soaked up at the Hill School. It was there that he cultivated his life-long attachment to the nineteenth-century French historian and critic Hippolyte Taine, whose historical approach to literature became the youthful intellectual's model. Taine made writers into vivid characters who were rooted in historical and social contexts—who represented and created their times, their cultures, and their peoples' identities. Wilson first found Taine's *History of English Literature* on his father's bookshelf, but reading him under some guidance seemed to convince the prep school idealist of the eternal, indispensable link between history and literature.[3] And if there was a single, primary thread to all of Wilson's extraordinarily diverse work as critic, journalist, poet, novelist, and memoirist, it was this furtive interdependence of history and literature, and his faith—a secular religion for him—that the reader-critic could become an artist-hero too.

From 1912 to 1916, Wilson went to Princeton University, his father's alma mater, where he lived at first in a dormitory financed by Edmund Senior's class. Although he harbored a good deal of contempt for the privileged elite who surrounded him, he was now also very much a part of it. He did not have their money, and he struggled to avoid their pretensions and assumptions of entitlement; his would be another kind of snobbery, wrapped in endless quotations from and judgments about great literature. He made many lasting friendships at Princeton, including F. Scott Fitzgerald, and played a leading role among the student-scholars, as opposed to the playboy-athletes. In this protected, class-conscious world of football rivalries, singing competitions, and social clubs with no pretense of merit, Wilson edited the same literary magazine his father had thirty years earlier.[4]

Two Princeton professors had lasting influence on Wilson's intellect and his career. The Scotsman Norman Kemp Smith, an authority on Descartes and Kant, introduced Wilson to Continental philosophy and became a model of the literary man interested in all subjects, "literature, science, ideas, and news—in everything that men were doing." Even more important, Christian Gauss, a professor of French and Italian literature, taught Wilson Dante and Flaubert, and drew him forever into the fold of French historical and literary culture. Gauss was not a flamboyant teacher, but a devoted and sensitive one. His lectures on Flaubert in Wilson's senior year made Wilson "want to write something in which every word, every cadence, every detail, should perform a definite function in producing an intense effect." The sheer range of Gauss's interests left an enduring impact on the young Wilson; the student greatly admired the professor's "highly developed sense of history," and his firm if understated lesson that an artist's "fidelity to a kind of truth" derived from the sheer "discipline of aesthetic form." And of course, Wilson was much impressed with Gauss's occasional stories of sipping coffee with Oscar Wilde in London cafés in the 1890s.[5]

In the summer of 1916, after graduating from Princeton, and while his university's own Woodrow Wilson ran for reelection as president of the United States by vowing to keep America out of the war in Europe, Edmund Wilson enrolled in a preparedness training camp in Plattsburgh, New York. He "loathed" things military, hated firing a gun, and later remarked that he "could not imagine commanding men," or "killing them—at least men I did not know and in cold blood." But the Armageddon across the sea had everyone's attention, and some of his friends were going into it. In August 1914, at the end of a summer bicycle trip in England with some of his Princeton friends, Wilson happened to be in London when World War I broke out. "The declaration of war on Germany came on a bank holiday," he wrote much later, and "was prolonged for a day or so." He declared himself "astonished" at the "popular enthusiasm: people riding on tops of taxis, cheering in the crowded streets, a mob around Buckingham Palace calling for the King and Queen ... singers in the music halls reviving the old banal Boer War song 'Soldiers of the Queen' ... I wondered if they thought the war was all going to be a tremendous bank holiday."[6] That youthful reaction touched off what became Wilson's long and growing disgust with mankind's instinctive cravings for violence and war; in it, one sees the early kernel of his introduction to *Patriotic Gore,* and his deep ambivalence even about "good" wars.

But in the spring of 1917, when the United States declared war and entered the mad but beguiling fray, Wilson enlisted in the hospital corps so as to avoid being drafted into the infantry. From August to October of that year, he spent most of his time at a base on the Detroit Fairgrounds, awaiting deployment to France and doing fatigue duty. He wrote to his Princeton buddies that he found the camp "unbearably dull," and that he felt surrounded by the "sorriest company of yokels"—his fellow servicemen, who held degrees from the University of Michigan—"with whom you cannot talk the real language." After Wilson arrived in Europe and was assigned to a hospital unit in the Vosges in northeastern France, his arrogance as well as his innocence dissolved into a more mature sense of the absurdity and waste of war. He was not at the front, and only occasionally heard the shelling. In December 1917, he wrote to Fitzgerald of his eagerness yet inability to get on with his writing, and of the "futility of prolonging the war." He said he felt only "terrible silence and weariness" in his desolate "part of France."[7]

Out of place in this irrational world of suffering and death, Wilson complained that his only subject was his "unseen, unrealized reality of the war." But he soon had more experience with the "wretched, ghastly ironies of war" than he needed. In 1918 he spent an entire month "dressing gas burns," and worked with "a lot of pneumonia cases . . . most of them delirious." He worked through entire nights preventing "wild men from jumping out of windows." The "hospital business" clearly tried his youthful soul, although he claimed he developed a "kind of Nirvana of apathy and cynicism" in order to thwart his own depression. At the "madhouse," he also served on burial detail, with soldiers "being buried perfunctorily before their families know they are dead," and piled up "like logs . . . in big common ditches." And he met French veterans wandering the local roadways who seemed half crazy. The constant encounter with death, and the effects of mustard gas on the deluded living, got his attention even more than he admitted. "You do well to memorize Wordsworth as an antidote," he wrote at the end of a letter in September 1918, as though he could almost anticipate the poetry of Wilfred Owen and Siegfried Sassoon of the surviving war generation, or a Pat Barker novel about soldiers' mental hospitals in the Great War. The cynical, bitterly antiwar introduction to *Patriotic Gore*, written four decades later and denounced by some reviewers at the height of the Cold War, must be seen first through a lens situated back in those hospital wards in a devastated town in France. The hospital orderly seems to have steeled himself by turning some of his letters into discourses on literature, by writing poems about the dead and dying and about flowers in his mother's garden, by taking bike rides into the countryside along the German border, and by buying all the books he could get from Paris on an allowance from his father.[8]

Wilson did some fast growing-up in France; innocence exploded while one was caring for soldiers gone mad and lifting corpses onto stretchers. As the war came to an end, he managed to escape the hopelessness of the hospitals and got a transfer to intelligence work at General Headquarters. He developed a disdain for rank and privilege, and argued that everyone should serve at least for a time as an enlisted man, a private like himself, with no greater status or honor than that of burying the cold bodies of the unlucky. He seemed to reach for this sentiment in a poem entitled "A Hospital Nurse": "I, catching fevers that I could not quench, / When twenty died for two that we could save, / Was laid with dog-tagged soldiers in a trench, / Glad of no meaner grave." And in a poem that may have been his attempt to reverse the meaning of Lincoln's Gettysburg Address, and that he wrote as an epitaph at the graves of American soldiers, Wilson peered into the ironic hollowness of the cause to save democracy: "All sullen and obscene, they toiled in pain. / Go, countryman of theirs: they bought you pride: / Look to it the Republic leave not vain / The deaths of those who know not why they died."[9] Wilson would see to it that these poems were published in a book of verse in 1953, just as he began to publish his essays on Civil War literature.

That young writer of 1918, steeped in eighteenth- and nineteenth-century literature, eagerly sailed back to the United States to throw himself into a journalistic and literary career. But this lover of the romantics and the Victorians, the young would-be critic so devoted to literature that he believed it could change the world, had learned a profound lesson about the myths and ironies at the heart of war. The lesson that lay latent but potent in Wilson's imagination for years was one that Paul Fussell identified in the writings of the Great War: "it is the war that wins," not armies or nations or causes. In a quatrain about American soldiers who committed suicide, written while still in France, Wilson seemed to plead against the fate that war controlled: "What agony was yours whom here offend / These bitter graves? Turn not in scorn the face / From those who, breaking, fell before the end, / Nor yet from those whom base war rendered base."[10] Americans have never liked to have their mythology about the Civil War rendered base; but the day would come when an older Wilson would do just that before he could sing odes to its literature.

When Wilson arrived on a troop ship in New York harbor upon his return to America in 1919, after nearly two years in the army, he remembered feeling relieved to be out of the "dry tempered fields of Champagne, ploughed over with so many conflicts." He welcomed the "rotten salty smell of the river," the sounds of "American voices," and the "swift shuffling . . . of an American train." Back in "my own native land," he was ready to plunge into the life of a Bohemian journalist in Greenwich Village. But first he had to get out of the military and have a reckoning with his father. Waiting days for discharge in a camp on Long Island, Wilson was touched when his father came for a visit and raised a loud protest over the delay. Disgusted with a slow-moving bureaucratic officer, the elder Wilson berated the young administrator for his "inefficiency" and an "outrage against tax-paying citizens." When the officer challenged him and told him to "be careful," Wilson Senior denounced the Espionage and Sedition Act, declaring it legally irrelevant. Much impressed with his father's "fuming," Wilson especially liked the irony that a story he had written in France about the blundering administrative side of army life had been held up by the army censors. He and his father had a warm reunion and much to talk about; for the first time, remembered Wilson, "I was . . . no longer afraid of him." And tellingly, Wilson recalled, full of excitement about socialism and stories about the Russian Revolution, "I was learning now from my father what the principles of American justice were."[11]

After the death of Edmund Senior, such memories stimulated for Wilson a moving remembrance of his father, especially of what he had learned from him about history and ideas, and about Lincoln. His father collected a "whole library of Lincolniana," wrote Wilson in fond tribute, "and he liked to deliver a popular speech called 'Lincoln the Great Commoner.'" Wilson initially had rebelled against such adulation of the sixteenth president, making "a point," he said, "of knowing as little as possible about Lincoln." As a youth and young man, he had viewed his father's earnest chatter about Lincoln as a "pose" and as patriotic "demagoguery." But when he saw "poor farmers and their wives" whom his father had represented coming from miles around to pay tribute at the funeral, Wilson gained a new perspective. In 1923–1924, he started reading some of the books his father had been recommending, in order to learn about his father's feeling of "kinship with Lincoln."[12]

In William Herndon's and Nathaniel Wright Stephenson's works on Lincoln, Wilson found a key to unlock both his understanding of his father and his own developing fascination for the history and literature of the Civil War era. It was in *Herndon's Lincoln*, Wilson claimed, that he found the "explanation" for his father's intense interest: "a great lawyer who was deeply neurotic, who had to struggle through spells of depression, and who—as it followed from this portrait—had managed, in spite of this handicap, to bring through his own nightmares and the crisis of society—somewhat battered—the American Republic."[13] Here was a way for a young literary man to comprehend his enigmatic, deceased father, as well as pursue the epic story of Lincoln and the Civil War. But this he would do later, after exploring the deep literary and philosophical roots of the ideas driving the upheavals of the post–Great War world.

. . .

In 1929, as the stock market crashed, the thirty-four-year-old Wilson suffered a mental breakdown. His ordeal came after nearly eight years of frenetic journalism and creative writing—publishing plays and poetry, working as a staff writer for *Vanity Fair,* and then serving as literary editor of the *New Republic,* where he wrote weekly book reviews and other cultural essays. His mental collapse was accompanied by the breakup of his first marriage, to the actress Mary Blair, and a descent into very heavy drinking and multiple sexual relationships. After spending a month in a sanitorium near Syracuse, New York, being treated for his alcoholism, Wilson managed to recover as the country's economy sank into the Great Depression and 20 percent of adults became unemployed. Great literature was still his subject, and *Axel's Castle: A Study of the Imaginative Literature of 1870–1930,* his first major work of literary criticism and a thorough investigation of the roots of Symbolism and Modernism (a book he worked on in the sanitorium), was published in 1931.[14] But the Depression and its myriad moral and economic challenges gave Wilson a new subject, and a new purpose for his life and work. In a sense, he found the first of two civil wars he would ultimately write about with lasting fame: he would investigate what history had to do with literature, and literature with history. The crisis of capitalism, through his chosen method of seeking its philosophical, literary, and historical roots, would lead Wilson eventually to the crisis of the American Union. But that would take two decades and another World War.

In 1930–1931 Wilson began reading Karl Marx and Friedrich Engels, and he made it his passionate business to try to understand the crisis of world capitalism by reading deeply into the historical origins of the intellectual tradition of socialism. The quest was personal, intellectual, and professional; the Thirties made Wilson into a great participant observer, a sometime activist and incessant traveler, a radical intellectual, and a historian-biographer in search of the meaning of history itself. The crises of the Thirties made him more than ever want to change the world with his pen, or at least study those who had tried to do so in the previous century. In this quest, Wilson became—for a period at least—a devoted socialist, and Marx became a genuine hero. In 1931 he railed against "money-making" as inadequate to "satisfy humanity," and appealed to *New Republic* readers to "take communism away from the Communists."[15]

That same year, Wilson went on the road to report firsthand on Depression America, which resulted in numerous brilliant essays such as "Frank Keeney's Coal-Diggers," where he declared solidarity with oppressed coal miners in Kentucky; "Detroit Motors," in which he exposed the drudgery of automobile assembly lines, as well as some of Henry Ford's worst contradictions between idealism and bigotry; and "The Jumping-Off Place," about Depression-era suicides. With savage, haunting prose, Wilson described the human toll of joblessness and hopelessness. He reported on "coroner's records" of suicides in San Diego in which he found "the last futile effervescence of the burst of the American adventure . . . [where] brokers and bankers, architects and citrus ranchers, salesmen of groceries and real estate . . . well-drillers, molders, tailors, carpenters . . . mostly Anglo-Saxon whites . . . and a sprinkling of Chinese, Japanese, Mexicans, and Negroes . . . ill, retired, or down on their luck . . . stuff up the cracks of their doors and quietly turn on the gas; they go to the back sheds . . . and eat ant paste or swallow Lysol . . . they slip off to the municipal golf links and there stab themselves with carving knives." And in Detroit he observed overproduced, unsold "dingy dirt-colored Ford cars" filling vast parking lots, and many of his [Ford's] workers "left helpless in the collapse of that system." With fierce ridicule,

Wilson saw in Detroit perhaps an eternal truth about American capitalism.

> Until we have succeeded in the United States in producing states-men . . . or engineers with . . . the will to prevent the periodical impoverishment of the people who work for Ford and the wrecking of their energies in his factories, we cannot afford to be too criti-cal of the old-fashioned self-made American so ignorant and short-sighted that he still believes that any poor boy in America can make good if he only has the gumption and, at a time when thousands of men, who have sometimes spent their last nickel to get there, are besieging his employment offices, can smugly assure the newspapers that "the average man won't really do a day's work unless he is caught and can't get out of it."[16]

Wilson started studying Russian, published in the *New Republic* the first chapters of his evolving intellectual history of socialism, and toured the Soviet Union for six months in 1935.

To the Finland Station: A Study in the Writing and Acting of His-tory, published in 1940, is many things at once: an ambitious intel-lectual history of ideas about social justice, from the French Revolu-tion to the Russian Revolution of 1917; a brilliant series of portraits of writers and suffering artists (especially Marx) trying to transcend time and change the world with their pens; a personal search for intellectual and literary heroes in a world where revolutionary social-ism seemed to be remaking history; and a meditation on whether the ancient exploitation of the masses for the benefit of the greedy few could ever be tamed, and a humane society imagined and invented. It was, in other words, about one of the most profound subjects of modern history and about those who refused to relinquish a vision of justice no matter how strong their chains or how stark their disap-pointments and contradictions.

Wilson's biographer Lewis Dabney called *Finland Station* "the biography of an idea, the idea that society can be remade by men in

accord with human aspiration." At heart, *Finland Station* is essentially about the nature, trajectory, and meaning of history. Does history
have a purpose, a pattern, or a discernible design? Is it going somewhere—to Valhalla, to hell in a handbasket, to a happy, laissez-faire,
capitalist land of prosperity, to an America beyond the next horizon
or in a suburban cul-de-sac, to God's kingdom, or to the Finland Station in Petrograd as V. I. Lenin arrives to lead the October Revolution
of 1917 in the name of the proletariat and the theories of Karl Marx?
Wilson really was driven to comprehend the wondrous dichotomy of
his subtitle: the "writing and acting of history."[17]

In *Finland Station,* Wilson exposed his flawed heroes—Taine,
Marx, and even an idealized Lenin. By 1940, however, he had abandoned all of his earlier appreciation for Joseph Stalin, and joined other prominent American leftists who came to judge Stalin for what he
was: a tyrant and a vicious murderer. Wilson later admitted, in a 1972
edition of *Finland Station,* that he had been "very naïve" about some
aspects and leaders of the Russian Revolution. He had written the
book in the 1930s, he said, with "a too hopeful bias." But the central
preoccupations or fascinations—whether a writer can move govern-
ments and make history, whether he can reveal how historical change
comes about in the lives of real people, and whether ideas provoke
action or the other way around—remained with him into mature age.
For a man who distrusted theory, and who had abandoned any religious faith of his youth, Wilson could never quite give up a *belief* in
history, even if it was largely a skeptic's pragmatic search for what
might be rather than what *is.* And in Marx, among others, Wilson
found an affinity, a companion among those "wounded" artists and
writers he kept writing about in works like *The Wound and the Bow*
(1947). He relished exploring Marx's youthful poetry, discovering that
Prometheus was Marx's favorite myth and that the young romantic
German had used lines from Aeschylus's *Prometheus Unbound* as an
epigraph in his doctoral dissertation. Whatever the ideology, Marx
challenged gods, monarchs, and the landowners of the Mosel Valley

alike with the great Greek Titan on his side. Aeschylus's Prometheus declares to Hermes: "I would never be willing to exchange my misfortune for that bondage of yours. For better do I deem it to be bound to this rock than to spend my life as Father Zeus's faithful messenger." And Marx had to rebel indeed against his real, educated, lawyerly father, and suffered genuine poverty to pursue his goals. Choosing philosophy over law, Wilson writes approvingly, as a journalist-artist who himself never made much money, about Marx who "reads gigantically, plans immense labors, writes poetry, philosophy, and makes translations." Detesting all gods, and choosing poverty and isolation in order to work out his "system," Marx simply "decides to change the world."[18] Wilson was only an occasional actor in history; he preferred observing and writing about it. But there was nothing quite as interesting as those who did both.

In *Patriotic Gore*, Wilson will not have a "Finland Station," a destination that drives the method of multiple biography and literary history. He will have given up the search for an ultimate design in history, although never for its meanings. History can have plenty of meaning even when we lose certainty of where its road maps can take us. But in *Finland Station* Wilson found a method and a critical voice more expansive than ever. It is hard to imagine how he would have even attempted the reading of Civil War literature if he had not first accomplished his own kind of Promethean feat in *Finland Station*.

.   .   .

In the wake of the Japanese attack on Pearl Harbor in December 1941, Wilson opposed American entry into World War II. He remained an opponent of the war, especially its escalating use of indiscriminate bombing of cities, even after revelations of Nazi death camps and Japanese atrocities in Asia. He trusted no one and no cause, he wrote, when it involved the "primitive animal instinct" that all nations cultivate in wartime. Wilson bitterly objected to the bombing of German cities and condemned the American use of the atomic bombs on Hiroshima and Nagasaki. In the emerging new age of world geopolitics, genocide, unfathomed new technologies of slaughter, the death and reimagining of empires as communist and Western-American "blocs" from the massive ruins of war, Wilson became ever more antiwar.[19] For this World War I veteran, now writing prolifically as a memoirist, as well as novelist, essayist, and weekly book reviewer for the *New Yorker* (as of 1943), a "good war" was no longer possible to imagine, in the future or even perhaps in retrospect. Wilson feared and detested the world of superpowers made by the most destructive half-century for the human species on record. This perspective drew Wilson back to his own country and into the nineteenth century to pursue with great passion the literature of the Civil War and its aftermath. His former flirtations with the socialist crusade were long gone; ideological causes seemed to him motivated now only by power, military might, and market-hungry nations. Total war had bred the madness of a Cold War, with the United States and the Soviet Union locked in absurd competition and perhaps mutual destruction. But Wilson, caring deeply about American culture and its historical journey, turned back to the great crisis of America's existence to see if it, too, had a profound meaning to convey through its literature.

How Wilson managed to navigate his turbulent personal life while remaining such a productive writer is not easy to explain. But by the 1940s, he was writing in both very dark but also occasionally light modes. His second wife, Margaret Canby, whom he married in 1930, died in an accidental fall in 1932. His famous marriage to the celebrated author Mary McCarthy, a tempestuous arrangement to say the least, lasted formally until 1946, when Wilson divorced and remarried again, this time to Elena Mumm Thornton, a woman with whom he managed to have a relatively stable and loving relationship. They divided their time between Wellfleet, on Cape Cod, and Talcottville, in upstate New York, where they lived in an old stone house he had inherited from his parents. The glamorous, bookish forty-year-old Elena may have had much to do with reviving the fifty-six-year-old Wilson from a crisis of morale; she was thoroughly European, born in France of a German father and Russian mother, but now an American citizen whose life had been completely reshaped by the dislocations of World War II.[20] Just as his own life had been rife with little civil wars, parts of which he converted into essays and fiction, Wilson now sought to harness the literary legacy of a very big civil war.

As early as 1947 Wilson wrote to an editor at Oxford University Press about a book project, "a fairly elaborate affair . . . I have been working . . . on for some time." It would begin with "the literature of the Civil War and go up through Edith Wharton." He intended to "excavate a period . . . little explored." With an ambition perhaps even greater than it took to write *Finland Station,* Wilson judged the "Hawthorne-Emerson-Melville generation" well-enough understood, but when it came to the post–Civil War era of American literature, he considered the literate culture "still quite in the dark." He was right; as he listed many of the relatively unknown writers he was reading (George Washington Cable, John W. DeForest, Francis Grierson, and many others), he predicted "many surprises" as he signaled his intention: "Everybody knows Mark Twain and Henry James; but one finds when one begins to read . . . that there are writers of the first importance whose work is today scarcely known. I propose to throw these into relief and to let lesser people, even though more famous, sink more or less into the background." That year, Wilson signed a contract with Oxford for his "Civil War book," with an advance of $2,000.[21] *Patriotic Gore* was still fifteen years away from publication—a fact that, with time, greatly frustrated his publisher; but in the late Forties, Wilson had already fashioned a typically mammoth plan of reading, and soon he produced drafts of essays on Lincoln, Ulysses Grant, and Harriet Beecher Stowe that would be published in the *New Yorker* in 1951–1952.

As he read, Wilson shared with friends his unusual appreciation of Civil War–era writers, defining the category somewhat broadly. "I have been reading up the literature of the Civil War—some of which is wonderful," he wrote to John Dos Passos in 1952. Some of his discoveries should be "classics," he complained, but suffered obscurity because "the Civil War has to some extent been a taboo subject." Southerners, he maintained, refused to read "Northern books," and too many Northerners sought to "forget the whole thing." Through exhaustive reading of diaries, fiction, speeches, and memoirs, Wilson had arrived at sudden realizations of the most vexing dilemma in the historical memory of his own country. He sent Dos Passos a list of books he thought should be required reading in schools and colleges. In 1953, writing to his friend Mamaine Koestler, who was the wife of Arthur Koestler and with whom Wilson had once fallen in love, he gushed with excitement about his new project. "It will certainly be one of my best books," he announced, "more like the *Finland Station* than like, say, *Axel's Castle*." Sending Mamaine another list of Civil War writers, and admitting she had "probably never heard of most of them," he instructed her about his original discoveries. "It was not a period when belles-lettres particularly flourished," Wilson offered, "and the novelists and poets who had been in it before they began to write never quite got over it or adjusted themselves to post-war America, where commercialism ran riot." As if to say that America, too, had produced its own kind of a Great War literature, Wilson celebrated his subject: "I don't know of any other historical crisis in which everybody was so articulate."[22]

In the Fifties, Wilson wrote to Supreme Court Justice Felix Frankfurter about his excitement in reading Grant, Stowe, and Oliver Wendell Holmes, Jr., and about his discovery of the extent to which the tangled roots of Civil War literature lay in Old Testament Calvinism. With Arlin Turner he shared his joy in finding the writings of Cable and other unusual Southern writers (Turner had just published a biography of Cable). Other friends eventually heard about his amazement at discovering so many good military memoirists. "My greatest surprise has been Sherman's book," he wrote to Chauncey Hackett, referring to William T. Sherman's *Memoirs*. "I had had no idea that he was such an interesting character—rather complex, even a little unbalanced." When *Patriotic Gore* finally appeared in 1962, it was this element of sheer surprise for so many reviewers and readers that gave the book its unique place in the Centennial. As in all of his writing, Wilson's discoveries were part of his passionate quest for writers who could teach him something. As early as 1953, if not before, Wilson had found his way to the heart of the problem in Civil War cultural memory through the recovery of innumerable voices and literary forms of expression long overlooked. He had discovered that the conundrum of how and why Americans had forgotten, suppressed, or simply romanticized the most violent upheaval in their history was, indeed, discernible after all in a unique literature crafted by its participants. Wilson urged Dos Passos to bring along his radical vision and follow him back into the nineteenth century: "It is a period that has always been hard to grasp because it is so hard to face—though so much is being written about it nowadays."[23]

Hard to face indeed. Wilson had his own personal reasons for making his countrymen "face" the Civil War. At Princeton in 1952, Wilson was given a chance to teach about his emerging discoveries. He led one of the Christian Gauss seminars, in which he delivered early versions of his essays on Lincoln, Stowe, Grant, DeForest, and Ambrose Bierce to a distinguished collection of faculty and fellows that included Saul Bellow, Leon Edel, John Berryman, and Paul Tillich. Wilson was never at home in academic circles, and he did not like to give public lectures; he spoke *to* people and not really *with* them. In his seminar, he simply read drafts of his evolving Civil War epic, but no doubt benefited from the discussions.[24]

Patriotic Gore is really two books in one, and it has always been read and criticized that way. The first book is the Introduction, which Wilson wrote at the very end of the process in 1961, and in the midst of various Cold War crises in the world. The second consists of twenty-six chapters, analyzing the works and illuminating the lives of approximately thirty writers. The book endures because of the unprecedented literary history it presented at the time of the

Centennial. Since its publication, only one book like it has ever been attempted: Daniel Aaron's *The Unwritten War: American Writers and the Civil War* (1973), a brilliant work in its own right which goes much further into the twentieth century, owes much to Wilson, and even makes him a subject.[25] Wilson's Introduction has been called everything from shocking to naïve to brilliant; some have considered it unpatriotic, even un-American. Many even dismiss it as an unnecessary appendage to an otherwise classic, if strange, work of historical literature.

Wilson charted a road into Civil War literature, with a side excursion into his own particularly blunt critique of the Cold War and of war itself. In a book of collected essays from the Twenties and Thirties, *The American Earthquake* (1957), Wilson had written a Postscript which explained his opposition to American involvement in World War II. One can imagine how this was received in Eisenhower's America of 1957, in the wake of McCarthyism and in the midst of Cold War fear of nuclear attack. He did not blame Franklin Roosevelt for duping Americans into the war, although he came close; he did seem to accept the theory that the United States had provoked Japan into the attack on Pearl Harbor. He acknowledged the "real fear of Hitler," but believed it only caused America "to ally ourselves with another tyrant equally atrocious" (Stalin). And above all, he suggested that Nazi mass murder was morally equivalent to American carpet-bombing of cities and the use of atomic weapons to kill civilians. "The Nazis smothered people in gas-ovens," Wilson wrote without hesitation, "but we burned them alive with flame-throwers and, bomb for bomb, we did worse than the Nazis." In every nation, Wilson had come to see the same impulse: "the irresistible instinct of power to expand itself, of well-organized human aggregations to absorb or impose themselves on other groups." Twentieth-century expansion and mass violence had made imperialists of every nation big enough to compete, Wilson believed. The same "sub-rational reason" lay at the root of the conquest both "of the South by the North in the Civil

War [and] of Germany by the allies."[26] Given that his cynicism was so deep, one wonders how Wilson managed to find brilliance, humor, and even the sublime in so many Civil War writers.

Wilson finished *Patriotic Gore* in the first year of the Kennedy administration, which he supported. At the time, he was living in Cambridge, Massachusetts, and giving lectures as the Lowell Professor at Harvard. But he was very discouraged by the Cold War, nuclear testing, U.S.-Soviet saber rattling, and the death of Ernest Hemingway by suicide. In the summer of 1961 he unloaded on Alfred Kazin: "the U.S.A. is getting me down. . . . I don't see how you still manage to believe in American ideals and all that." By the fall—as he told two of his closest confidants in the writing of the Civil War book, Daniel Aaron and John Dos Passos—he was struggling mightily with his Introduction, making it ever longer as he also searched for yet one more book by Kate Chopin on microfilm. He was convinced that "nobody is going to approve of" his antiwar Introduction, and that the United States had fallen into "more of a mess" than in the Depression. He wished, he said, that he could spend his "declining years somewhere else."[27]

Only with this backdrop can we begin to understand the apparent incongruence between Wilson's widely discussed and controversial Introduction and the nearly eight hundred pages of literary history in *Patriotic Gore*. According to his good friend Jason Epstein, Wilson had always had an "anarchic streak" regarding war and nationalism, bred by his experience of 1918–1919 in those French hospitals. The alienation Wilson felt from what he called the "United States of Hiroshima" produced a belligerent, blasphemous screed against his country's sense of history, and especially its foreign policy. Some of his historical judgments and moral equivalences can still seem disturbing today. But it is not merely a perverse diatribe full of prickly opinions; at times, it is a weirdly brilliant exposition of "anti-war morality."[28]

In its mesmerizing opening pages, Wilson invites his readers to appreciate his unusual collection of writers who left an all but unknown trove of "speeches and pamphlets, private letters and diaries, personal memoirs and journalistic reports." The writers, he says, will play their parts in a "drama" as "character[s]," and will thus present their ideas better than their poetry or fiction has "been able to do." Then he abruptly stops and launches into his "general point of view" on war. Wilson scorches all forms of nationalistic pieties, all excuses for mobilizing societies for war, all manipulations of history to justify conquest. Recalling a Walt Disney nature film in which a sea slug devours smaller sea slugs by natural instinct, he urges a "biological and zoological" approach to the human obsession with war. We should ignore the "war aims" pronounced by nations, he suggests, and understand that the "difference . . . between man and other forms of life" is that man has invented what he calls "'morality' and 'reason' to justify what he is doing." "Songs about glory and God, the speeches about national ideals," insists Wilson, are only the "self-assertive sounds which he [man] utters when he is fighting and swallowing others."[29]

A more direct condemnation of humankind's "war-like cant" could hardly have been more provocatively fashioned than in Wilson's infamous "sea slug" metaphor. He spared no one in the withering assault, not the French in their revolution nor the Russians in theirs. He judged Americans, if anything, the worst offenders: they were "self-congratulatory grandchildren of a successful revolution" whose "appetite" must be fed by ever more self-aggrandizing slogans, such as the "American Dream, the American way of life, and the defense of the Free World." Although Wilson claimed privately not to be a "pacifist," he rejected virtually all ideological reasons for war— even, seemingly, self-defense. But he would also contradict himself, of course. In response to a letter challenging his Introduction just after the book came out in April 1962, he declared that "in the case of resistance movements, I approve of the use of force if I sympathize with the people resisting."[30] Sometimes the smaller sea slugs had the right to fight after all.

In essence, Wilson simply wanted Americans to admit that, historically, they had been "devourers" too, and experts at "talking cant." He surveyed America's westward expansion, the killing and displacement of Indians, and the ever-replenishing theory of manifest destiny, in which he included the North's "repression of the Southern states when they attempted to secede from the Union." Indeed, he offered an explanation of the coming of the Civil War borrowed almost completely from the Lost Cause tradition, accented with his own brand of biological determinism. Northerners' concern to preserve the Union, he maintained, had nothing to do with freeing slaves. When the "militant North" (meaning abolitionists) made a "rabble-rousing moral issue" out of slavery, it provided what all wars need: "myth" and "melodrama" for which men are willing to die. In language that no diehard Lost Cause advocate of the turn of the twentieth century or neo-Confederate of the early twenty-first could improve upon, Wilson said Lincoln's government sought to "crush the South not by reason of the righteousness of its cause but on account of the superior equipment which it was able to mobilize and its superior capacity for organization."[31] Robert E. Lee, in his farewell address to his troops at the surrender in 1865, had used the phrase "superior numbers and resources" as an explanation for Confederate defeat—a fact Wilson surely knew.

Although Wilson's views of the roots of Southern secession, and for that matter the nature of Reconstruction, were inevitably rooted in some old mainstream histories still popular in the 1950s, his apparent Southern sympathies did seem jarring to some readers. Given Wilson's radical proclivities and his voracious reading, one might think he would have read W. E. B. Du Bois on Reconstruction, or at least have encountered John Hope Franklin on the whole of black history or Kenneth Stampp on slavery. But no such evidence emerges in the book. On the contrary, Wilson all but casts a vote for "white Southerners" of the early 1960s, people "rebelling against the federal government, which they have never forgiven for laying waste their country, for reducing them to abject defeat and for the needling and meddling of the Reconstruction." As he pushes on in defense of the poor benighted South, his language sounds badly out of tune with historical interpretations of today and very much in tune with twenty-first-century white political resentment. "When the federal government sends troops to escort Negro children to white schools and to avert the mob action of whites, the Southerners remember the burning of Atlanta, the wrecking by Northern troops of Southern homes, the disfranchisement of the governing classes and the premature enfranchisement of the Negroes." Here we have, in nearly full flower, the old "tragic legend" of Reconstruction and the nobility of Confederate defeat against overwhelming odds.[32]

Why, for Wilson, was the South a sea slug worth defending? How could he find Yankee piety disgusting, yet not see all the foolish piety dripping from Lost Cause legends? One answer is that he needed the Confederacy to play the role of the devoured in his drama—the little, misguided David to the huge and imperialistic Goliath of the United States, preparing for its twentieth-century career of war and expansion. Another is that Wilson really did not believe slavery was the primary cause of the sectional crisis; he believed slavery had never been anything but a "pseudo-moral issue," and the purpose of his book, he contended, was to "remove the whole subject from the plane of morality." And last, we might understand Wilson's apparent Southern sympathy by looking at his use of analogy. A favorite was his comparison of the plight of Hungary in the Soviet invasion of 1956 with that of the seceded Southern states invaded by Union armies. Moral equivalence is a dangerous rhetorical tool, but Wilson employed it happily and sometimes recklessly. "In what way," he asked, "was the fate of Hungary, at the time of its recent rebellion, any worse than the fate of the South at the end of the Civil War?"[33] Well, the outcome for the Hungarian worker crushed under a Russian tank and the white Georgian farmer killed during Sherman's march might be identical. But Wilson needed to learn more about Reconstruction to make the link between the strangleholds that the Soviet army and the Union army had on their respective foes. The Soviet army really did occupy Budapest a great deal longer and with much more lasting consequences than Yankee troops ever interfered in the lives of ex-Confederates.

Yet Wilson pushed his analogies even further. In a beguiling comparison, he argued that the three great leaders of the modern "impulse to unification"—Lincoln, Bismarck, and Lenin—all became heroic, but they detested "dictators" who supported their respective causes. Each was "confident that he was acting out the purpose of a force infinitely greater than himself," Wilson intoned. Bismarck believed in "God," Lenin in "History," and Lincoln in some kind of democratic combination of the two. All three, though, according to Wilson, were mere agents of the "power drive" that moved nations and history over and over into mass violence and conquest. It is remarkable how Wilson could write so freshly and so cynically at the same time; the lumping of these three world leaders together, today, seems jarring at best. Unfortunately, one of Wilson's analogies clangs in the modern ear, although it is consistent with his argument. He likened our wonderment over whether "Germans really knew about the gas chambers and the other mass killings" by the Nazis to the American "state of mind in regard to what the United States government is getting ready to do to a possible enemy" with nuclear weapons.[34] His point, again, was that Americans just did not like to look closely at their own violent past and present. In 1962, only a few months before the Cuban Missile Crisis made everyone look at the prospect of nuclear extermination, such a test of the imagination may have been a good thing.

Wilson hated piety and cant as much as Robert Penn Warren did; he just did not always excoriate it quite so artfully. Wilson invoked Warren's *Legacy of the Civil War* as a way of ending his Introduction to *Patriotic Gore,* calling it the "most intelligent comment . . . that has yet been brought forth by this absurd centennial." "A day of mourning," Wilson wryly offered, "would be more appropriate" to commemorate the Civil War anniversary. He liked Warren's notions of the "Great Alibi" by which Southerners had long blamed everything violent or backward about their region on the North and on their defeat, and the "Treasury of Virtue" by which his fellow Northerners, with "insufferable moral attitudes," had justified and sanctified all subsequent American wars. The two ideas fit nicely into Wilson's scheme of not only spreading around blame for the Civil War (a scheme he shared, for different reasons, with both Warren and Catton), but also of maintaining his primary focus—the "panicky pugnacity" of the two sea slugs in the Cold War.[35] Before settling in to restore Harriet Beecher Stowe and Ulysses Grant and their host of odd companions to an American literary pantheon, Wilson had first tried to settle a score with his demons of war and nationalism, and perhaps some other demons from his personal life as well.

• • •

Upon publication in the spring of 1962, *Patriotic Gore* became a literary sensation. It was the rare book that seemed to make virtually everyone in the thinking-literary class stand up and take notice. If Abraham Lincoln, according to H. L. Mencken, had become an American institution—a "solar myth"—then to the young Garry Wills, Edmund Wilson had also reached the status of an institution—a "lunar myth"—among the "entire tiny group of literate Americans." Nothing quite like this book had or ever would intervene in the Centennial observance. Indeed, one reason so much attention was paid to *Patriotic Gore,* as one reviewer after another remarked, was that it was so "genuinely serious," so startlingly unusual amid the "flapdoodle," the "dressed up" "vulgarities and tomfooleries" of Centennial books, pamphlets, reenactments, facile speeches, patriotic commissions, pursuits of minutiae, and other Blue-Gray sentimentalism. The literary class, from critics to historians to poets and novelists, seemed grateful that someone had spent all those years going back to explore whether the Civil War had actually left any serious cultural stamp on the country. Most confessed that the answer was a profound and surprising yes. Right when it seemed that the Centennial might produce only some worthy narrative histories at best and a great deal of commercial claptrap at worst, an eight-hundred-page epic about American "writers," many of whom the educated classes had never read or even heard of, burst on the scene to save the day. It was as though a writer with a mind more expansive than anyone else's had gone and found a story where most believed there was no story. The Civil War, as important as it loomed in national history, had not produced a *War and Peace* or an *All Quiet on the Western Front,* so why go looking? If there was no American *Iliad,* why search for puny substitutes? A British reviewer, J. E. Morpurgo, combined Wilson's *Patriotic Gore* and Catton's *Coming Fury* in order to declare the Centennial in America useful after all. "Suddenly," wrote Morpurgo, "and in the midst of the banalities of the Centennial, two books appear which stand out from all the others, two books which will not allow the Americans to cry silence to their national conscience."[36]

Many impulses drove the enormously positive response to *Patriotic Gore* in 1962, but none more than the public's encounter with Wilson's sense of discovery. "*Patriotic Gore* is not really much like any other book by anyone," gushed Elizabeth Hardwick. She admired Wilson's ability to find large, new "subjects," such as the Civil War's literary "harvest," of which she seemed utterly unaware. Continuing her tribute, Hardwick found Wilson's "willingness to learn peerless," his "grubby . . . industry" and his humble "curiosity" astonishing. She simply gave herself over to Wilson's portraits of the famous Lincoln or the forgotten Kate Chopin or Albion Tourgee. Could one writer-critic ever pay a greater tribute to another than Hardwick when she said: Wilson "does not, as many others do, seem to stand aside and view himself—at the least without displeasure—in the act of forming his own opinions. 'Here am I on the state of Israel; here am I on the American Indian; here am I as an old friend of Scotty Fitzgerald; here am I as an old radical; here am I on the horrors of war."[37] Certainly some might dispute that claim, especially regarding Wilson's legendary arrogance, but Hardwick captured several truths: Wilson ventured where others would not tread; he read more widely than anyone else; and he kept redefining the very idea of literature.

In *Patriotic Gore*, Wilson chose his subjects within the big subject—the meaning of the Civil War and of war itself within individual lives—in his own idiosyncratic ways. He included many obvious writers (Stowe, Lincoln, Oliver Wendell Holmes, Jr., and Ambrose Bierce) and sidestepped some obvious ones who make only cameo appearances (Nathaniel Hawthorne, Mark Twain, Walt Whitman, and Henry James). Who knew that the travel writings of Frederick Law Olmsted, who was much more famous as the designer of Central Park in New York, or the works of the poet John T. Trowbridge, provided such vivid depictions of slavery and the ruined South both before and after the war? Who had read the diary of Charlotte Forten, the romantic, educated young black woman who went South during the war to work among freedmen, or the important *Army Life in a Black Regiment* by Thomas Wentworth Higginson, the Massachusetts abolitionist who became a soldier overnight and a student of slave musical culture? Who understood by the mid-twentieth century that such Confederate soldiers as Richard "Dick" Taylor, son of President Zachary Taylor, and John Singleton Mosby, notorious cavalry raider and bandit, had written such fascinating and richly literary memoirs? And did anyone but the rare specialist know that Mosby, who had captured and killed many of Grant's men during the war, became a good Republican friend of the general and president by the end of Reconstruction? How many white Southerners, or anyone else for that matter, understood just how complicated proslavery ideas were when comprehended in the "diverse" writings of William J. Grayson, George Fitzhugh, or Hinton R. Helper, the last of whom tried desperately to get the South to modernize its agriculture if not

its racial views? Did even the most literate Americans in either section know about the advanced racial imagination of a Northerner like
Albion Tourgee and his now classic book *A Fool's Errand*, or about
the remarkably progressive and prolific Louisianan George Washington Cable, whose novel *The Grandissimes* and whose nonfiction
works *The Silent South* and *The Negro Question* earned him a forced
exile to New England for his safety? Indeed, how many Americans
even today know of Tourgee's complex personal critique of the Ku
Klux Klan or of Cable's early and forthright engagement with racial
mixing, well before the works of William Faulkner? This list goes
on: How many literate Americans were at all aware of the eloquent
Confederate women diarists—Mary Chesnut, Kate Stone, and Sarah
Morgan—who left such extraordinary visions of the tragedy of war,
rendered with wit and haunting despair? Some of Stone's writing,
especially about her experiences in 1865, comes as close as anything
by an American woman to the wailing of Hecuba in Euripides's *The
Trojan Women*. Who knew indeed? These writers and more provided
the wave of surprises that made *Patriotic Gore* such a revelation in
the season of Centennial fatigue.

Wilson overwrote some of his portraits, self-indulgently over-
quoted some of the writers, and often provided his chapters with
lumpy and awkward titles, all of which greatly frustrated his editor at
Oxford, Sheldon Meyer, who tried heroically without success to get
Wilson to make major cuts after the book was finally submitted in
1961. The book wanders from soldiers to poets and diarists, and back
to soldiers once again, without obvious organizational logic. Eventually, in the self-appointed role as judge of taste and significance,
Wilson seems to just follow his whimsy. He would wear out most
readers with his overblown discourse on John W. DeForest, former
soldier and author of *Miss Ravenal's Conversion to Secession* (which
Wilson judged to be the book in which American realism had been
born), and leave many dumbfounded as to why an obscure poet like
Henry T. Tuckerman occupies more space than Whitman or Herman

Melville. But in his inclusion of numerous relatively unknown writers, and the sheer virtuosity of insights, some leaping off the page and others subtle, Wilson provided a feast for all who came under his spell. As the historian Richard Current commented in a review, Wilson seemed "naïve" in some of his historical understandings, as long-winded and disjointed as an "anthology," and narrowly limited in his judgments of Southerners because of a single-minded fascination with Alexander H. Stephens, the vice president of the Confederacy. But Current loved the book nonetheless, claimed Wilson's "fascination will infect any reader," and said the work was "not nearly long enough." And Lewis Dabney, Wilson's eventual biographer, wrote a review in which he addressed the question of the complexity and cacophony of *Patriotic Gore*'s cast of characters. "Reading it," wrote Dabney, "is indeed a little like being set down in a room packed with people, each and every one of whom wants your ear for however long it takes to tell of himself or of others, of great or sorrowful events. . . . Putting himself on the sides of his characters, Wilson also speaks over their shoulders in his own voice."[38]

Dabney's image works as a way of understanding the book and its impact. It portrays writers as historical actors through some frequently sparkling biographical portraits, and the critic is there when we need him, reminding us how the wielders of words and ideas are the drivers and reflectors of history. Thus, such major critics as Irving Howe and Alfred Kazin called Wilson the "American Plutarch."[39] The writers' lives, as well as their works, are always Wilson's combined subject. The book can be exasperating, exhausting, and rewarding, often within the same chapter. It does have a structure of a sort—it moves by the logic of a loud and contentious conversation, spilling into violence, with many voices and shifting points of view. Most of the voices are either participants in the bitter debates that led to war, warriors themselves, or veteran-participants who lived to tell of the war in memoir, fiction, or public orations. They are women who were writing in their diaries at home, and men who held high office.

They are all witnesses to an epic event full of convulsion, blood, and sacrifice, and from which Americans are always expecting a redemptive, progressive story. But the unsentimental Wilson steadfastly refused to give them that. Such redemption hardly intrigued him at all, unless of course that was the grain in or against which his subjects wrote.

Wilson tries very hard not to be a partisan himself, and therein lies one secret of the book's success as well as some of its flaws. He is equally excited by the terse, captivating prose of Grant's *Memoirs* and by the blunt and eloquent honesty of Chesnut in her novelistic *Diary from Dixie.* He stands in awe of Lincoln's unique brilliance with language and political philosophy, while at the same time he breaks fully with establishment Lincoln lore in portraying him as a ruthless, power-driven, "extremely ambitious" war maker.[40]

Wilson's portrait of Lincoln, still worthy of a careful read today amid the flood of books on the Illinoisan, is as much intellectual biography as it is literary work. Wilson wanted to puncture the myth and legend of Lincoln as the "folksy and jocular countryman swapping yarns at the village store . . . presiding with a tear in his eye over the tragedy of the Civil War." In a memorable line some have used to dismiss Wilson's rendering of Lincoln, he declares: "The cruelest thing that has happened to Lincoln since he was shot by Booth has been to fall into the hands of Carl Sandburg." But after lampooning the myth-makers, Wilson himself declares a deep fascination for how Lincoln labored to forge "his own legend," and for how the president's sense of Divine Providence and a faith in the power of "history" to work its way through chosen individuals became the nation's dominating epic of the Civil War. Wilson both pillories and respects the power of that epic, of the myth itself. He seems irresistibly drawn to the "poem that Lincoln lived," as well as to the poetry of Lincoln's transcendent rhetoric. On the latter count, Wilson left no doubt and anticipated a later revival of scholarly study of Lincoln, the man "who could summon an art of incantation with words, and . . . practice it magnificently."

Lincoln's writing "style," wrote Wilson, "was cunning in its cadences, exact in his choice of words, and yet also instinctive and natural." On Lincoln as well as many others among his writers, Wilson weaves to and fro between the language and the life. With Lincoln, he seems to cast his fierce irony and his disdain for legend momentarily aside as he concludes with a telling biographical claim: "He [Lincoln] must have suffered far more than he ever expressed from the agonies and griefs of the war, and it was morally and dramatically inevitable that this prophet who had crushed opposition and sent thousands of men to their deaths should finally attest his good faith by laying down his own life with theirs."[41] Perhaps that final sentence came from Wilson's well of remembrance of how he had first encountered Lincoln in those early, misty conversations with his father.

As the Irish intellectual Conor Cruise O'Brien, a man who appreciated independence of mind and the role of the provocateur, remarked in a review: perhaps it was "healthy" for Americans with their historical self-righteousness to have to digest Wilson's "cool leveling together of the angel Lincoln and the demon Lenin." And Wilson treats Robert E. Lee as only a marginally interesting symbol of his generation, a cavalier who upheld his family tradition and "sense of responsibility" as a soldier, one of the "paladins . . . too proud to need hope."[42] Wilson's gazes and prejudices were largely nonpartisan, but ideologically he was not convinced that the war was really fought for or against slavery—an odd conclusion in the face of how much he acknowledged Lincoln's fervent antislavery convictions. He simply could not help admiring the South's principled stand against centralization, industrialization, and commercialization, which for Wilson were the major and unfortunate outcomes of Union victory.

The astute and patient reader of *Patriotic Gore* has to step in close and then back up again, as when viewing Impressionist paintings, as a means of seeing Wilson's recurring themes. Above all, the book is shot through with Wilson's quest to reveal and explain the competing myths of Northerners and Southerners caught up in this struggle for national and regional existence. Like Warren, Wilson was convinced that people live by myths—the stories from which they draw meaning and identity—as they experience history, and he was devoted to comprehending the relationship between the two. Since the war came in 1861, and then in its long aftermath in American culture, Northerners and Southerners of all backgrounds have lived some grand myths. Wilson did not much sympathize with the abolitionist piety of Yankees, their stern religious certainty that they knew what was best for the country in its great westward expansion. He managed a rather long, unsympathetic treatment of the tortured Calvinist guilt and hypochondria of Calvin Stowe, but much preferred the brilliant probing of Stowe's long-suffering wife, Harriet, on the slavery question, in the art of her magnificent characters in *Uncle Tom's Cabin*. Wilson found most proslavery writers, especially Fitzhugh, largely contemptible and backward, but he grudgingly admired the *art* with which some Southern memoirists defended their cause of military resistance, state sovereignty, individual liberty, and anticentralization.

The war may not have produced a literary *Iliad*, but it certainly had produced the swirling myths that forge competing epics in national memory: the righteous, abolitionist North acting out its destiny, saving the Union by purging the land of its sins in the necessary blood that John Brown had prophesied on the Christian gallows of Harpers Ferry; and the noble, Southern aristocratic defense of the old republic, its ordered, limited government and its honorable, even gallant bulwark against the leviathan of capitalism and the alienation of industrialization. And both the Northern and Southern epics enlisted God or Providence on their side; the apocalyptic destruction of slavery or its humane, eternal improvement might be the divine plan. The house divided had been sundered over rival, incompatible stories, which, since the war, had thrived as folk epics. Some reviewers called Wilson a "myth breaker" or "Civil War debunker," but those likely did not read past the Introduction. Wilson understood myth as astutely as any literary historian could; he also enjoyed finding and analyzing the true artfulness of mythmaking. To Wilson, myth was not something to be lampooned or wished away in favor of an accurate history. It was to be breathed in, appreciated, countered by careful exposure. Myths can be dangerous, but also strangely fascinating in their uses and abuses. As Warren aptly said of *Patriotic Gore,* its great aim was to prompt us to "criticize our myths and, even, to enrich them."[43] Perhaps this is why Wilson stumbled into a rather nostalgic companionship with Alexander H. Stephens, and wrote one of the most unusual and important chapters in the book.

The sympathy with which Wilson wrote about the Confederate vice president—about his frailty and physical sufferings, and his incarceration for several months after the war—is at first astonishing. In Stephens, though, Wilson had found an irresistible character and what Dabney called a "literary ancestor of sorts." Embedded in Stephens's turgid, 1,455-page apologia for the Confederate cause, published in two volumes (1867 and 1870), Wilson found the complete lyrics of the Southern version of the war song, "Maryland, My Maryland!" Sung to the tune of the German Christmas carol, "Tannenbaum, O Tannenbaum," the Confederate version of the words told the story of the first federal troops who marched through Baltimore in 1861 and who clashed with hostile secessionist crowds. Wilson used a portion as an epigraph for the book and plucked his title from it:

> The despot's heel is on thy shore,
>   Maryland!
> His torch is at thy temple door,
>   Maryland!
> Avenge the patriotic gore
> That flecked the streets of Baltimore,
> And be the battle-queen of yore,
>   Maryland! My Maryland!

Wilson's editors were "rather startled," they diplomatically remarked, when Wilson informed them that "Patriotic Gore" would be his title.[44] They were also puzzled by his fascination with Stephens, as well as with other previously unknown writers.

Wilson admitted that Stephens, an ardent states' rights advocate, wrote like a "merciless old ideologue," and that his "gigantic book" had been forgotten for good reasons. The book "endured as a great cold old monument," said Wilson, "which few people have cared to visit." Structured in hundreds of pages of dialogues between Stephens and three kinds of Unionist politicians, Wilson admitted that the two tomes were largely unreadable. But he seems to have read them almost in their entirety anyway, calling the books a "mausoleum some day to be opened." There readers would find, "laid away by the last traditionalist of the eighteenth century South," all the odd but hardly lost arguments against what Stephens called the "Monster . . . the Demon of Centralism, Absolutism, Despotism." Wilson confessed to his own quirky "sympathy" with Stephens's unrelenting rant against big government and in defense of state allegiance and authority over federal power. Stephens delivered his case like a medieval monk savoring and defending the true faith of state sovereignty, including his adamant resistance against Jefferson Davis's attempts to centralize authority in Richmond in order to try to win a war for the Confederacy. Stephens was proud of his insubordination in the name of principle as the former vice president of a colossally failed cause. Again, Warren saw penetratingly into Wilson's game. The critic's heart, said the poet, always answered "most deeply . . . [to] some courageous manifestation of the old virtues."[45]

Wilson always had a weak spot for utopians; but in this case the utopian was a man out of time who could vehemently defend racial slavery as the natural order, even as he based all of life on the sanctified principle of individual liberty against the state. Wilson seemed to admire more than he criticized Stephens's antimodernism. The former Confederate leader argued that citizenship could exist only at the state level, never the federal. Wilson seems all but seduced by the sincerity of this bizarre intellectual and his fierce sense of principle. He allows Stephens several pages to make the case that Lincoln's Emancipation Proclamation was unconstitutional—merely an act of tyranny and the theft of legal personal property. Even Stephens's claim of illegality about Lincoln's call for troops in the wake of the firing on Fort Sumter in 1861 merits a long and sympathetic discussion. Reading Stephens carefully, Wilson remarks, allows one to "understand why the South regarded Lincoln as a bloody tyrant and even why Booth should have wanted to kill him." Stephens's prolonged attack on Lincoln, his former colleague in the U.S. Congress, as "the founder of a centralized state" deserved respect, Wilson believed. It provided a "corrective to the immense amount of mush that has been written about Lincoln."[46] Well, the mush on Lincoln has continued to flow from publishers over the decades; but one wonders what Wilson would think of the way Stephens's ideas about Lincoln and federal power have found a secure home in the libertarian wing, if not the center, of the twenty-first-century Republican party.

Wilson all but lost his sense of irony in writing about Stephens's defense of slavery; he had apparently never encountered this organically conservative, hierarchal view of racial slavery, rendered in such florid language, by such a confident "theorist of the perfect system for organizing human beings." The modern critic could not stop gazing at those remarkable passages in which Stephens portrays slavery as a feudal structure of "reciprocal duties and obligations" between master and slave, and where the old slaveholder admitted that it was Southern whites who had failed in holding up their side of the equation by not improving or perfecting human bondage. Wilson quotes at such length that a modern reader might become captivated by Stephens's sweeping vision of the "immutable features of the harmony and order of the universe," with all of God's creatures "in the vegetable and animal kingdoms ranging from the stateliest trees of the forest to the rudest mosses and ferns . . . [to] distinctions and grada-

tions in the races of men, from the highest to the lowest type." To Stephens, it was the North that attempted to disrupt and overturn this
divine and natural order of the races, and hence it is the abolitionists'
"higher law" doctrine that ran roughshod over the true higher law
of the universe.[47] Wilson exposes just how much Stephens's proslavery ideas, while militantly philosophical, were invested in racist doc-
trines, although he can never quite characterize them as such. The
abstract intellectual, reading the classics and trying to teach Latin to
his prison guard, while theorizing the perfect society where all white
men would be left free with their "liberties," absorbed Wilson much
more than the slavemaster who argued for the preservation of his
section's interests in human chattel.

In the end it is Stephens's "intransigence" about principle, his role
as an "impossibilist," that best represented the "death of the old political South" and that, in Wilson's lights, should be read and understood.
Stephens spent the last ten years of his life, until he died in 1883, serving as a U.S. congressman for Georgia. He was a tiny, frail, invalid of
a man who would sit in his seat, cloaked in robes or blankets like a
"queer looking bundle," as a colleague described him. Always the por-
traitist, Wilson made much of Stephens's persona as a withered body
and fiercely active mind. "It was as if he had shrunk," wrote Wilson,
"to pure principle, abstract, incandescent, indestructible." Perhaps.
But just how indestructible ought Stephens's ideas be in the modern
world? Wilson seemed willing to hold the frail old Confederate's hand
and hear him out. "This issue presses hard on our time," he summed
up. "There are moments when one may wonder today—as one's living
becomes more and more hampered by the exactions of centralized
bureaucracies of both the state and the federal authorities—whether
it may not be true, as Stephens said, that the cause of the South is the
cause of us all."[48] For Wilson—tax resister, staunch opponent of most
Cold War foreign policy and military expenditure, and a believer in
the old "needless war" interpretation that saw the origins of the Civil
War in raucous and misguided political fury rather than in any moral

dimension of slavery—these were, by and large, consistent if harsh conclusions.

But as he ended his long chapter on Stephens, in one of the most revealing sentences in the book, Wilson cautioned his reader to look inward in contemplating this most divisive story in American experience. "There is in most of us an unreconstructed Southerner," he suggests, "who will not accept domination as well as a benevolent despot who wants to mold others for their own good, to assemble them in such a way as to produce a comprehensive unit which will satisfy our own ambition by realizing some vision of our own; and the conflict between these two tendencies—which on a larger scale gave rise to the Civil War—may also break the harmony of families and cause a fissure in the individual."[49] If it took reading a thousand pages of Alexander H. Stephens to find those tragic truths about the human condition, and to grasp that America's many civil wars are never really over, so be it. That Wilson found such an insight by suggesting the unreconstructed Confederate as the essential American is a measure not only of his iconoclasm, but of the fact that he had not thought through the racial implications of the idea.

.   .   .

But why didn't Wilson read Frederick Douglass? Or any other African American writer besides the diarist Charlotte Forten? Why not William Wells Brown? Martin Delany? Frances Ellen Watkins Harper or Elizabeth Keckley? Or, for that matter, Booker T. Washington, who was born a slave and published his classic narrative in 1901? Why didn't Wilson pursue the abolitionist mind quite as fervently as he did the Confederate, secessionist mind? "I don't think Wilson cared very much about race relations," recollected Alfred Kazin in 1997. "He did say to me once he thought Jimmy Baldwin's essays were fantastically brilliant, and he was happy and proud as a liberal about that sort of thing, but he didn't pay much attention to what we now call minority writing, and he was terrible about the Jews during World War II, because he was against the war."[50] Kazin hastened to point out that

Wilson was anything but anti-Semitic; he had learned Hebrew and loved Orthodox Jewish liturgical culture. But as for the great American dilemma of race and the legacies of slavery and emancipation? Just not much interested?

Many distinguished white reviewers respectfully but directly thrashed Wilson for his admiration of Confederate apologists. Marcus Cunliffe argued that Wilson's sympathy for the "bullied South" had led him to "under-estimate the respects in which slavery poisoned Southern life." Irving Howe could hardly stomach the way Wilson identified with Stephens, and judged the critic complicit with the doctrine of states' rights as the "handy slogan" that masked the "moral shame of the South." The Southern literary scholar Louis Rubin wished that Wilson had read more Southern political writers, especially the secessionists; he might then have seen more clearly how much their cause relied on the defense of slavery and their own callous "lust for power." Warren worried that Wilson's metaphor of the "unreconstructed Southerner" representing the "independence of character" in all of us led too easily in modern times to Southern governors like Orville Faubus of Arkansas, blocking any kind of racial progress and demonstrating only the "near bankruptcy of leadership on the question of race in the South." And the literary scholar Marius Bewley brilliantly exposed the implications of Wilson's soft spot for secessionists and Confederate antistatism. Why didn't Wilson speculate further on what kind of "nation" might have emerged from "Stephens's philosophy of racial inequality and subordination," asked Bewley? In the long run, was Stephens really a better defender of "civil rights" than Lincoln, as Wilson implied? Could Stephens's republic, with its "cornerstone of slavery," have "discouraged the Nazis," or have provided "another political asylum for discredited European fascists"?[51] Would that Wilson had been forced to answer these questions in open debate.

But none of these same critics wondered much about why Wilson had left out most black writers. Among white intellectuals generally of the 1950s and early 1960s, nineteenth-century African American culture remained invisible. Slave narratives were mostly not in print, and almost nowhere to be found on college reading lists. Frederick Douglass's classic *Narrative*, first published in 1845, had just come back into print in 1960, introduced by the distinguished but isolated black historian Benjamin Quarles, and published by Harvard University Press at the very moment Wilson was in Cambridge, Massachusetts, lecturing from his chapters for *Patriotic Gore*. Moreover, most of Douglass's writings had been edited and published in five massive volumes by Philip S. Foner from 1950 to 1955. These were the years, now apparently so stunted and ignorant, when the writings of former slaves were still under suspicion of unreliability. Harriet Jacobs's remarkable narrative, *Incidents in the Life of a Slave Girl* (1861), now a famous and widely taught text, was virtually nowhere to be found in 1961. Could a genre ever have been imagined for "study in the writing and acting of history" more ideal than the American slave narratives? We know this today; neither Edmund Wilson, nor the many smart people who read, admired, and reviewed him, knew so then. And might any creations quite like Douglass's hundreds of editorials in his abolitionist newspapers and his thousands of orations over fifty years have been fashioned any better as material for Wilson's own definition of the "literature" in which he found his Civil War?[52] The past is the past—but every time we say it cannot be changed, we realize that it changes us as we endlessly revise it. Wilson's own genius emerged from a profound mixture of his traditionalism and distaste for theory about literature, along with an incomparable zest to learn languages and read new, nontraditional literatures. Hence, a degree of puzzlement at his ignorance of black writing is in order. Perhaps he could not get beyond that old, lethal assumption that a people for whom slavery and forced illiteracy had been the central historical experience just could not have produced literature.

It is a shame Wilson never met Douglass in his transcendent oration "What to the Slave Is the Fourth of July?" (1852), a work that should rank as the rhetorical masterpiece of abolitionism. Wilson would have feasted on the rhetorical structure (it reads and sounds like a symphony in three movements) and would have found even better illustrations of just how much abolitionists owed to biblical narratives and cadences in their arguments against slavery than the ones he uncovered in Harriet or Calvin Stowe, or even in Julia Ward Howe's "Battle Hymn of the Republic." It is a shame Wilson did not encounter Douglass's apocalyptic rhythms in language and argument before he wrote off all the pieties of abolitionists. What a surprise discovery Wilson might have given the literate class in America by examining in one of his forty-page chapters the genius of Douglass's three autobiographies as windows into the meaning and legacies of the Civil War. What a *character* portrait Wilson might have given us of the former slave who became a *writer*—the hero as artist in a world that declared him outside the community of letters because of his race and his servitude! Instead of Lenin arriving at the Finland Station with the works of Marx careening in his head, we might have had Douglass leaving the Baltimore Station on his escape to freedom, with his one precious book *(The Columbian Orator)* in his pocket; or we might see Douglass arriving at the Rochester Station about to rewrite the Declaration of Independence in an artful attack on American hypocrisy, or at the B&O Station at New Jersey Avenue and C Street in Washington, D.C., about to meet with Lincoln to urge the president to let his people go. He might then have gained an even deeper measure of Lincoln's own "religious mysticism" about the Union, as well as a reason to see that aggressive "centralism" and "despotism" were not the only results of Emancipation. Wilson might not have liked Douglass at all—too florid and bombastic, too righteous or millennial, too easily dismissed as a pleading partisan. But who in his book was not a partisan, which Wilson respected? Would that Wilson might have stumbled into some of Douglass's "prison" and "tomb" metaphors or the voice he gives to the terrors of the fugitive slave in flight, honed from twenty years in bondage—and maybe, just maybe, the critic's tender mercy for Alexander Stephens in his jail cell for six months in Boston with his books and his bedbugs might have been tinged with just a touch more irony.[53]

This is relevant perhaps only because it reminds us just how far 1961 is from 2011, but also how close. We cannot blame Wilson for not reading Douglass; we can, though, use the fact as a measure of the distance we have traveled and as a reminder that the Civil War was actually *about something* beyond all the blood of the war years, the disappointments and faltered experiments of Reconstruction, the rise of the centralized state, and the corruption and greed of the Gilded Age. About more than gore.

At the centennial of Wilson's birth in 1995, a conference was convened at Princeton University to explore the writer's many legacies. The volume of essays and conversations emanating from that conference contains a fascinating set of exchanges about Wilson and race. Occurring at a time when "multiculturalism" and contentions over a changing "canon" surged as intellectual and curricular issues in the academy, several scholars and writers debated "omissions in *Patriotic Gore*" and whether the topic of race had been one of the "great man's limitations." Randall Kennedy, an African American law professor from Harvard, pointed out that Wilson had been an extraordinarily active critic in the 1920s and 1930s without apparently ever noticing the Harlem Renaissance or once discussing the work of Langston Hughes, Sterling Brown, or Zora Neale Hurston. He had published literary chronicles of the 1940s and 1950s without so much as a mention of Richard Wright or Ralph Ellison. Baldwin had merited a page of admiration in *The Bit between My Teeth* in 1966, and Wilson had written favorably about Haitian writers and movingly and at length about American Indians, publishing *Apologies to the Iroquois* in 1960.[54]

Yet Kennedy, not a literary scholar by training, was most exercised about *Patriotic Gore*. The virtual absence of black writers from the text, Kennedy asserted, ranked as "one of the most egregious oversights in the history of literary studies." The absence of Douglass in particular, said the law professor to the room full of literature professors and critics, was a "major intellectual failing." And they reacted primarily with unguarded scorn. "I'd be interested in what Randall Kennedy thinks of *Patriotic Gore*," sniffed Yale's David Bromwich, "and what's in it, not what's not in it." Jed Pearl, art critic for the *New Republic*, said Kennedy did not understand the very nature of imaginative literature, and called the accusation of "racism not on the basis of what is included . . . but on the basis of what is not . . . perverse." Pearl dismissed the question of race by simply ranking *Patriotic Gore* with Francis Parkman's history of the French and Indian Wars as the "two greatest works produced about the cultural experience of this country." Kennedy demurred, suggesting that none other than the historian C. Vann Woodward, present in the room, had really missed something in claiming that no book had ever gone "deeper into the meaning . . . of the Civil War" than *Patriotic Gore*.[55]

Then Nobel laureate Toni Morrison rose from the audience to speak. She was "uncomfortable" about the "intrusion of race and the possibility of racism" into the discussion. She spoke in defense of artistic freedom, suggesting that Wilson might not have understood Frederick Douglass very well anyway. "I am very happy that Wilson chose to be brilliant about what he did know," said Morrison to what must have been a riveted audience, "and I have always admired him for that." She chastised Kennedy and reversed the story. Morrison said she would never want to be held to a standard that judged her books negatively fifty years hence because they did not adequately develop "white people as major characters." Let Wilson be Wilson, she implied; let every writer be who he or she is, without "that burden of inclusiveness."[56]

Such a debate about Wilson's *Patriotic Gore* is one we might expect in 1995, and perhaps again in some other form with new kinds of intensities, at the Sesquicentennial. That it did not happen in 1962 to any significant extent was placed in a longer perspective in a brilliant short essay for the same Wilson conference by the black novelist David Bradley. Author of the historical novel *The Chaneysville Incident* (1975), Bradley described mixed feelings of admiration and "sorrow" when confronting the question of race in Wilson's work. He called Wilson a "courageous . . . intellectual treasure," a "brilliant thinker," and a "brave traveler" in many of the world's literatures. But he wondered about Wilson the man and the "things" he had "left unspoken." "One can only be so gracious," offered Bradley as a black American, "and still tell the truth." He wondered how Wilson could occupy the post he did in New York in the 1920s literary world and never acknowledge Alain Locke's book *The New Negro*, when many other white artists and critics surely had. He quoted from a long letter by Wilson in 1925 where the critic commented, disturbingly, on meeting members of the Ku Klux Klan who were guests at his own home in Red Bank, New Jersey. Bradley wondered how Wilson could write to a friend that his wife, Mary Blair, was about to appear in a play by Eugene O'Neill about racial mixing, without the slightest mention that she was playing next to Paul Robeson.[57]

Mostly, Bradley too was troubled by *Patriotic Gore*, and to a degree he hung Wilson on his own words, drawn from *Finland Station:* "One cannot reproduce the whole history and yet keep the forms and proportions of art. One cannot care so much about what has happened in the past and not care what is happening in one's own time. One cannot care about what is happening in one's own time without wanting to do something about it." Bradley acknowledged *Patriotic Gore* as a great book, but called it an "opportunity lost" and asked for the possibility of a "more complicated reading" of it. He wondered if Wilson had not been a grand man of letters "searching for something among all the tribes save one." Bradley's nuanced, mournful critique of Wilson was one that only a great, flawed writer might inspire in a time that had seemed to pass that writer by. Bradley asks: "What could be gorier than slavery?"[58] Although Wilson had always understood how the present intruded on the past, in this case his blind spot had been exposed.

. . .

Patriotic Gore should ultimately be judged for what is in it. The book prompted many American writers and critics to take notice, and indeed to write essays on the Civil War's place in American culture that, without Edmund Wilson's challenge, they never would have written. The book inspired a virtual genre of review essays about the meaning of the Civil War like nothing else published during the Centennial, or perhaps even since. As the reviews poured forth, Wilson showed a bit of defensiveness in responding to his friends and critics. He was especially sensitive to all the outrage over his Introduction. He effusively thanked Warren for his review, which pleased him "more than anything else that has been written about *Patriotic Gore,* because it got deeper into the book." Indeed it did. But Wilson felt a need to explain his "moral indignation," saying that he wanted to "remove" the Civil War "from the old melodramatic plane." To Max Eastman, he admitted that his Introduction was "inadequate," but said he was "supplementing it with a kind of pamphlet, which I'll be sending you in due course." In 1963, Wilson published his strident, polemical attack on federal taxation, *The Cold War and the Income Tax: A Protest,* which reads like a thoroughly presentist, antiwar addendum to *Patriotic Gore.*[59]

With Kazin, who generally loved the book, Wilson had a running dispute and demanded to be better understood. "I do not think you quite understand my point of view," he wrote to his friend. He insisted that World War II and the Civil War were not, essentially, "moral battles"; Americans, he maintained, would not have fought to "defend the Jews," nor did Yankees fight to "liberate Negroes." He wanted to take politics and morality out of the story of the Civil War. "I think we ought to train ourselves to disassociate our views of war from these moral attitudes," he lectured the disbelieving Kazin, who would have been right to ask: Who was the real romantic or utopian now? Wilson revealed his obsession for imposing his wish-fulfillment on the past. "In the case of the Civil War," he fumed, "I believe that the most embarrassing policy the North could have adopted with the South would have been to allow them to secede. They would have been stuck with their unworkable economy and would have had to come to terms with the modern world . . . just as at present the most embarrassing thing we could do with Russia would be to abandon nuclear testing."[60] Many of Wilson's critics saw the holes in his arm-chair zoological lessons of history, and concentrated on the eight hundred pages about literature and the war.

But Wilson did not lose his sense of humor about the attention and furor his book had stimulated. Sometimes it was manifested in a self-protective arrogance. On May 11, 1962, Wilson and his wife, Elena, were among 168 guests at a White House dinner given by President and Mrs. Kennedy in honor of André Malraux, the French writer and diplomat who had just won the Nobel Prize. The attendees at this "big cultural blowout," as Wilson called it in his irreverent and hilarious journal entry, included Allan Tate, Robert Lowell, Robert Penn Warren, James Baldwin, Thornton Wilder, Saul Bellow, Tennessee Williams, and many more. The guests were seated in groups of ten, and Wilson was placed at Kennedy's table. The president had read a review of *Patriotic Gore* and pressed the author on why he had chosen his title and what "conclusions" he had "come to about the Civil War." "I answered that I couldn't very well tell him then and there," remembered Wilson, "and referred him to the Introduction." Kennedy remarked that it was unusual for an author not to want to talk about his book, and then the subject changed. As they were all saying goodbye at the end of the glorious evening, which conclud-ed with a performance by the violinist Isaac Stern, Kennedy again said something about Wilson's not discussing his book and joked, "I suppose I'll have to buy it." Wilson answered, "I'm afraid so." Wilson ended the journal entry by noting that at the after-party Warren and Tate had showered him with compliments about *Patriotic Gore*, which he "waved away but much enjoyed—especially since they are both Southerners."[61]

In June 1962, Wilson crafted an imaginary "Interview with Edmund Wilson," and published it in the *New Yorker*. In the dialogue, he is visiting London for what may be one last time and he especially wants to dine at the Café Royal. He and his interlocutor discuss various English authors and playwrights, some of whom Wilson likes and some he "abominate[s]" for their "fraudulent cleverness." He gets to hold forth on nuclear weapons and the "animal rivalry" between the United States and the Soviet Union—like "a couple of gorillas beating their breasts." He tries to remain "cheerful," he tells his interviewer, since "there's no real way of getting rid of the horrible American cities except to have them vaporized." When asked about his new book and whether it is on the "American" Civil War, as opposed to the English, Wilson answers: "Yes the North and the South—Lincoln and Lee and all that." Then, queried as to whether he actually remembers the Civil War, Wilson lampoons the Centennial's popular excesses, gets in a dig at his critics, and declares his thoughts on the conflict's meaning all in one satirical moment. "Oh, very well," he answers. "I was a drummer boy at Gettysburg, one of the big battles. But later on I came to realize that the South ought to have been allowed to secede from the Union—that was the great issue rather than slavery you know—and I deserted and took refuge in upstate New York, which had always been rather disaffected. I became what is called a Copperhead."[62] One can almost hear Red Warren howling while reading those lines, knowing that Wilson had revealed something largely true about himself.

Many critics rambled through *Patriotic Gore* to divine its impact and discovered a Civil War they had never known. Despite the book's iconoclasm and its unnecessary heft, Daniel Aaron described it as a "nutritious discourse" that "discloses unwelcome truths about ourselves and our country. . . . It uncovers or discovers what we forgot or never knew about our literary culture." Parts of the book read today as anachronisms. Wilson's long concentration on the Southern poet Sidney Lanier, for example, in his ninety-page chapter on Civil War poetry, seems odd at best. Warren, for one, really slammed Wilson for missing the depth and power of Melville's *Battle Pieces.* And Wilson's historical grasp of the Reconstruction era is mired in outdated (even for 1960) notions of the period as a time of sinister exploitation and oppression of the South by radical Republicans. Both David Donald and Robert Penn Warren chastised Wilson for this enduring misunderstanding of Reconstruction, Warren going so far as to write a long footnote in his review, suggesting that "a much tougher line than the one pursued" by the North "might have done more good . . . if it had . . . been more consistent and comprehensible."[63] It is remarkable that a book of literary history could solicit such serious contemplations on the meaning of the entire epoch of the Civil War and Reconstruction. Even when wrongheaded, *Patriotic Gore* was the kind of book that provoked attention. And it still should today.

If the book has one further overarching theme, it is Wilson's claim that the Civil War, though it destroyed so many lives, literally made the careers of some Americans and ushered in a new, modern, money-obsessed commercial age. Wilson charted the rise and wreckage of this age through literature, a new chastened literary style born of the war, and especially two unusual writers—Ulysses S. Grant and Oliver Wendell Holmes, Jr. Grant and Holmes captivated Wilson for different reasons, but his portraits of both are lasting achievements even as they serve to refute the central intention of his Introduction: to remove the Civil War from the "moral plane," to lift it out of myth and peel it down to its reality. With Grant and Holmes, Wilson did peel the war down to its bloody horror, and they all but tricked him into stepping out on his own moral plane—paradoxically, the antiwar terrain on which hero-warriors could still be celebrated.

Like Gertrude Stein and others before him, Wilson fell for Grant the writer, as well as for his seemingly imperturbable, stoical Americanness in this most American crisis. That Grant had managed to finish writing the two volumes of his *Personal Memoirs* as he was dying with throat cancer—one of the most remarkable deathbed writing stories of all time—was, to Wilson, "another of his victories." At times, Wilson's study of Grant is even better biography than it is literary history. Wilson describes Grant writing in those last days: "Humiliated, bankrupt, and voiceless, on the very threshold of death, sleeping at night sitting up in a chair as if he were still in the field and could not risk losing touch with developments, he relived his old campaigns." Wilson had discovered a center for his long book, and his characterizations of Grant's literary deathbed are no less moving or powerful than those of Bruce Catton in his *U.S. Grant and the American Military Tradition* (1954). Wilson shows no evidence of having read Catton, but we might wish that the literary critic and the popular historian had met and talked. Catton, too, found inspiration in describing Grant in the final days of writing: "Now the man is fighting to get the job done while the light lasts. . . . The writing becomes skeletonized as if pain and the rising mist made it impossible to get every word in . . . [and] going back along the old road he somehow found himself."[64] Both writers seemed endlessly surprised by the fascinating literary ride that Grant, the great horseman turned author, gave them along that road.

Moreover, Wilson found Grant's spare, direct prose "perfect in concision and clearness, in its propriety and purity of language." Wilson was a man of a million literary judgments, yet he seems never to have said this about any other writer. He is also impressed with the way Grant, "without conscious art, conveyed the suspense" in describing his campaigns and the drama of the war. "The reader," writes an enthralled Wilson, "finds himself involved—he is actually on edge to know how the Civil War is coming out." Wilson is so taken in by Grant's portrayal of his meeting with Lee in the surrender at Appomattox that he simply says, "It is impossible to summarize this scene," and then quotes at great length from the general's unsentimental remembrance of his conversations with the far better-dressed Virginian. Grant arrived clad in a mud-splattered uniform with no ceremonial sword to match that of his opponent. That "this ideal of the powerful leader, with no glamour and no pretensions," emerged from such a transcendent moment moved Wilson to call the scene "perhaps something new in the world"—the commoner as the winning general in the biggest war ever, with no "epaulettes."[65] For a writer so contemptuous of sentiment, he seems in this instance to have simply given in.

Wilson is further struck by how Grant admits to losing composure when he faced the wounded and dying in field hospitals. After seeking cover in a house full of badly wounded men, Grant recalled: "The sight was more unendurable than encountering the enemy's fire and I returned to my tree in the rain." The old hospital orderly from World War I admired Grant's unromantic willingness to admit that it was "after the battle," not during, that war leaves its lasting marks on the psyche. And he stressed how this great and sometimes ruthless warrior detested "the sight of blood." Wilson uses a book entitled *Campaigning with Grant*, by Horace Porter (a staff officer on the Overland Campaign of 1864), to illustrate with realistic eloquence how Grant personally struggled when witnessing the death and suffering he daily ordered his men to endure. In a lull in the terrible Battle of the Wilderness in May 1864, Porter remembered, Grant was riding past scenes of "unutterable horror . . . forest fires [in which] the dead were roasted . . . and every bush seemed hung with shreds of blood-stained clothing." Grant rode past a line of wounded along the roadside; one particular young, "strikingly handsome" soldier caught the general's attention because of "the blood flowing from a wound in his breast, the froth about his mouth . . . tinged with red and his wandering, staring eyes . . . unmistakable evidence of approaching death." Grant stopped, "visibly affected," and then a galloping officer rode by and splattered mud all over the dying man's bloody countenance. Grant began to dismount to attend to the soldier, but Porter leaped from his horse to wipe the young man's face. As they rode away, said Porter, the general kept looking back at the dying, youthful face.[66]

With Porter's help, Wilson made genuine war literature out of Grant's magnificent memoir, and, in turn, made Grant himself into an unforgettable character. But he also knew that the real war was still not quite attainable to Grant, or even Bierce, DeForest, or other early realists. Something was deflected and missing in these nineteenth-century writers. As Grant, at the end of his moving remembrance, turned to the mission of sectional reconciliation—predicting an era of "great harmony" between North and South—Wilson acknowledged that the general had made it possible for his readers to "forget a good deal of the Civil War," and that his "very objectivity" and terse style served to "eliminate its tragedy."[67] Wilson may have so admired Grant because he was both the antimythic and the mythic character all at once. And by giving in so thoroughly to this great performance of writing—recreating and celebrating it as he did—Wilson showed just what a deeply *moral* event the Civil War had been. His brilliant chapter on Grant is a moral testimony about the costs of war, as well as about how cheaply we sometimes purchase the complex consequences of its aftermath. So determined was Wilson to rid all discussion about the war of its moral cant, he sometimes could only replace it with a half-intended, literary form of moral grandeur. What the Grant chapter demonstrates is that the war had enormous moral consequences, in its scale of death and suffering, as well as for those aims and purposes Wilson preferred to dismiss.

In Holmes, Wilson seems to have thought he had discovered an aristocratic, scholarly Grant, and a kind of ultimate survivor of the war. To a degree, perhaps he even found in Holmes an alter ego, a man as detached as he could get from the "pulse of the machine" in his own age, just as Wilson had become in his alienation from Cold War America. Myth and reality also collided in Holmes, especially in relation to the war that had ravaged him physically and emotionally, and that in turn seemed to condition his habits and shape his memory for the rest of his long life. No one more famously contributed to the myth of soldiers' valor and devotion than Holmes did in his 1895 Memorial Day address, "Soldier's Faith"—a speech quoted over and over in the decades since, to serve both hawkish and dovish persuasions.[68] At the same time, no one had more thoroughly exploded the romance of war than Holmes did in his despairing testimonies from the front in 1861–1864.

In diaries and letters, Holmes left a vivid trail of his youthful immersion in the terrors of war. He enlisted at age twenty in April 1861, in a "spirit of romantic chivalry" (says Wilson), eager to sacrifice for the "crusade" of Union and abolition. But combat and several brushes with death soon gave a "paralyzing stroke to his idealism." Holmes was badly wounded in the chest at Ball's Bluff in October 1861, and as he came to believe he was dying, his New England Christian faith dissolved. After a long convalescence, he was back with his regiment at Antietam, on September 17, 1862—the bloodiest day of the war—when he was again desperately wounded, with a bullet through the neck that only narrowly missed his jugular vein. Sent home again for six more weeks of recovery, he followed "duty" back to the front once more, only to be wounded yet again—this time in the heel—near Fredericksburg in May 1863. Holmes nearly quit more than once, and his letters and diary became a confused catalogue of horrors and disillusionments—of seeing the dead piled in heaps, and trees shot into pieces. He survived the Virginia campaign of 1864, through all the carnage of the Wilderness, Spotsylvania Court House, and Cold Harbor, writing to his mother and father about the escalating "butcher's bill" and "all the fatigue & horror that war can furnish." "I started in this thing a boy," he wrote his parents when he was mustered out in July 1864; "I am now a man."[69] But a vastly different man.

In the aftermath of this central experience of his young life, Holmes threw himself into studying the law, tried desperately to forget the war, and refused as best he could to even read about it. Serving first on the Supreme Court of Massachusetts and later appointed by

Theodore Roosevelt to the U.S. Supreme Court, Holmes converted his past agony into an almost ruthless ambition and a Puritan work ethic. An atheist as a result of the religious crisis he had undergone in the war, he nevertheless maintained a staunch set of Calvinist habits and behaviors—anxiety about his elite ("elect") status, about measuring up to his inherited superior Brahmin talents, and, as Wilson puts it, about "working hard and working uphill." Wilson admired all of this in Holmes, as though he were somehow seeing what his own father had wanted for himself and his son. But most of all, he admired Holmes's splendid "isolation" from "the whole turbid blatant period that followed the Civil War—with its miseries of an industrial life that was reducing white factory workers to the slavery which George Fitzhugh had predicted, with its millionaires as arrogant and brutal as any Carolina planters, with the violent clashes between them as bloody as Nat Turner's rebellion or John Brown's raid upon Kansas." Holmes became Wilson's own ideal of a sort, "the one" survivor "who was never corrupted" by the war he had "with him all his life." Wilson, too, exhibited a nearly superhuman work ethic; he had floundered through many corruptions of his own, and had often struggled to earn enough money. Perhaps through Wilson's deep reading of Holmes's letters, we can best see that, as one critic has suggested, Wilson played the role of "historian of the fate of American Calvinism."[70]

After 798 pages, Wilson had long since decided that the Civil War had, in the long run, not really been worth it; the Gilded Age, and future Gilded Ages to come, had rendered the field hospitals and graves of the 1860s unworthy of Lincoln's grand eloquence at Gettysburg or in the Second Inaugural. Even more, Wilson seemed to find in Holmes this very interpretation of the Civil War that he himself had embraced. Describing Holmes, Wilson wrote: "The Northerners had to kill the Southerners in order to keep the South in the Union. And thus, at least, Holmes is never misleading. He does not idealize Lincoln; he does not shed tears about slavery. He does not call the planters wicked; he merely says that they are not truly civilized." All the actors had played their parts, and the curtain would come down on that "bleakness" that neither Holmes nor Wilson could ever quite dispel.[71] It was this bleakness underneath any higher sense of redemptive outcome to the Civil War that Wilson insisted upon. Human beings, through nations, act out their violent aims in history; the writer-hero remains to meditate on such essential tragedies in the human condition.

But Wilson loved paradox, and even seemed to relish his own contradictions. In Holmes he found a harsh hero as artist; a legal philosopher who hated facts and loved abstract ideas as he interpreted the Constitution as an evolving "experiment"; an American who had little interest in seeing his own country and rarely read newspapers, but who devoted his life to a national institution. In Holmes, Wilson found, it appears, even his own kind of patriotism—a devotion to old republican ideals embodied by America's "Last Roman," a man born and educated to lead, by "moral courage," with his pen and through action. Like Stephens, Holmes became a kind of secessionist, too—seceding from all that was stultifying in society itself. And if "businessmen" were the real victors in the Civil War, as Wilson believed, Holmes apparently tried to remain as removed and ignorant of their universe as he could in his scholarly perch on the Supreme Court. As though stepping outside of history were itself a moral act, Wilson seemed to cynically follow Holmes (according to Norman Podhoretz) in acts of "private salvation."[72] One way of reading Wilson on Holmes, as *Patriotic Gore* comes to an abrupt end, is to conclude that there is no point in taking ideas out into the cold, brutal world to try to change anything. But that would be forgetting so much of the rest of the book.

As Robert Penn Warren concluded, Wilson was less a historian and more the "moralist—a rather peculiar moralist" who knew that the world was changed by human "self-interest" and by "ideals." Warren appreciated *Patriotic Gore* as a moral "work of art" probing one American Civil War survivor after another—men who, as an aggregate, helped to explain the "tragic depth" of that event. As Warren beautifully put it in tribute to Wilson, there is no higher calling for the artist than to show us how to "criticize our myths." Learning history can have no better use, patriotism no deeper purpose. "They also serve," Wilson wrote, "who only stand and watch. The men of action make history, but the spectators make most of the histories, and these histories may influence the action."[73] Or so we can hope.

James Baldwin, February 1963, as *The Fire Next Time*
was published. Private collection, courtesy
Picture Research Consultants.

· CHAPTER FOUR ·

"This Country Is My Subject"

James Baldwin

To accept one's past—one's history—is not the same thing as
drowning in it; it is learning how to use it. An invented past can
never be used; it cracks and crumbles under the pressures of life
like clay in a season of drought.

—James Baldwin, *The Fire Next Time*, 1963

ON September 24, 1964, aboard an Alitalia flight from Europe
soon to land in New York City, the intercontinental commuting
writer James Baldwin scratched out a handwritten letter to his friend
Mary Painter, an economist working at the United States Embassy in
Paris. It was a volatile, tense, and increasingly violent time in the daily
developments of the Civil Rights Movement, in which Baldwin had
become a famous player. Indeed, by 1963–1964 Baldwin's words, as
speaker and essayist, as well as his photograph, had become ubiquitous in the American and European press. Fearing for his own physical safety and hounded by reporters to make pronouncements on
race at every turn, Baldwin periodically fled to parts of Europe or to
Istanbul, Turkey, to find some peace and quiet to write. The stressed
passenger was listening to a loud American woman's voice on the
plane, and he could not bear it. "Those voices!" he complained. "How
did Americans get them?" He was very anxious about the racial and
historical situation, less than a year after President Kennedy's assassination, a full year after the March on Washington, in which he had
participated, and little more than two months since the passage of
the 1964 Civil Rights Act. A year after the killing of black children
in Southern churches and of Civil Rights workers across the South,

the prominent grassroots leader Medgar Evers, a friend of Baldwin's, was murdered by Klansmen in Mississippi in June. All still seemed frightfully uncertain to Baldwin; he felt an "unshakable burden of apprehension." "Returning to America has never made me joyful," he told Painter, "but never before has it made me so sad." Baldwin did not fear for his own ability to keep rising to the challenge as an activist, he wrote; "it is simply that I no longer feel that the challenge is worthwhile. It is a doomed nation, a doomed people—if I were not an American I would say *Tant mieux, Qu'il crève* [all the better if it were to die]. Maybe, then, whoever is left will have learned something." As he ordered another whiskey and asked Mary to "hold my hand," he concluded this odd but compelling letter: "But I *am* an American and cannot shrug my shoulders."[1]

The Civil War Centennial and the Civil Rights Movement were at once awkwardly intertwined and deeply segregated. Sometimes they seemed to exist on different planets orbiting different suns. Other times the two planets veered off course and collided. Partly of his own emerging political will, but also from the exile's need to return to his personal and literary homeland, Baldwin strode into the breach between these two historic phenomena like no other writer. In an atmosphere of historical commemoration, as well as book and magazine publishing, dominated by Civil War nostalgia and minutiae, Confederate symbolism, the pathos and heroism of military narratives, and North-South reconciliation, Baldwin provided a thoroughly public, often strident voice of dissent. He was not the spokesman for "Negro history"—the carefully researched, well-written, and largely unknown story of the crucial roles of blacks in the shaping of American history from slavery to freedom. A growing number of talented professional historians had been writing that story—for relatively small audiences, and with only marginal impact on mainstream curriculums—for two or three decades. In a memorial culture about the Civil War era, a culture riddled with white-supremacist notions of the meaning and legacy of Reconstruction and bitterly unwilling to surrender Jim Crow, who really listened to Baldwin's demands for an alternative history? Even racially liberal or moderate whites, often themselves the products of genteel segregationism, and stymied by their own educational, imaginative, and Cold War restraints, could not forge a genuine place for blacks at the table of the Centennial feast. Moreover, many blacks themselves lacked the power or will to demand a place at that national table. In the midst of this toxic but fluid convergence of Civil War mania and civil rights revolution, Baldwin wrote and shouted his way into the room. Less as an artist and more as a preacher and polemicist who could deliver history and ideas with what his biographer James Campbell calls a "quicksilver intelligence," Baldwin became unavoidable by the early Sixties.[2] Millions of whites read or heard him; it is difficult to know how well or to what ends they listened. What is clear is that the throngs of serious readers attracted by the works of Warren, Catton, and Wilson on the Civil War theme at least had to decide whether to listen to or dismiss Baldwin.

When the weary Baldwin return to New York in the fall of 1964, the year after the centennial of Emancipation, he was acutely aware that he had been throwing himself into the Civil Rights Movement for at least seven years, often willy-nilly and with great harm to his artistic talents, trying in his unique if futile way to redeem the nation and especially to make his countrymen face their history. In what became a trademark pattern, Baldwin would make a public statement in which he all but gave up the struggle; and then in a subsequent statement he would fight back, at least rhetorically, with unbridled passion. Earlier that year he had "bitterly bewailed . . . the lot of an American writer—to be part of a people who have ears and hear not, who have eyes to see and see not!" And in a piece to be published soon after his arrival back in the United States that autumn, Baldwin declared himself fed up with Americans' insistence on seeing their history through the sunny lens of "progress." "I become so unmanageable," he wrote, "when people ask me to confirm their hope that

there has been progress—what a word!—in white-black relations."
Yet he could still conclude with his own demand on the nation's historical consciousness: "The American Negro really is a part of this
country and on the day we face this fact, and not before that day,
we will become a nation and possibly a great one."³ From a distance
of nearly fifty years, it is easy to forget that in 1964 such a claim was
startling, threatening, even unacceptable to millions of Americans. It
is still sobering in the twenty-first century to wonder how much that
claim, and the claims of other nonwhite, non-Christian groups, challenge the comfortable worldview of the White Republic.

By 1964, Baldwin's picture had been on the cover of *Time* magazine
(May 17, 1963); long features had been written on him in *Life*, *Esquire*,
and many other magazines. For sheer fame, Baldwin was probably
the most prominent writer in America during that period. He had
been elected to the National Institute of Arts and Letters that year; he
had lectured all over the country, toured the South and parts of West
Africa, been to dinner at the White House, and given almost endless television interviews. For better or worse, Baldwin had become
what Robert Penn Warren and others called the "voice" of the "Negro
Revolution," virtually as prominent as Martin Luther King, Jr., Malcolm X, or any other black leader.⁴ How the lonely, emotionally dis-
traught, little Jimmy Baldwin of the late 1940s to mid-1950s, who had
been living in self-exile in Paris and who had been born and raised in
poverty in Harlem and struggled very publicly with his homosexuality in a society that considered it illegal and unnatural, had attained
this kind of cultural and political celebrity tells us much about Baldwin himself. But it also says much about how the Civil War Centennial era was experienced on opposite sides of the color line in America. By the late Fifties and early Sixties, most Americans who cared
still did not really comprehend how slavery, the African American
experience, and the Civil War and Reconstruction fit into the same
epic story. Baldwin spent the Centennial mostly in America, flying in
airplanes and riding buses, doing countless interviews, engaging in

many public debates, and especially laboring as an essayist, recording his interpretation of the civil rights revolution and what it meant in the sweep of American history. Although he hardly needed to declare it explicitly, Baldwin made himself into an alternative African American voice responding to the cacophony and orthodoxy of Centennial popular culture.

Baldwin wanted desperately to be loved—by his family, by his father, by his friends, by his lovers, by the world at large; he also wanted to find a way, if possible, to love his country, and to be loved by it.[5] If Robert Penn Warren felt the Civil War in the emotional furniture of his psyche, Bruce Catton narrated its drama as though he had lived it in a Union regiment, and Edmund Wilson spent a huge swath of his career breathing in its literature and puncturing its myths, then James Baldwin embodied it. Yet he did so not as the clash of Blue and Gray, or as the consequence of secession, disunion, and reunion. Baldwin's Civil War was a deeply internal battle against the fear and rejection caused by racism, homophobia, and what he came to analyze as America's mythic sense of its own invulnerable, self-righteous, unexamined or even unknown history. If emancipation of the slaves and the reimagination of the American republic were the central results of the Civil War epoch, then Baldwin used his own experience, his own sense of self, as a kind of emotional and intellectual testing ground of those results. The tests brought tormented hope and terrible despair.

Baldwin only occasionally wrote directly about the Civil War; his subject, rather, was America's enduring dilemma with race and its searing effects on his own life. Baldwin's subject, like that of the other three writers to varying degrees, was also the centrality of alienation, violence, and hatred in the human condition. Also like the other three, Baldwin wanted to know what really constituted "tragedy" in American experience, and why his fellow countrymen spent so much energy trying to deflect or deny it. As an artist he was thoroughly engaged, even consumed, by his search to understand and remake

American historical memory. As we contemplate the multiple "legacies" of the Civil War, one place we can find many of the most potent is inside the interior world of James Baldwin, in those letters and essays he wrote from the "regions" of his "mind."[6] If, without the Civil War as a great pivot in the trajectory of American history, it is impossible to imagine our aspirations for the maximization of freedom and equality—racial, religious, sexual, gender, or any other form—then the war for union and emancipation never really ended for James Baldwin the writer. In his work we might find ways to test whether it has ended for us.

• • •

Born James Arthur Jones on August 2, 1924, at Harlem Hospital in New York City, Baldwin never knew his real father, who, it appears, abandoned him and his mother, Emma Berdis Jones. Baldwin's mother had emigrated from Maryland to New York after World War I. In 1927 she met and married David Baldwin, also a recent arrival from the South. The man who thus became James's stepfather, and the "father" immortalized in *Go Tell It on the Mountain* (1953) and other writings, was born in New Orleans and followed thousands of other blacks in the Great Migration to northern cities in search of jobs and better lives. But he was a deeply embittered man who worked in a deadening day job at a bottle factory out on Long Island, and then served in the evenings and on Sundays as a storefront preacher of a stern and angry Christian Gospel. Seeking vengeance against the "white devils" he had encountered seemingly at every turn of his desperate life, Baldwin's father was a violent and ultimately mentally unstable man who, with the small, sensitive, religious Emma, had eight more children. As a child, James feared and sometimes loathed his father. "Part of his problem was he couldn't feed his kids," Baldwin recollected, "but I was a kid and didn't know that." Young Baldwin knew his grandmother, his stepfather's mother, Barbara Ann Baldwin, who was a former slave and lived with them until she died in 1933. His grandmother provided vivid memories for young Jimmy;

for a few years she served as protector of the little boy against the abusiveness and anger of his father.[7]

It is telling to note that beginning in a drab and overcrowded house at Park Avenue and 131st Street, hard by the elevated railroad tracks connecting downtown Manhattan with all points north, little Jimmy Baldwin grew up as the third generation removed from slavery. His parents and grandmother were migrants from the Jim Crow South, and eventually Jimmy wound up helping to nurture and raise his eight younger siblings, as the entire family tried to cope with the hell of urban poverty. In a brief poem Baldwin later wrote, "Imagination," he might have been remembering the anguish as well as the life-affirming circumstances of the household at Park and 131st:

> Imagination
> Creates the situation,
> And, then, the situation
> Creates imagination.
> It may, of course,
> be the other way around:
> Columbus was discovered
> by what he found.

Trying to sidestep the drunks, addicts, pimps, and abusive police who at least once attacked him in the streets outside his home, Baldwin, who was very small and who believed, with his father's urging, that he was ugly, escaped as best he could into books. By age thirteen, Baldwin claimed, he had read everything worth reading in the Harlem libraries and he soon ventured downtown to the main New York Public Library on 42nd Street, an imposing two-block-long building with giant stone lions out front. More than once, the young, diminutive Baldwin would cross Fifth Avenue to enter that magnificent library of his dreams while a white policeman yelled at him that "niggers" should stay uptown where they belonged. As newborns kept appearing in the house, "I took them over with one hand," Baldwin remembered, "and held a book with the other." He fell in love with language and stories, especially *A Tale of Two Cities*, by Charles Dickens, and *Uncle Tom's Cabin*, by Harriet Beecher Stowe. His opinion of Stowe's classic antislavery novel would later drastically change, but as a youth Baldwin relished books that would transport him to new worlds and offer characters he could almost see.[8] His "situation" created both the need for and the character of his imagination, but he would not stay there any longer than he had to.

Language both saved and tormented James Baldwin. He learned to use it fluently for many purposes; it became his boyhood means of imagining his way out of the Harlem ghetto, as well as his means to first embrace and then reject the intense, stultifying religion of his father and his neighborhood. When writing his compact "Autobiographical Notes" at age thirty-one in 1955, after publishing his first novel and living abroad in France for most of seven years, Baldwin reflected on the "price a Negro pays for becoming articulate." He had been reading Shakespeare carefully in the early 1950s, and there in *The Tempest* he found, as many writers have before and since, a personal resonance; the play became central to his self-portrait. "You taught me language," says Caliban to Prospero and Baldwin to us, "and my profit on't is I know how to curse"; "The red plague rid you for learning me your language," Caliban concludes the accusation. Language opened for Baldwin an awareness, he claimed, of all that he loved and hated. Reading, layered with experience, made him comprehend that he "hated and feared white people," and that he "hated and feared the world." But because he could write, he would use language in order to prevent the world from exercising "a murderous power over me." If he remained in a "self-destroying limbo," Baldwin wrote as a maturing artist, "I could never hope to write."[9]

These were the reflective but controlled reminiscences of a thirty-one-year-old who had been writing plays, stories, and now novels and essays since the age of twelve. But perhaps the most revealing element of his self-perception as a writer-artist in that 1955 sketch was Baldwin's "prime concern" about the importance of history. His Caliban may have felt the curse of language and needed to purge it by constant striving, and by writing and rewriting against publishers' rejections; but very little in the imagination really mattered, Baldwin concluded, unless one learned how to "take a long look back." "I think that the past is all that makes the present coherent," said the young novelist who would constantly make his own personal present his passionate subject, "and, further, the past will remain horrible for exactly as long as we refuse to assess it honestly." The "most crucial time" in his own development, Baldwin maintained, came when he began to feel like a "bastard" or an "interloper" in the history he learned and felt. But he also learned that he would have to appropriate and make his own story out of and within what he called "these white centuries." He wrote as a Negro, he said, about being a Negro, because, like all writers, he had to draw "the last drop, sweet or bitter," from his "own experience." The "Negro problem" was his problem as well as the country's, and he never tired of using that word "country," with all its possible ironic meanings. A country *is* its history and its myths, Baldwin clearly understood, and any writer's work had to be forged through the "history, traditions, customs, the moral assumptions and preoccupations of the country." As Baldwin summed up his loves and hates in his "Autobiographical Notes," he announced what might be considered the theme of his artistic life: "I love America more than any other country in the world, and, exactly for this reason, I insist on the right to criticize her perpetually."[10] In the decades ahead, as Baldwin personally threw himself into the history that was happening in his country, the love would ebb and flow, die and then flicker again to life.

. . .

Before James Baldwin could ever understand the meaning of Emancipation in American history and life, he had to find liberation in his own life. He had some help, especially from teachers and mentors who offered creative buffers against his rigid father. At his elementary school, P.S. 24, the principal, a black woman named Gertrude Ayer, nurtured Baldwin's zest for writing and instilled confidence in the boy. And a white teacher, Orrin Miller, from the Midwest, took Baldwin under her wing as long as he would stay there, and introduced him to plays, films, and even May Day marches. At Frederick Douglass Junior High School, P.S. 139, Jimmy flowered as a writer-to-be, producing short stories and other articles for the school magazine, the *Douglass Pilot*. At Douglass, Countee Cullen, the Harlem Renaissance poet, served as advisor to the literary club and as a mentor to Baldwin. Around 1940, Baldwin met the black artist Beauford Delany, who lived in Greenwich Village; this life-long friendship began with the elder painter teaching the youngster how to "see" as an artist, and, most important, introducing him to the blues and to jazz, which were forbidden fruit in his father's house in Harlem. Delany served as the first true model of an artist in Baldwin's personal life, and he seems to have been the first to convey aesthetic sensibility to the boy. Good fortune struck again when Baldwin was accepted at DeWitt Clinton High School, a prestigious institution in the Bronx where most of the students were white—Jews, Italians, and all manner of other ethnicities. At DeWitt Clinton he competed with boys who turned into lasting friends, such as Sol Stein (who became a writer and the editor-in-chief of Stein and Day Publishers), Emile Capouya (who likewise became a writer, and the publisher of the *Nation*), and Richard Avedon (who became famous as a photographer). Here again, Baldwin wrote short stories for the school magazine, and remembered Countee Cullen leaving him with advice to do three things if he wanted to be a writer: "Read and write—and wait."[11] Baldwin managed to do the first two, but rarely ever the third.

Baldwin had escaped the clutches of his father's uneducated anger by day, but not by night. And he was an active member of the Baptist church before escaping it. At age fourteen he experienced the "religious crisis" that he wrote about with such power in *Go Tell It on the Mountain* and *The Fire Next Time*. Knowledge and education had challenged as well as fortified Baldwin. He plowed these memories into scene after scene of *Go Tell It on the Mountain,* his first novel, which took him many years to complete. In that book, the young John Grimes is sent by his teacher to the front of the classroom to write on the blackboard the letters he had memorized. Terrified at being singled out, "on the edge of tears," and certain the teacher is about to demonstrate his errors, he is amazed when she simply tells him to "speak up" and then announces to the whole class that John is a "very bright boy" and should "keep up the good work." Baldwin converts this scene into a self-revelatory commentary: "That moment gave him, from that time on, if not a weapon at least a shield; he apprehended totally, without belief or understanding, that he had in himself a power that other people lacked; that he could use this to save himself, to raise himself; and that perhaps with this power he might one day win that love which he so longed for." A black boy in Harlem had found a new kind of food for life. The text continues:

> This was not, in John, a faith subject to death or alteration, nor yet a hope subject to destruction; it was his identity, and part, therefore, of that wickedness for which his father beat him and to which he clung in order to withstand his father. His father's arm, rising and falling, might make him cry, and that voice might make him to tremble; yet his father could never be entirely the victor, for John cherished something that his father could not reach. It was his hatred and his intelligence that he cherished, the one feeding the other.[12]

But before brains and rage could combine to save him, Baldwin first had to deal with sin and faith. Intelligence was not nearly enough yet to control the sexual and religious confusions churning in his body and soul.

In order to understand Baldwin's view of his country and of history at any time in his life, we need to appreciate his ever-turbulent effort to understand and define himself. For Baldwin, history and the self would always be intertwined. And to know him as a writer, we can do no better than to start by looking at the African American churches in which he first found the rhythm and power of language, but also from which he spent a lifetime escaping even as he knew he never could. As Baldwin once told an interviewer, he was "born a Baptist." When he was fourteen, he had a life-altering conversion experience at a Pentecostal church in Harlem called Mount Calvary. A school friend, Arthur Moore, took Jimmy to meet Mother Horn—Bishop Rosa Artemis Horn, the spiritual leader of this "holy roller" congregation. Wracked with sexual guilt from a confusing and terrifying encounter with a heavy-breathing man in a hallway, from threats by pimps in the streets, and the gnawing guilt his father incessantly imposed on him for going to movies and reading books, Baldwin found a temporary home-away-from-home among the shouting "saints" at the church. Sin was suddenly very real and now had to be contained and defeated; he was for the first time, he said, "afraid of the evil in me." He "fled into the church" to escape all the racial "humiliation" he encountered on the streets, all the "wages of sin" he saw every day "in every wine-stained and urine-splashed hallway, in every clanging ambulance bell, in every scar on the faces of the pimps and their whores."[13] He also discovered some tough, loving attention, and what he admitted he liked most: power.

Young Jimmy was much taken in by the sermons and shouts that seemed to flow directly out of those Old Testament stories about the "whirlwinds" and "plagues" afflicting Egypt, and the "judgment trumpets" sounding forth. Sometimes the saints up by the altar would claim to actually see a "garden trampled by many horsemen, and the big gate open." "Signs" were everywhere and people were being saved on the "threshing floors" of the Baptist and Pentecostal churches around Harlem. One Saturday night, Baldwin (as portrayed in the figure of John Grimes) found himself down on that floor, for hours apparently, the "dust in his nostrils, sharp and terrible, and the feet of the saints shaking the floor beneath him." Baldwin eventually wrote—in fiction and nonfiction—about this experience with an extraordinary combination of sublime respect and vicious contempt. Part Three of *Go Tell It on the Mountain*, "The Threshing-Floor," is as riveting a tale of religious suffering and conversion as has ever been captured in fiction. It is also the tale of a young man's desperate yearning for love—sought from an older-brother figure, Elisha, but also hopelessly from his father, and from the world at large.[14] To understand Baldwin, one should never read his critique of his experiences in the church, written long afterward, without first reading his fictional account of the conversion. Only by writing a story about it, by making his very personal story into art, did he begin to comprehend as well as purge what his father's religion had done to him. Religion was for him his teenage crucible, as his sexuality would be for his early adult years. Both were wars within him, and he would spend some tormented years trying to find their meaning as a fledgling writer.

In 1938–1941, the same three years he attended Clinton High School, Baldwin became a popular boy preacher in several churches around Harlem. He studied the Bible and worked hard on his sermons; most of all, he mastered the craft of the preacher—calling the fallen to the altar, and taking them by exhortation from sin to hope and salvation. The saints liked him; he purchased whole days full of love by what he eventually called his "gimmick" in the "church racket." In *The Fire Next Time*, he recollected that conversion experience with a guarded reverence for its mystery. "The anguish that filled me cannot be described," he wrote. "It moved in me like one of those floods that devastate counties, tearing everything down." He felt "unspeakable pain," screaming and writhing on the floor covered in dust. "I was on the floor all night," he remembered in 1961. And before Baldwin condemned the church and its methods, he honored it; he had to "disengage" himself "from this excitement," but on "the blindest, most visceral level, I never really have." He loved and hated his teenage preaching feats. The drama of the theater, the sheer spirit of the faith, always moved him. "There is still for me no pathos," Baldwin admitted, "quite like the pathos of those multicolored, worn, some-how triumphant and transfigured faces, speaking from the depths of a visible, tangible, continuing despair of the goodness of the Lord. . . . Nothing that has happened to me since equals the power and the glory that I sometimes felt when, in the middle of a sermon, I knew that I was somehow, by some miracle, really carrying, as they say, 'the Word'—when the church and I were one." All those cries of "Amen!" and "Yes Lord!" felt like acts of love that helped him to mask what he later called "the shabbiness of my motives." It was the corruption of the church, the fancy cars and houses of some of the ministers, that drove him away, he claimed. In addition, it seemed to Baldwin that the deep love for the Lord that many of the worship-ers felt was a measure of the despair and self-hatred in their own desperate lives. He could remember the church suppers fondly, but the place only seemed to make him hate his suspicious, bitter, anti-intellectual father even more. Baldwin later thought that his slow exit from preaching and the church dated from the time he turned again to reading major works of literature.[15]

After graduation from high school, Baldwin followed many other young men in the summer of 1942 and found a job working at army depots and defense plants in New Jersey. He told this story in one of his finest pieces, the essay "Notes of a Native Son," first published in *Harper's* in 1955. World War II was now in full force, and Baldwin found himself living in a rented room near the town of Princeton, among white men from the South and the North. Jim Crow stalked the public establishments and the minds and habits of white Jerseyites. "I knew about Jim Crow," he admitted, "but I had never experienced it." In "bars, bowling alleys, and diners," as well as from his coworkers, he encountered almost daily hostility. "We don't serve Negroes here" became so common a response to his presence that the angry nineteen-year-old began to give as good as he got, and it nearly resulted in his death. One night, he and a white buddy saw a movie, *This Land Is Mine*, starring Maureen O'Hara and Charles

Laughton, about the German occupation of France, and afterward went out for a hamburger at the "American Diner." When the counterman refused to serve him, Baldwin and his friend stalked out after a verbal altercation. The streets were crowded with white people, Baldwin remembered in dramatic prose, and he walked right into and through swarms of them, a rage roiling inside his head. Then he described how his anger took over from his head to his body: "I felt, like a physical sensation, a click at the nape of my neck as though some interior string connecting my head to my body had been cut." He snapped, and with utterly reckless abandon surged ahead of his friend and into the most upscale restaurant he could find, and immediately sat down at a table for two. A frightened, sensitive white waitress came up to him and spoke her assigned part—"we don't serve Negroes here"—and then after forcing the girl to say it once more, young James grabbed a glass of water and heaved it at her, missing the waitress but smashing the glass into the mirror behind the bar. As his "frozen blood abruptly thawed," Baldwin kicked his way past people and ran for his life, his white friend providing a decoy.[16]

From this story, Baldwin brilliantly fashioned the lesson of his youth: his life was in danger, in part from the oppressive powers around him, but primarily from the "hatred" in his "own heart." He characterized this dilemma unforgettably as "some dread, chronic disease, the unfailing symptom of which is a kind of blind fever, a pounding in the skull and fire in the bowels." There are many remarkable literary depictions of what racism can do to the human mind and soul, but few any better than this. It was as though in leaving his father's Harlem, Baldwin had discovered the real power of that sickness he could hardly fathom in his father. And by 1955, he was already beginning to speak for the whole race. "There is not a Negro alive," he insisted, "who does not have this rage in his blood—one has the choice, merely, of living with it consciously or surrendering to it. As for me, this fever has recurred in me, and does, and will until I die."[17]

Baldwin rarely wrote of any lesson of youth without its being passed through the tortured memory of his father. And from that well of woe and inspiration came some of his best writing, as well as one of the most perceptive ways of seeing the longer inheritance of historical memory to which Baldwin came to understand himself as an heir. In the summer of 1943 he came back home to Harlem; the physical labor and the racism in New Jersey were too much for him (he could hardly lift a pickaxe), and, most important, his mother was pregnant again and his institutionalized father was dying. In "Notes of a Native Son," Baldwin transcendently wrapped the story of his father's death around his New Jersey labor experience. His father had been "eaten up by paranoia" and finally lay dying, mute and insane. Baldwin wrote hauntingly about his father, a man imprisoned in "an intolerable bitterness of spirit," as though he could have been a model for August Wilson's character Harold Loomis in the play *Joe Turner's Come and Gone.* Yet no redemption in this life awaited David Baldwin. His son the writer would leave such heartbreaking memories of him as this: "I do not remember in all those years that one of his children was ever glad to see him come home." Or the equally painful: "When he tried to help one of us with our homework the absolutely unabating tension which emanated from him caused our minds and our tongues to become paralyzed, so that he, scarcely knowing why, flew into a rage and the child, not knowing why, was punished."[18] All writers have subjects about which they simply must write; this was surely one for Baldwin.

"This bitterness was now mine," Baldwin wrote in retrospect. What he feared most was that the only real inheritance he possessed from his father was this cup of hatreds. And these were old, practiced, historical hatreds, earned by slaves in fields, convicts on chain gangs, menial laborers in dank factories, countless men and women bent under Jim Crow's daily humiliations, and generations of Sunday worshipers shouting away their pain. "I saw that this had been for my ancestors and now would be for me an awful thing to live with and that the bitterness which had helped to kill my father could also kill me." On the day of his father's funeral, the stark joylessness of which he described with eloquent precision, his mother gave birth to her ninth child, James tried to "celebrate" his nineteenth birthday, and Harlem picked up the shattered pieces after the horrible race riot of late July 1943. Baldwin transformed these simultaneous events into nonfiction art with perfect pitch. All in one essay, one finds the over-whelming impact of a distant world war on a frightened home-front population conditioned to distrust all authorities, the irrepressible force of violence ready to explode at any moment in a ghetto on the brink of self-destruction, and a desperate young man's realization in the hollow bleakness of his father's dead face that this old man's bit-terness might be understandable after all—since it had now become his own. His father, concluded Baldwin, as he remembered riding in the hearse over glass-strewn streets, had believed that in racial mat-ters "poison should be fought with poison"; but now the son could say that maybe it "was better not to judge the man who had gone down under an impossible burden." The challenge, of course, was to unbur-den himself of this inheritance. So, almost like a mantra, Baldwin kept reminding himself: "the dead man mattered"; "bitterness was folly"; "hatred could destroy."[19]

Baldwin remembered precious few genuine conversations with his father. In "Notes of a Native Son," he recalled an incident that had occurred when he was about seventeen and about to cease his preaching, walking home from church with his father in their "usual silence." His father asked abruptly, "You'd rather write than preach, wouldn't you?" Astonished at the honesty and vulnerability of the question, he answered, "Yes"—and then he declares the scene "awful to remember," since "that was all we had *ever* said." With his father gone, and after he himself had been fired from yet another job, in a meat-packing plant, Baldwin moved to Greenwich Village, where from 1943 to 1948 he worked as a dishwasher, a janitor, and an eleva-tor operator, while living a bohemian life in cafés. In these crucial years, Baldwin developed some personality traits and habits that only worsened with age: he was always broke and borrowing money, erratic and usually late, self-dramatizing and wearing every personal problem on his sleeve, and prone to sometimes volatile, unpredictable, drunken rudeness. But he had vulnerable charm to spare, and could collect friends by his mere presence and capacity to talk all night.[20]

Baldwin careened between despair in his personal relationships— sexual liaisons with men and women, as he strove to affirm and overcome guilt over his homosexuality—and the joy of meeting many writers and artists, including Marlon Brando and especially Richard Wright, author of *Native Son*, who befriended and mentored the young writer. Wright furnished recommendations to publishers for Baldwin's early version of *Go Tell It on the Mountain*. The manuscript had no success at first, but Wright helped him to obtain fellowships and grants that kept him alive. Wright's extraordinary kindnesses make Baldwin's later fiercely critical (and painfully Oedipal) essays on the older writer all the more ironic. In 1946, a very close black friend named Eugene Worth committed suicide by jumping off the George Washington Bridge, a haunting episode Baldwin would use in his later novel, *Another Country*, which is based directly on these Greenwich Village years. By 1947, Baldwin had begun to publish reviews and essays, honing his skills as a rather audacious, sometimes brutal critic of his elders in such journals as the *Nation, Commentary, Partisan Review,* and the *New Leader.* But he was still unable to finish his novel; and fearing for his well-being (he was harassed in the streets) and his sanity (he believed he was fated for a "similar end" to Worth's), with little money and few plans, Baldwin "resolved to leave America." He moved to Paris in the fall of 1948.[21]

"I left America," Baldwin wrote, "because I doubted my ability to survive the fury of the color problem." He also left for deeply personal and professional reasons. "I think my exile saved my life," he later wrote. His years in France and other parts of Europe, as well as in Istanbul, transformed Baldwin, helped him to produce his first three novels, and made him, along with Ralph Ellison, among the greatest essayists on matters of race and writing of the civil rights era. From 1948 to the late 1950s were also years when Baldwin was plagued by occasional emotional breakdowns, a heavy drinking habit, and constant stress over money. He moved often, living in hotel rooms and friends' apartments when he could. He suffered under, thrived on, and wrote eloquently about the "aloneness" required of the artist. In an essay entitled "The Creative Process," Baldwin developed an idealistic and romantic view of the role of the writer in any civilization. The writer, Baldwin asserted, "must never cease warring" with a kind of heroic loneliness, and must be an "incessant disturber of the peace." As he found his subjects—race, sexuality, the nature of his country's history, and humanity's general inability to face its history—Baldwin found his voice. And he found his workable combination of loves and hatreds. "Societies never know it," he wrote, "but the war of an artist with his society is a lover's war, and he does . . . , at his best, what lovers do, which is to reveal the beloved to himself, and with that revelation, make freedom real." But this "war" had a "price"; and Baldwin began paying it in France, England, Sweden, Switzerland, Corsica, Turkey, and then eventually back in the United States.[22]

Baldwin wandered—first all over Paris, living in various residences, and then to other parts of Europe—in search of companionship and the repose to write. In France, he learned quickly just how American and how Negro he really was. And deciding just who and what he was became a consuming preoccupation, even as Baldwin learned to see the world and write as a cosmopolitan individual. He had to get out of America to know how he might fit back into it. "I wanted to prevent myself from becoming merely a Negro," he wrote in "The Discovery of What It Means To Be an American" (1959), "or, even, merely a Negro writer." Baldwin yearned to know how his *specialness* could "connect" him to other people, rather than "dividing" him from others and from himself. He would often claim he had found reconciliation of all his warring and paradoxical selves, even when he had not. As he later said to an interviewer about his decision to move abroad, "I no longer felt I knew who I really was, whether I was really black or white, really male or female, really talented or a fraud, really strong or merely stubborn. . . . I had to get my head together to survive and my only hope of doing that was to leave America." If there is such a thing as an emotional and intellectual "inner civil war" among young, questing, ambitious artists, Baldwin provides a classic case. In this turbulent stew of personal identity confusion and the desire to find what he had to say about America's story, Baldwin, the wandering *artiste*, wrote about what he knew. "I was not expected to know the things I knew," he recalled of his early Parisian years, "nor to say the things I said . . . or to do the things I did. I knew that I was a black street boy and that knowledge was all I had. . . . All I had, in a word, was me, and I was forced to insist on this *me* with all the energy I had."[23]

In two novels, *Giovanni's Room* (1956) and *Another Country* (1962), Baldwin explored sexuality as few ever had in American fiction. *Giovanni's Room,* which was turned down by several publishers before Dial Press finally accepted it (Knopf called it "repugnant" and Baldwin's own agent urged him to "burn" it), is about the failed and melodramatic love affair between a blond, well-bred, white American expatriate, David, and Giovanni, an Italian bartender in Paris. The novel explores the homosexual world of closeted secrecy and shame, and a passion first achieved and then denied. It also probes the American problem of Puritanism versus freedom and adventure, society's prudish bounds versus human nature and desire. But its deepest theme is how true love can become a tragic casualty in a world where a man (David) proposes marriage to a woman to try to overcome his more natural attraction to men (Giovanni). David cruelly abandons Giovanni, who dies horribly by the guillotine, and then finds his relationship with his fiancée crumbling and his life in confusion and misery, as he cannot suppress the inclination that his society and mind tell him is wrong but that nature and truth tell him is his essential identity. Remarkably, the *New Yorker* reviewed *Giovanni's Room* right next to Bruce Catton's *This Hallowed Ground,* which came out the same year.[24]

In the longer and even more complex book *Another Country,* which became a major bestseller in the United States, Baldwin drew richly from his Greenwich Village experience to explore heterosexual, homosexual, and interracial relationships, all coiled around the theme of the human costs of rejected or socially prohibited love. The sex scenes, though restrained, may have helped to sell the book as well as to get it banned in a few places, but Baldwin's characters, especially the men, are constantly trying to comprehend their sexual natures as their lives demonstrate how historical and social pressures thwart their humanity. A leading black character, Rufus—whose story occupied the first fifth of the book, and who is tortured by racial (rather than sexual) dilemmas—like Baldwin's real-life friend, Eugene Worth, kills himself by jumping off the George Washington Bridge. Lovers are constantly being torn apart, rather melodramatically, over race and sexual preferences; they are all in pursuit of true love, which always seems to slip away in politically and socially charged circumstances; and sometimes they descend into madness. The book, which received decidedly mixed reviews, lacked structure and almost any sense of plot. *Another Country* seemed to be Baldwin's long, tortured way of expressing his roiling "interior world" where fears and prejudices about race and sexual identity continually defeated the incessant human desire to overcome them, to cast away the past, and to simply be loved. When Baldwin became preachy in his fiction, it often spoiled the art. But what sometimes flashes through are brilliant moments about the fated connection of the individual human heart with the collective human story. Early in *Another Country,* David muses about the meaning of the Garden of Eden. "Perhaps life offers only the choice of remembering the garden or forgetting it," he says. "Either, or: it takes strength to remember, it takes another kind of strength to forget, it takes a hero to do both. People who remember court madness through . . . the pain of the perpetually recurring death of their innocence; people who forget court another kind of madness . . . ; and the world is mostly divided between madmen who remember and madmen who forget. Heroes are rare." As Baldwin turned to his "country's" problems with remembering, a peculiarly American brand of innocence would look rather puny in a long view that started with the beginning of time.[25]

Working on multiple projects at once, borrowing money from editors and close friends, and stuffing manuscripts into his duffle bag to travel in search of a new place to write, Baldwin teetered on the verge of what had to have been mental breakdowns, from the mid-1950s into the 1960s. He was a prolific and self-conscious letter writer; and if nothing else, his letters were often his therapy and his way of capturing the attention of those he most needed. Baldwin became a "commuter," returning to the United States occasionally, especially when he could manage a grant, a publisher's advance, or an appointment at a writer's colony. By 1957, he was saying he felt like "a stranger everywhere." He made some very close American friends, first Mary Painter (in Paris), and then David Leeming (in Istanbul), who would become one of his authorized biographers. To Leeming he wrote letters about being nearly suicidal, about how "life is the very greatest artist," and about his conviction that this was almost killing him. At one desperate moment, Baldwin spewed self-pity and anger at his friend, saying, "I may not have every right, but I certainly have every reason for my terrified and terrifying tantrums." And on another occasion he all but apologized to Leeming for appearing as no more than "a difficult, troubling, living tormented man." Baldwin also wrote extraordinary letters to his mother back in Harlem, whom he addressed as though she were the pages of a diary. From Corsica in 1956 he wrote of his feelings one night at "three o'clock in the morning," when he had just returned from a dinner with the mayor of the village; he was lonely and listening to Ella Fitzgerald and Mahalia

Jackson records, and finding that his best thoughts came "out of sorrow." One can only imagine how Emma Baldwin reacted to reading her son's description of his "really peculiar, terrifying demoralization," and his confession that he "became a writer out of loneliness" in order to conquer his loneliness, only to discover the "paradox" that it had the opposite effect. He wanted to be an "example" as a writer, and he knew he "must not . . . fail." The "bill" was coming in for his "journey's cost," and he understood the "price will not go down." Above all, he wanted his mother to know that his emotional crisis was "altogether interior," and nothing for which she should be "ashamed." Desperate to finish *Another Country,* and resisting coming to New York again until he did, Baldwin dramatically assured his mother: "though the war is not over, I am yet holding my own."[26]

Mary Painter supported Baldwin lovingly and endured many of his melodramatic missives. While in the midst of trying over and over to finish *Another Country* without success, Baldwin wrote to Painter with pages of reflections on his desperate solitude. "My life doesn't seem to have any foundations," he lamented, "except whatever foundations I can create by working. And I'm just terrified." "The microbe of human loneliness infects everything I see," he continued. "One begins to suspect that the world we know, the world we make, is nothing but a series of desperate stratagems designed to outwit and to deny the dark." Here was his romantic artist's "aloneness" pouring forth from reality, and not as mere metaphor or theory. "I think life is more important than art," said Baldwin in the middle of a long soliloquy; "the problem is how best to sustain life." He desperately desired, he told Painter, to "make articulate . . . those worlds which bang in me." And from Istanbul, likely in 1961, Baldwin desperately reached out for love from his oldest source of pain. He felt "helpless," he told Mary, but "driven" to finally find "the return of that moment from which this whole, bloody, tangled thing began, when my father's eyes & the world's eyes told me that I was despised." He vowed to Mary Painter, as though she were his conscience, that he would "descend into the heart of my confusion and make peace with it before I die."[27] These anguished cries could have emanated from James Joyce's *Portrait of the Artist as a Young Man*, which Baldwin had avidly read shortly after his arrival in Paris. Joyce's character Stephen Dedalus also struggles mightily to overcome stern religious, sexual, and familial restraints, and has to leave his country to pursue his art. But amid what he called his "confusion" and his interior "war," Baldwin increasingly had a very good reason to return to America, to get outside of himself if he could, and get close to history. It was time to turn his attention to history as well as art—and that, too, would have its price.

· · ·

Baldwin did not attend college, and it is difficult to know precisely how he came by his historical knowledge. He voraciously read American, French, and English fiction; Henry James was his model and his literary hero. But he also read a good deal of history, before and after he left New York, and perhaps on some of those afternoons following all-nighters in Paris cafés. What is clear is that from his earliest writing he exhibited a keen and passionate, if sometimes inchoate, sense of history. For Baldwin, not unlike Warren, Catton, and Wilson—though the young black writer came by it with very different experience—history was epic in its sweep, mythic in its power and substance. A sense of history emerged from and drove the narratives woven into the head and the heart, into action and art, into human nature as well as imagination, and into the best and the worst in human affairs. History made people agents and victims, often both at once. Baldwin ventured bold, sometimes vague, but frequently refreshing claims to speak for and about history; untrammeled by formal research, he converted his individual experience and his sense of the past into a kind of political art. Baldwin worried about how Americans remembered or forgot the Civil War, the Reconstruction era, and the agonizing past-present of the Jim Crow society, but primarily he was driven to play the Jeremiah, constantly calling his readers to wake up, face the past, and thereby try to imagine a new future. This redemptive quest—very much at the heart of that "war" he wrote to his mother about—both made and unmade him during the era of the Civil Rights Movement.

Especially in the genre of the essay, which he mastered in the Fifties, and almost no matter what topic he addressed, Baldwin played the historian in his own populist, artistic way. He developed early a sharp sense of how people used history as a political weapon or as a comforting cloak for policy and behavior; and however he learned to employ the past, he surely understood how others had used it on him. In a 1957 letter on his first tour of the South, he reflected on the much-discussed matter of "public opinion" in the civil rights struggle—the question of how much "change" people would bear. People, he believed, were more fearful than evil. "Most people are not wicked," he wrote. "They are cowards and they are afraid to move alone and they can't bear too much reality." As for public opinion, he declared that "the public . . . doesn't have an opinion, it only has reflexes and fears and taboos and shibboleths, and habit, which are their substitutes for memory."[28] Baldwin had not, so far as I know, needed to read much anthropology or philosophy to know how historical memory functioned in the world, through the virulent mixture of myth, prejudice, and story.

In many of the essays in *Notes of a Native Son* and *Nobody Knows My Name,* as well as in numerous subsequent pieces, Baldwin laid down an artist's analysis, forged out of the cauldron of the Civil Rights Movement, of the nature and meaning of American history during the very years of the Civil War Centennial. Without formal training, Baldwin shows us that the philosophy of history, and indeed intellectual history, for better or worse, belong to all of us. Public memory, in the myriad ways it is forged, is far larger than the history written by historians. We might wish otherwise, but in vain. "History," Baldwin wrote in 1965, "as nearly no one seems to know, is not merely something to be read. And it does not refer merely, or even principally, to the past. On the contrary, the great force of history comes from the fact that we carry it within us, are unconsciously controlled by it in many ways, and history is literally present in all that we do. It could scarcely be otherwise, since it is to history that we owe our frames of reference, our identities, and our aspirations."[29] Americans, in particular, Baldwin believed, tended to think with a set of myths, ingrained by schooling and social conditioning, that under most circumstances governed them. Baldwin understood that people generally tend to think *with* their memories much more than *about* them.

In forms and language reminiscent of W. E. B. Du Bois's *The Souls of Black Folk* (1903), Richard Wright's *Twelve Million Black Voices* (1941), and Ralph Ellison's essays in *Going to the Territory* (1986), Baldwin discussed history as though it were a set of forces in the warp and woof of a nation or in the bloodstream of a people. History was omnipresent, potentially omniscient, a power that had to be harnessed and resisted, studied and used. But first, people had to know its stories, face its terrors, and not merely expect history to please and entertain them. Facts were essential, but they always had to be judged; history had didactic lessons, but those lessons were always embedded in the stories over which we fight. Myths were history's disguises and its stock in trade. As Baldwin matured and became an activist, few matters concerned him more than the nature and power of history; sometimes he flayed away at it as though trying to slay a dragon with sheer exhortation, but sometimes he wrote about it with lasting insight. Both impulses are at work in a passage he wrote in 1979: "Perhaps . . . we have no idea what history is, or are in flight from the demon we have summoned. Perhaps history is not to be found in our mirrors, but in our repudiations; perhaps the other is ourselves. History may be a great deal more than the quicksand that swallows others, and which has not yet swallowed us; history may be attempting to vomit us up, and spew us out; history may be tired." In such passages, it is as though Baldwin did not always know where his thought was going, but he followed it nonetheless. He could leave a public audience alternately enlightened and exasperated. Whatever it took, he would try to make Americans see a past they did not want to see—a past of slavery and racism, travail and triumph, universal guilt and responsibility. The problem, he said in a 1962 essay, is that in America "words are mostly used to cover the sleeper, not to wake him up." Hence, we tend to possess too much "adulation" for our founders and elders, too much reverence for a stable and reassuring past.[30] Baldwin's aim was to destabilize the complacency at the heart of American historical consciousness; his best weapon was usually the anguish in his own life, which worked especially well in essays, if not in fiction.

In the hothouse of the civil rights era, whenever Baldwin philosophized about history, it was often for a white audience. When he employed the words "United States" or "the country," which he did constantly, he often meant white America and what he considered to be its master myths. At the tender age of twenty-four, in one of his first published reviews, he took on the meaning of "the American Myth." In a scathing dismissal of the book *Raintree County*, by Ross Lockridge, Jr., Baldwin called the work "as banal and brave and cheerful as *The Battle Hymn of the Republic*." Americans loved their history in the "sunlight in which they always seemed to be bathed." And invoking Abraham Lincoln without using his name (a common practice over the generations), he warned that "if it [the United States] is the last best hope, we had better find out more about it." By 1951, he was complaining about the tendency to compare "history in America to a kind of tableau of material progress," as though he had looked at one too many school textbooks. "American Negroes are better off because some are able to drive a Cadillac," Baldwin scoffed. "The history of the Negro in America is a heavier weight than this celebrated vehicle is able to carry." In that same year, embedded in his essay "Many Thousands Gone," he offered this remarkable statement of the American habit of turning painful or embarrassing history into cheerful progress: "Americans, unhappily, have the most remarkable ability to alchemize all bitter truths into an innocuous but piquant confection and to transform their moral contradictions, or public discussion of such contradictions, into a proud decoration, such as are given for heroism on the field of battle."[31] Baldwin generally had no use for that word—"progress"—which he all but hated.

In 1956, at the invitation of *Partisan Review*, Baldwin wrote an essay about William Faulkner's public embrace of segregation. "After more than two hundred years in slavery and ninety years of quasi-freedom," said Baldwin, it was "hard to think very highly of William Faulkner's advice to 'go slow.'" Blacks could not merely sit around waiting for white Southerners to work out their "high and noble tragedy." That a white Southern artist of Faulkner's talent would "leave the 'middle of the road,' where he has, presumably, all these years, been working for the benefit of Negroes," was nothing more than an "up-to-date version of the Southern threat to secede from the Union." Baldwin brilliantly played out several Civil War metaphors in this blistering assessment of the Squire of Oxford. Despite all Faulkner's conflicted feelings about racial "equality," Baldwin trusted that he would go with his people and "fight for Mississippi." Inadvertently, Faulkner provided Baldwin a perfect target and a specific means by which to demonstrate how much he understood the stakes in Civil War memory. He invited Faulkner, in effect, to come join the rest of the national "Republic"—as had, he pointed out, another Southerner, Robert Penn Warren. Here was an angry young black voice confronting the Lost Cause tradition, just as Du Bois and Frederick Douglass once had confronted it for earlier generations. Baldwin wondered why Faulkner could not utter a word about "desegregation that does not inform us that his family has lived in the same part of Mississippi for generations, that his great-grandfather owned slaves, and that his ancestors fought and died in the Civil War." He reminded Faulkner that "slaveholding Southerners" were not the only people to die in the war: "Negroes and Northerners were also blown to bits." And poignantly, for Bruce Catton's legions of readers, Baldwin insisted that "references to Shiloh, Chickamauga, and Gettysburg" did nothing to help anyone understand the history and human ravages of segregation.[32] Baldwin used Faulkner to demonstrate the frozen state of American memory, and to insist that African Americans had a centennial to recognize as well.

Baldwin simply would not allow Faulkner, the white South, or any other sentimental Americans, to own the Civil War's legacies. All Faulkner had proven, Baldwin argued, was that he could employ the war's lasting "legend" as well as anyone—put simply, "that the North in winning the war left the South only one means of asserting its identity and that means was the Negro." Baldwin captured the character of Civil War memory; by five years, he elegantly anticipated Warren's notions of the Southern and Northern myths of the "Great Alibi" and the "Treasury of Virtue." White Southerners had always been able to claim the moral ground as "underdog," said Baldwin, and to insist that they had only fought for "blood and kin and home." And the North had escaped "scot-free"; by "freeing the slave it established a moral superiority over the South which the South had not learned to live with until today." The North's "moral superiority" was "bought ... rather cheaply," Baldwin believed, and now the most famous white Southern writer of all time was urging the nation to let the region determine its own time to do once and for all what they never had done on their own: "freeing themselves from the slaves."[33]

By the late 1950s, as the Centennial arrived, Baldwin was referring to the Civil War as the source of the "deepest, most lasting bitterness" in American memory. He even used his newfound distaste for *Uncle Tom's Cabin,* its lack of depth about slavery while it continued to dominate the institution's popular remembrance, as a way of portraying the Civil War as the dividing line in the national story that kept whites and blacks willfully ignorant of each other's lives. This fated circumstance in American memory, the inability to really face the war and its consequences, Baldwin argued, made people of both races treat "History" as a kind of "terrifying deity ... to which no sacrifice in human suffering is too great." In 1959, in the opening piece of *Nobody Knows My Name*—sounding very much like Warren, who was about to write *The Legacy of the Civil War,* like Wilson, who was wrestling *Patriotic Gore* into shape, and like Catton, who was about to publish *The Coming Fury*—Baldwin confessed to his own deeply American sensibilities, as he demanded that his countrymen join forces "to free ourselves from the myth of America." Until now, he proclaimed, echoing especially the Kentucky poet, they had not risen to this challenge because they lacked "a sense, in a word, of tragedy."[34]

• • •

In July 1957, Baldwin boarded a ship in France to sail to New York. He had been back to the United States a few times in prior years, but this would be a new and longer journey, an end to his foreign "havens" and the beginning of what would be thirteen years of a very public and perilous life. He could hardly have known it yet, but he had embarked on what Caryl Phillips has called "the second act of Baldwin's literary life." He had moved to Europe, Baldwin wrote in the opening pages of *Nobody Knows My Name,* to see if he could "be a writer" and "be free." He had certainly accomplished the first goal, but was not yet certain of the second. The thirty-two-year-old writer came back to his country, he later said, to "bear witness," to be an active member as well as chronicler of the Civil Rights Movement emerging all over the American South.[35] From Paris, Baldwin could not feel, touch, or see the history reshaping his homeland; so, with commissions from *Harper's* and *Partisan Review,* he went South for the first time in his life.

Baldwin traveled to Charlotte, North Carolina, in September 1957 to meet and interview black students, who were the first to shoulder the burden of federally sanctioned integration in that city's schools. From his time abroad, Baldwin felt "alchemized into an American," but now he was in the Deep South, meeting black and white people he seemed to know but not know. "The South had always frightened me," he wrote in a tender essay, "A Fly in Buttermilk," about his visit to

Charlotte. He had been advised by older black friends and academic giants, such as the sociologist Kenneth Clark in New York and the poet Sterling Brown in Washington, D.C., that the South he entered now was not the same one he might have encountered a quarter-century earlier, with "Negroes hanging from trees" or "when conductors on streetcars wore pistols." The older friends had heard Booker T. Washington speak in the Teens, had followed the Scottsboro case in the black newspapers of the Thirties, and had played pivotal roles in the Supreme Court's *Brown v. Board* desegregation decision of 1954. Now, suddenly, Baldwin felt the weight of that past in his own anxieties and reactions; it was as if he saw haunting legacies or specters rising up in his path. "These had been books and headlines and music for me," the traveler wrote, "but it now developed that they were also a part of my identity." Initially, Baldwin went South as though to another foreign country. In Charlotte he met a Negro educator who had spent all his life laboring to create a viable education for black college students; the educator forced the writer to admit that he had never been to college and, most humiliating of all, that he did not know how to drive a car.[36]

But in interviewing a young black teenager, identified as "G" (Gus Roberts), along with his white school principal, Baldwin found the voice he would need not only as a reporter, but as a witness. Baldwin's essays about the South were as novelistic as they were journalistic, and the combination gives them their power as literature. The boy's lonely devotion to his books and to his homework in the hostile world of his all-white school, and his mother's courageous determination to send her son to "walk through mobs" to get a better education, genuinely moved Baldwin. He wrote honestly about how the boy's black school had taught him "nothing," due to the indifference of teachers and the inadequacy of resources, and he may have seen himself in the boy's "fanatical concentration on his schoolwork" and his "silence" used as "weapons" of survival. But it was in the "eyes" and the "strained laugh" of the young white principal that Baldwin found his theme—the old, tortured guilt and responsibility of white Southerners for the racial system that they had always assumed was natural and permanent but that now seemed questionable. Baldwin had long had a driving fascination for the mind of the oppressor. The white educator had "never dreamed of a mingling of the races," but here he was every day keeping the peace in his school as a handful of black youngsters "integrated" his classrooms. Baldwin made the white man's "eyes" almost a character. He portrayed this man as an example of the South's white racial tragedy. When the black interviewer asked the white educator how he could possibly deny a Negro child's right to simply have a little of what he (the principal) had, "the eyes came to life then, or a veil fell, and I found myself staring at a man in anguish. The eyes were full of pain and bewilderment and he nodded his head. This was the impossibility he faced every day." Segregation had "worked brilliantly in the South and . . . in the nation," Baldwin concluded. "It has allowed white people, with scarcely any pangs of conscience whatever, to create, in every generation, only the Negro they wished to see." Now, "struck by the look in his eyes," Baldwin thought this one white man, though not really ready to see, might be looking at a new world, and might have a repressed conscience coiled up behind those anguished eyes. Their conversation ended when the white man said, "I don't want to think about it," and turned the matter over to "the Creator" to "find a way to solve our problems."[37]

Baldwin had not come South to turn the story over to Jesus, but he surely discovered that he had encountered a spiritually inspired and religiously led movement. He next traveled to Atlanta, and over the course of nearly two months to Little Rock (Arkansas), Nashville (Tennessee), and Tuskegee, Birmingham, and Montgomery (in Alabama), as well as to other towns in between. Little Rock, of course, was the site of the more famous school integration events, and in Montgomery the famous bus boycott had only recently concluded with federally ordered desegregation of the buses. He described pressing his face against the window of the airplane as he prepared to land in Atlanta on the "rust-red earth of Georgia." As trees came into sight, Baldwin, the novelist with journalist's pad in hand, could not help thinking "that this earth had acquired its color from the blood that had dripped down from these trees. My mind was filled with the image of a black man . . . hanging from a tree, while white men watched him and cut his sex from him with a knife." That nightmarish image in "Nobody Knows My Name," perhaps Baldwin's greatest single essay, placed him in the extensive tradition of African American writers who could not go for long in their careers without crafting some artistic remembrance of a lynching.[38]

In Atlanta, Baldwin met Martin Luther King, Jr., the young minister who had been thrust into national prominence when he served as a leader of the Montgomery Improvement Association from his Dexter Avenue Baptist Church during the bus boycott. King was holed up in a hotel, trying to write. When Baldwin arrived for his appointment, he found a reserved but gracious King. The New Yorker was frankly awed by the Georgian. He found King "tremendously winning"; but what was most compelling was that when he came to write about his Southern encounters, he placed King in a historical continuum, and—typically for Baldwin—he wondered openly about the famous minister's "private" emotional and physical situation. King would never be "confused with Booker T. Washington," Baldwin hastened to declare, meaning that King would never be a compromiser or accommodationist. While remembering this episode in 1961, the writer said that the reverend had convinced him "segregation was dead." But admiring King's courage to tell it like it really was on the ground, Baldwin drew a harrowing conclusion: "The real question which faces the Republic is just how long, how violent, and how expensive the funeral is going to be" (that is, the funeral for segregation). King was likewise small, and even younger than Baldwin. And the traveling poet remembered King "rather as though he were a younger, much-loved, and menaced brother"; "he seemed very slight and vulnerable to be taking on such tremendous odds."[39] Baldwin could never hang out in a bar drinking the night away with Martin Luther King, but he never missed a chance to collect a friend whom he hoped would collect him.

In Montgomery, Baldwin felt swept up in an epic historical contest of wills between powerful interests and ordinary people led by a brilliant Baptist preacher. In private letters he worried about whites who would not tolerate "defeat," as well as about the daily crisis of "morale and tactics" in the black community. He feared that in the end he might be watching a "bloody, suicidal comedy," but also assured Mary Painter: "We shall never be again as we were (and everybody knows it)." Baldwin attended Sunday worship at King's church. As a former preacher himself, Baldwin judged King a "great speaker," and found his charismatic as well as intellectual connection with his congregation breathtaking. He met Coretta King, whom he admired, at a church basement reception, and listened while the reverend explained to his parishioners that racism was a "disease" and nonviolence its cure. Baldwin took a ride on one of the recently desegregated buses; now he himself was a character in the drama. The bus driver gave him a "hostile" look and no answer when he asked the price. Baldwin was stunned by the "offended silence" maintained by the whites as blacks entered the bus and sat wherever they chose. The silence struck him, he wrote, as "nothing so much as . . . a really serious lover's quarrel."[40] But the author, always more skilled at seeing into tangled human hearts than into material and political reality, soon found out that segregation was much more than a lover's quarrel.

One evening Baldwin went out walking from his shabby but boisterous Negro hotel, looking for some dinner. He suddenly felt good and almost relaxed as he strolled in the calm Alabama autumn air. He remembered feeling comfortable around the blacks with whom he mingled on the sidewalks for the first several blocks; he felt an "unfamiliar peace" with the folk among whom he could "logically have been born." After a while, though, he came upon a restaurant and without thinking opened the front door. Suddenly, he found himself in a "Marx Brothers parody of horror." All the whites in the restaurant were struck dumb as they looked at the small black intruder. "The messenger of death could not have had a more devastating effect" than his startling appearance where no black person knowingly tread. In his 1972 memoir-manifesto, *No Name in the Street*, Baldwin wrote a tight, exquisite, even hilarious remembrance of this tragicomic episode. As the customers sat "paralyzed," a waitress, "one of those women, produced, I hope, only in the South, with a face like a rusty hatchet, and eyes like two rusty nails—nails left over from the Crucifixion," rushed to stop Baldwin and "barked . . . what you want, boy?" Baldwin was directed around to the side of the building, to the "colored entrance," which to this Northerner's horror, led to a "small cubicle with one electric light, and a counter" with some stools. Through a "window" with "cage wire mesh," out of sight of any of the white customers inside, Negroes could order food. Baldwin ordered a hamburger and a coffee in great discomfort, as another local black man entered, ordered, and ate quietly as though he had practiced this ritual a thousand times. The two black men looked at each other in stone silence. Baldwin could not eat, and threw his hamburger into a bush as he went back into the streets, leaving his compatriot behind in the "colored" cage. "They had been undergoing and overcoming for a very long time without me, after all," the observer recorded, as he wretchedly sensed a gulf of history that he felt he could not cross and only half comprehended.[41]

In all his work in the South from 1957 into the Sixties, Baldwin seldom missed an opportunity to make an essayist's art out of the historical aura and social change he found around him. He recognized Montgomery, for example, as the "cradle of the Confederacy, an unlucky distinction which no one in Montgomery is allowed to forget." The "White House" that had served as the Confederacy's first home still stood, and one of the black ministers told Baldwin that "people walk around in those halls and cry." This meant white people, of course. The black Yankee relished noting that the bus boycott had succeeded in the face of such misty-eyed Lost Cause sentiment. He remembered and described Southern people as though they were all creatures marked and weighed down by the past. "Every black man," Baldwin wrote, "whatever his style, had been scarred, as in some tribal rite; and every white man, though white men, mostly, had no style, had been maimed. And everywhere, the women, the most fearfully mistreated creatures of this region, with narrowed eyes and pursed lips . . . watched and rocked and waited." He also exoticized the land itself: "the great, vast, brooding, welcoming and bloodstained land, beautiful enough to astonish and break your heart . . . seems nearly to weep beneath the burden of this civilization's unnameable excrescences." He saw the South's unspoken (by whites) sexual past in the colors of all the faces of black people. "The prohibition . . . of the social mingling," Baldwin argued, "revealed the extent of the sexual amalgamation." He described "girls the color of honey, men nearly the color of chalk, hair like silk, hair like cotton, hair like wire, eyes blue, grey, green, hazel, black, like the gypsy's, brown like the Arab's, narrow nostrils, thin, wide lips . . . every conceivable variation."[42] To Baldwin, the Jim Crow South tried to hide many secrets, but they were visible all around if one's eyes were truly open. And the past, like Spanish moss, hung on everything and everyone.

In "Nobody Knows My Name," Baldwin explored for his predominantly white readers what segregation meant to the human heart in the South; he had done the same in *Notes of a Native Son* with regard to poverty and racism in Harlem. He helped those readers grasp why black parents would want their children to risk life and limb to go to a white school for an education by which they might "defeat, possibly escape . . . impossibly help one day abolish the stifling environment in which they see, daily, so many children perish." He demanded that his readers see the "Negroes whom segregation has produced and whom the South uses to prove that segregation is right." Above all, Baldwin's aim was to expose the "myth" to which white Southerners, and peo-

ple across the nation as their enablers, clung. He portrayed segregation as a deeply historical, all but fixed tragedy, laden with "longings"
and "taboos" and "guilt" born of the loins as well as of interests.[43]

Baldwin had returned to a society gearing up for the Civil War
Centennial, which was fashioned in many sectors as a Blue-Gray "celebration," and as a national reunion in which citizens of Cold War
America could renew their allegiance to the country that had not only
survived civil conflict once before, but had grown greater and more
powerful because of it. Such was Bruce Catton's beautifully crafted
narrative message to his loyal readers. Now the country found itself
embroiled in a new civil conflict directly related to the first, although
huge swaths of the populace seemed unwilling or unable to face it.
"History," as Baldwin might have put it, had once again risen up and
blindsided a nation that had rendered itself willfully ignorant of the
causes. This was a perfect mixture for Baldwin's disposition and his
art. In his writings from and about the South, Baldwin uncovered layer after layer of alternative universes—counterparts to the national,
public-memory landscape that so many Americans preferred to see.
The more Baldwin immersed himself in the Civil Rights Movement,
the more he seemed compelled to expose what he variously called
the "evasion," or the "dreadful paradox," or the "lie" at the heart of the
nation's attempt to commemorate 1861–1865. Why was the country
in such a new and, for many, surprising racial crisis? "It is because
the nation," Baldwin declared, "the entire nation, has spent a hundred years avoiding the question of the place of the black man in it."
Sweeping statements of this type became Baldwin's stock in trade;
they worked for increasing numbers of readers and auditors because
he embedded them in such artful storytelling. Critics raved about
Nobody Knows My Name. Irving Howe thought Baldwin had arrived
at a "masterly use of the informal essay," and had discovered a unique
way of writing about race, "more in a voice of anguish than revolt,
and concerned less with the melodrama of discrimination than the
moral consequences of living under an irremovable stigma." And

Charles Poole thought Baldwin could "write about bigotry as if it had never been written about before."[44]

This American habit—the nation's inability to know or see the racial history of slavery and its brutal aftermath—emerged as a Baldwin trademark subject. Once again, the writer found the story where most whites would not look: in the "eyes" of the people he met, this time those of an old black man, who, in Atlanta, "looked into my eyes and directed me into my first segregated bus." Baldwin could not forget the eyes of that man in a bus station, the most symbolic setting of the Jim Crow South. "I never saw him again," Baldwin wrote, "but it made me think . . . of Shakespeare's 'the oldest have borne most.'" And it made him think of a blues song: "Now when a woman gets the blues, Lord, she hangs her head and cries. / But when a man gets the blues, Lord, he grabs a train and rides." The poet had found his material, and he made magic of it in prose. The old man had provided Baldwin with lessons for the journey. "He seemed to know what I was feeling," Baldwin continued. "His eyes seemed to say that what I was feeling he had been feeling, at much higher pressure, all his life. But my eyes would never see the hell his eyes had seen." Then Baldwin gave his readers a definition of that hell, as if to say: How could your Centennial celebrations account for this? "This hell was, simply, that he had never owned anything, not his wife, not his house, not his child, which could not, at any instant, be taken from him by the power of white people. This is what paternalism means." Yes, Baldwin portrayed his old black man as a victim, a symbol of countless poor, debt-ridden sharecroppers who might have ended up in cities with marginal jobs in the Jim Crow economy. But Baldwin took a certain wisdom from his encounter: "The rest of the time I was in the South I watched the eyes of old black men." As the country's Civil War tourism and readership continued "feeding," as the writer Russell Baker put it, "on a thin gruel of romance," Baldwin insisted that Americans remember the nameless man who directed him to a Jim Crow car with his old and knowing eyes.[45]

When Baldwin returned to New York in the fall of 1957, he spiraled into depression for a while; he was now a nomad in the Civil Rights Movement, a chastened, unemployed writer with books to finish and a new vocation he feared but could not avoid. He returned to France in the summer of 1958, and spent the next two years traveling from place to place, desperately trying to finish *Another Country.* He became involved in theater and film, as a playwright and screenwriter, with mixed success. By 1960, he was back in the United States for an extended stay, and thoroughly back in the Movement. As Baldwin's own celebrity grew, he continued to meet, and especially to party with, all manner of American writers, artists, actors, and singers. Baldwin's "party" was a moveable feast of good times, long nights, and extensive drinking.[46] At times, he was simply a man with no address, too many friends, and a persistent desire for love.

In 1960, though, he was back in the Deep South to cover and to some extent join the sit-in crusade. He interviewed students in Tallahassee, Florida, and used those conversations as the basis for his essay "They Can't Turn Back," a moving tribute to the courage and sacrifice of the young people who were leading the Movement and with whom he developed a complicated camaraderie (like their elder civil rights leaders, some accepted and some rejected Jimmy's homosexuality). He had landed once again in the lair of the Jim Crow beast, places where white folks had constructed "an entire way of life on the legend of the Negro's inferiority." But these young activists, deeply Christian and believers in the Ten Commandments, were demanding recognition of their full humanity, which had never been accorded their parents. It was because they were "so closely related to their past" that the students in the sit-ins, and soon on the Freedom Rides, were able to "face with such authority a population ignorant of its history and enslaved to a myth." For all those wondering about what had gotten into these young people, Baldwin proffered his ever-ready answer: "What has 'got into' them is their history in this country."[47] Baldwin tried to make poetry of almost all his travels in the South;

he wanted to throw the nation's master mythology into convulsion by exhibiting the inner, personal worlds of the everyday heroes he found, facing down the beast.

By 1961, when *Nobody Knows My Name* was published to critical acclaim and bestseller status, Baldwin was garnering nearly as many speaking engagements as Malcolm X, whom he met that same year, along with Malcolm's mentor, the Nation of Islam leader Elijah Muhammad. Baldwin spoke at a major rally of the Congress of Racial Equality in Washington, and later CORE sent him on lecturing tours of the South. As faux soldiers prepared for the much-ballyhooed reenactment on the hundredth anniversary of the First Battle of Bull Run in July, Baldwin sat for an interview with Studs Terkel in Chicago. When Terkel asked about the "bitter" title of *Nobody Knows My Name*, Baldwin responded: "It is meant as a kind of warning to my country." "This country is my subject," Baldwin stated as the radical patriot-critic he had now become. "I'm not mad at this country anymore—I am worried about it." Baldwin relished talking about the "sexual paranoia" of white Americans, and how closely related whites and blacks were, as "kissing cousins"; but it was the fate of the nation that he made his theme in his conversation with Terkel, and in a hundred other interviews. He complained that Americans were "badly educated," and did not know their history—a topic that Terkel pushed, resulting in Baldwin's off-the-cuff definition of what it means to have a "sense of history": "You read something that you thought only happened to you, and you discovered it happened a hundred years ago to Dostoyevsky. This is a very great liberation for the suffering, struggling person, who always thinks that he is alone. This is why art is important. Art would not be important if life were not important, and life is important." And finally, Terkel prodded Baldwin on his claim that Americans possess no "sense of tragedy," which stimulated this remarkable explanation: "People think that a sense of tragedy is a kind of . . . embroidery, something irrelevant, that you can take or leave. But, in fact, it is a necessity. That's what the Blues and Spirituals are all about. It is the ability to look on things as they are and survive your losses, or even not survive them—to know that your losses are coming. To know they are coming is the only possible insurance you have, a faint insurance, that you will survive them."[48] To Americans of the World War II and Cold War generations, before the Vietnam War was really on the radar, and a year and a half before the Cuban Missile Crisis, this kind of respect for tragedy might have seemed un-American.

. . .

In 1962, Baldwin was a guest at the same legendary Kennedy White House dinner for writers that Wilson and Warren attended, though no record seems to survive of any conversations among the three. Baldwin was already an outspoken critic of the civil rights reticence and Cold War policies of the Kennedy administration, and engaged with myriad other subjects on which he was constantly asked to pontificate. Perhaps too often, he obliged. At the dinner, Baldwin was nervous about the seating arrangements, but was relieved when Diana Trilling arrived at his table. He went to an after-party at the home of the historian Arthur Schlesinger, Jr., where he got into a nasty exchange with Joseph Rauh, a white liberal civil rights activist. According to Schlesinger, Baldwin "baited Rauh . . . by sarcasm and insult into confessing that his concern for civil rights was a cover for prejudice." Jimmy became well-known for taking over the room at parties, often with such confrontational tests of the guests' racial sincerity.[49]

That summer of 1962, accompanied by his sister Gloria, Baldwin toured West Africa, visiting Senegal, Guinea, and Sierra Leone. And after his return from the African trip, an experience he found both exhilarating and sobering, he published a long essay entitled "Down at the Cross" in the November 17 *New Yorker*, the piece that would soon become *The Fire Next Time*—the work for which Baldwin is most widely remembered. As a literary and political phenomenon, *The Fire Next Time* "shook the American rafters," writes the critic

Claudia Roth Pierpont. If *Nobody Knows My Name* was meant as a warning, *The Fire Next Time* was Baldwin's attempt to hurl Jeremiah's thunderbolt down on his countrymen in their slumber. The 20,000-word essay showed an angrier Baldwin, searching for the largest possible audience, and was written in a self-consciously prophetic mode. In the *New Yorker* the piece appeared, with some controversy, surrounded by numerous advertisements for mink coats, Rolls Royces, and expensive French perfumes displayed by beautiful white models. Those juxtapositions—what Robert Penn Warren called a "grisly comedy"—have never vanished altogether from that magazine, but the combination of the good life of the white upper class with Baldwin's tale of personal woe, familial longing, and potential national and racial apocalypse seems bizarre even as an artifact today. Baldwin was happy to take the money; he received a much larger fee from the *New Yorker* than he had been offered by Norman Podhoretz at *Commentary,* to whom he had originally promised such an essay. In the book, as a preface, Baldwin included the brief essay "My Dungeon Shook: Letter to my Nephew on the One Hundredth Anniversary of the Emancipation." To the fourteen-year-old James, his brother Wilmer's son, Baldwin put his sense of history on display as an uncle's dire cautionary tale about race in America. The piece had been prompted by a disturbing visit to a classroom in Dakar, Senegal, where he and his sister had watched as a French-produced history textbook was read aloud among Senegalese students; its opening line declared: "Our ancestors, who came from Gaul . . ."[50] Aghast, Baldwin angrily warned his nephew that this must not be his ultimate fate in America; he would not learn a history rooted in sentimental colonialism and twisted lies about white supremacy.

By the Sixties, Baldwin had developed close relationships with his burgeoning extended family. His nephew was his namesake, and in what had emerged as the Baldwin style, he wrote "My Dungeon Shook" as a very personal story. He remembered holding his nephew in his arms when James was a baby, and asked him to try to understand the racist world into which his father and grandmother (Baldwin's brother and mother) had brought him. "Your countrymen," Baldwin told his nephew, "do not yet really know that you exist." Looking right past the nephew, Baldwin lectured white Americans at the Emancipation Centennial. "This is the crime of which I accuse my country and my countrymen, and for which neither I nor time nor history will ever forgive them." Poverty, hopelessness, and racism were "destroying . . . lives" every day in urban ghettos, and most Americans were blissfully ignorant. "It is the innocence that constitutes the crime," Baldwin proclaimed.[51] He all but begged his nephew, and all the young blacks that James represented, not to internalize the self-perceptions that the larger society imposed upon them.

As though he were now in a junior high school classroom and making an inspirational speech, Baldwin preached: "Trust your experience, know whence you came. If you know whence you came, there is really no limit to where you can go." But watch out for "those innocents," he warned, who were "trapped in a history they do not understand." Then, like the former preacher he was, as if delivering the altar call to the fallen, Baldwin switched course: the unforgiven, whose sins must first be named and faced, might yet be redeemed with a ferocious "love" that could "force our brothers to see themselves." He left all the black nephews and nieces with a history lesson. "This is your home, my friend, do not be driven from it; great men have done great things here, and will again, and we can make America what it must become." Sounding now like Frederick Douglass or Langston Hughes in their more buoyant moments, Baldwin concluded: "You come from sturdy, peasant stock, men who picked cotton and dammed rivers and built railroads, and, in the teeth of the most terrifying odds, achieved an unassailable and monumental dignity. You come from a long line of great poets, some of the greatest poets since Homer. One of them said, *The very time I thought I was lost, My dungeon shook and my chains fell off.*"[52] Baldwin had invited his sophisticated white reading audience to listen to a sermon about a monumental history they did not know; the slave poets who created the spirituals provided the chorus.

The middle section of *The Fire Next Time* was Baldwin's creative account of his meeting with Elijah Muhammad, leader of the Nation of Islam, at the minister's home in Chicago. On a hot late-summer night in 1962, Baldwin accepted an invitation to dine at Muhammad's house on the South Side. He had already met and appeared on television with Malcolm X. But he was "frightened" about this gathering. Nine or so male and an equal number of female Nation of Islam devotees and attendants were assembled on opposite sides of a large room, the women all in white and the men in perfect dark suits; they provided a disciplined, if tense, reception for the writer, who of course was not served the alcoholic drink he needed (though he kept his forbidden cigarettes in his pocket). Baldwin knew yet did not know these people. He understood their zealotry, the desperation of their pasts, and even the sources of their open hatred for the "white devils." He had stood and listened to numerous Nation of Islam speakers at the corner of 125th Street and Seventh Avenue in New York. But his worlds no longer intersected much with the streets that had produced his hosts. Tuning out as a matter of course when he came near a "pulpit or a soapbox," he had begun to listen to Nation of Islam orators when he saw that the police paid close attention to them. He had come to know that the Nation of Islam message was essentially one of "power" for the powerless.[53]

Baldwin himself had long been quite adept at using the nonspecific rhetoric of "white people" and "the American Negro." He employed the terms frequently and sometimes with willful vagueness. He astutely placed the Nation of Islam's historical growth in the context of black Americans' deep disappointments from the World War II era, when a "certain hope died," as black men in uniform endured being called "nigger" in the armed forces, were Jim Crowed at segregated USOs, and saw German prisoners-of-war being treated better than they themselves were on American soil. Seven years earlier, in

"Notes of a Native Son," he had written poignantly about Harlem's wartime anguish in the early Forties, "the churchly women and the matter-of-fact, no nonsense men," with "children in the army" writing home "bitter letters" about the racism they faced. He had captured the collective black "directionless [and] hopeless bitterness" in parents, wives, and girlfriends over the indignity and danger their loved ones encountered at war. He described a "peculiar kind of relief when they knew their boys were being shipped out of the South, to do battle overseas."[54] More than anything, perhaps, Baldwin understood hatred, both the kind of resentment bred in the lower working class and the nihilism of the desperately poor. And he knew full well why it was easy to recruit drunks, addicts, and former prisoners from ghetto streets with new forms of religious and messianic drugs.

But he was not comfortable meeting Elijah Muhammad, a man who reminded him so much of his stepfather. His treatment of Muhammad and his black separatist sect in *The Fire Next Time* probably reached a wider white audience than anything yet written on the group. The portrayal was a combination of spiritual respect and what one might call experiential camaraderie; it also artfully mixed parody, satire, and disdain for Muhammad's demagoguery and the cult-devotion of his acolytes. Baldwin described Muhammad's version of the creation story: black people were not only first in the world, but originally "perfect"; despoiled and polluted by the white minorities, blacks with the true faith, Islam, would soon rise to control their own land and nation, and ultimately drive whites away. American blacks had a special, chosen role to play. Baldwin masked his contempt for these ideas remarkably well, but did offer a comment: "Heavenly witnesses are a tricky lot, to be used by whoever is closest to Heaven at the time. And legend and theology, which are designed to sanctify our fears, crimes, and aspirations, also reveal them for what they are." Baldwin felt as if he failed virtually every test question he faced at Muhammad's simple but exquisite dinner. He fumbled when trying to answer a query about what religion he embraced, replying: "I?

Now? Nothing. I'm a writer. I like doing things alone." And as for separating from and properly hating whites, he failed miserably; as Baldwin left for the evening, Muhammad's driver in a big blue car gave him a ride to a section of Chicago where the writer planned to have drinks with several "white devil" friends.[55]

Baldwin used his evening with the leader of the Nation of Islam for one other major purpose: to scold white America for its complacency and show why it had better pay attention to black rage. In sensitive, novelistic tones, ever observing eyes and faces, he humanized Muhammad before undressing his ideology. "The central quality in Elijah's face is pain," wrote Baldwin, "and his smile is a witness to it—pain so old and deep and black that it becomes personal and particular only when he smiles. One wonders what he would sound like if he could sing." Always the student of paradox as well as the moralist, Baldwin then reversed sympathies. Hatred, however justified, he argued, led to dehumanization of whole groups of people and, as recent history had demonstrated, to mass murder in the name of race. His meeting with Muhammad made him more than ever concerned about the "spiritual wasteland" Americans risked creating in their domestic crisis over civil rights, and in the Cold War's standoff between two superpowers that could now destroy the planet with nuclear weapons. Suddenly he was Citizen Baldwin, reminding his readers that the simplest of principles are the hardest to hold. "Whoever debases others debases himself," he declared. "That is not a mystical statement but a most realistic one, which is proved by the eyes of any Alabama sheriff—and I would not like to see Negroes arrive at so wretched a condition."[56] Some faiths were worth keeping.

The Fire Next Time ends with Baldwin's signature—in this case some unforgettable pages calling whites and blacks alike to change their history or face a world increasingly dominated by the kind of bleak, walled-off, racial and cultural tribalism he had witnessed that night at Muhammad's dinner table. In a culture awash in Civil War books, commemorations, paraphernalia, and imagery of nineteenth-century white men in Blue and Gray, Baldwin threw down such markers as this: "I am called Baldwin because I was either sold by my African tribe or kidnapped out of it into the hands of a white Christian named Baldwin, who forced me to kneel at the foot of a cross." He rarely missed an opportunity to either carry or throw down his "cross." But he continued:

> I am then both visibly and legally the descendant of slavery in a white, Protestant country, and this is what it means to be an American Negro, this is who he is—a kidnapped pagan, who was sold like an animal and treated like one, who was once defined by the American Constitution as "three-fifths" of a man, and who, according to the Dred Scott decision, had no rights that a white man was bound to respect. And today, a hundred years after his technical emancipation, he remains—with the possible exception of the American Indian—the most despised creature in this country.

So here was Baldwin's challenge, especially to his white audience: learn some history, let it hurt and make you guilty if it must, crawl out of your sloth, and, as he put it, embrace the "torment and necessity of love," while using the "Negro past" to remake "this otherwise shapeless and undiscovered country."[57]

Thousands of white readers not only endured but, at least in the early Sixties, seemed to welcome the beating Baldwin gave them. Self-flagellation among white liberals became one part of the cultural milieu during the Civil Rights Movement, and no one tapped its nerves quite like Baldwin. Henrietta Buckmaster, the white author of a popular book on the Underground Railroad, wrote a typical review of *The Fire Next Time* in which she acknowledged the reason for the book's impact. "No billowy sentiments . . . cushion the bounce we are given," she wrote. "It is a book for white readers. . . . We white people, in the confusion of our educated nonsense, have waited a long time for such a book and we had better not bungle our chances now or fail to grasp this tow rope to shore." Baldwin likely nodded with approval at such a review. But on many occasions he reacted to white liberals—in social and public situations—with an unpredictable and sometimes lethal brew of gratitude, insult, and outright contempt. He seemed to alternately enjoy and loathe meeting, as he once said, "another group of masochists." And when he was asked about the significance of the Black Muslims, his reply too typically came as a shot from the hip. They served "one extremely useful function: they scare white people. Otherwise, they are just another racist organization and the only place they can go is to disaster." Baldwin was not without black critics on this and other matters. The novelist and jazz and blues historian Albert Murray argued that too many white intellectuals and friends of civil rights "assume that Negro writers" have no "literary ambitions," and that "Negro literature is simply incidental to protest." Moreover, Murray (in an essay about Baldwin) challenged black writers to "start asking themselves why these people are happiest when Negroes are moaning and groaning about black troubles and miseries. It is undeniable that these friends also tolerate and seem to enjoy being insulted, accused, bullied, or *baldwinized*" (italics mine).[58] Baldwin had, indeed, started his career by attacking a writer like Richard Wright for writing only about black misery as a form of protest—but by the 1960s he had become, perhaps by necessity and choice, just what he had decried.

The Fire Next Time also stimulated serious critical reviews. In the *New York Review of Books*, F. W. Dupee admired Baldwin's virtuosity with language and style, especially in the autobiographical mode, but not some of the book's "speculative fireworks." "Ideas shoot from the book's pages as the sparks fly upward," said the reviewer, "in bewildering quantity and at random." And Dupee likely spoke for many silent readers when he called Baldwin out for "imputing" motives for the "behavior of entire populations."[59] But in 1962–1963, eloquent anger and spiritually undergirded warnings were Baldwin's chosen methods. He had assumed a self-consciously prophetic stance, not that of a cultural critic, and such an approach carried its costs. His book could not possibly please, at one and the same time, the readers of the *New York Review of Books* and the members of the Student Nonviolent Coordinating Committee, as well as other black intellectuals; but a measure of the work's significance is that it became the traveling companion of all of them.

The *New Yorker* edition of the essay sold out, and soon *The Fire Next Time* was at the top of the nonfiction bestseller list, where it stayed for forty-one weeks. Many people in the early twenty-first century can still describe what they felt on their first reading of the book. Baldwin and Catton (with *Terrible Swift Sword*) simultaneously attracted countless readers in 1963, the centennial year of Gettysburg, Vicksburg, and Emancipation—but one wonders if their legions of fans were ever reading the same books. The works represented two variations on tragedy, and two quite different modes of history: one narrative, elegiac, and ultimately triumphant, if bloody and sacrificial; and the other confrontational, admonishing, philosophical, and sweepingly if darkly romantic. Catton placed people in a national narrative of a difficult but heroic past that anticipated a better and victorious present; Baldwin harked back to a "beautiful," "terrible," and largely unknown past that might explode in a horrible present. Baldwin's ending—"God gave Noah the rainbow sign, No more water, the fire next time!"—is the most famous line in the book, but it needs to be read through the many pages in which he called for a mutual, racially shared, and genuine sense of American history and tragedy. White guilt was a potent weapon in 1962–1963, and Baldwin exploited it; but he also aimed higher, and this is why the book lasts. Blacks and whites, he argued, were bound in a mutual fate, carved, like it or not, from shared if painful experience and mixed blood; if whites had to take a whacking in order to know this, so be it. If they had to face utterly uncomfortable realities in their own family histories, all the better, he believed. "The Negro came to the white man for a roof or for five dollars or for a letter to the judge," he wrote in a Baldwinesque generalization. "The white man came to the Negro for love." "Historical vengeance" might be what lay down the racial road Americans found themselves traversing, but the "relatively conscious whites and the relatively conscious blacks," Baldwin imagined, might yet join together before it was too late, "end the racial nightmare," and—his deepest wish—"achieve our country."[60]

By 1963, Baldwin's celebrity status had secured him a multiple-book contract with Dial and then Dell, and even members of his family enjoyed the publishers' largesse. CORE sent Baldwin on a lecture tour all over the South, where he spoke in church pulpits and school classrooms. He met James Meredith and Medgar Evers in Mississippi and joined Evers on an investigation of a lynching. He also went west and maintained a breakneck schedule of speeches at colleges and universities in California. Baldwin, now the "literary voice of the Civil Rights Movement," spoke outside and inside, in small halls and in huge arenas, and he made television and radio interviews into his own genre, answering questions rapidly almost before they were asked. Baldwin had become, at the age of thirty-eight, the mass-market voice against racism and for a new history. In a remarkable essay published late that year in the *Saturday Review,* but first delivered as an address entitled "A Talk to Teachers," Baldwin kept up the drumbeat for an alternative historical consciousness. Zooming right past the scholars, he summed up in his own way the history of slavery in America: "Black men were brought here as a cheap source of labor. They were indispensable to the economy. In order to justify the fact that men were treated as though they were animals, the white republic had to brainwash itself into believing that they were, indeed, animals and *deserved* to be treated like animals." Before black-studies programs had emerged, before virtually any public school offered something resembling black history, Baldwin suggested a new curriculum that would liberate whites as well as blacks. "If you are compelled to lie about one aspect of anyone's history," said Baldwin, "you must lie about it all. . . . If you have to pretend that I hoed all that cotton just because I loved you, then you have done something to yourself. You are mad." Before we dismiss this as shoot-from-the-hip hyperbole, which in part it was, it is worth remembering how widely Americans as late as the early 1960s still saw slavery through images drawn from *Gone with the Wind,* or from the enduring stereotype of the faithful "Little Black Sambo."[61]

After Baldwin's California tour, and in the midst of the civil rights marches against Sheriff Bull Connor's dogs and fire hoses in Birmingham, Alabama, *Time* magazine put Baldwin on its cover and provided a revealing portrait of the author, including substantial quotations from his recent writings. *Time* described Baldwin as "a nervous, slight, almost fragile figure, filled with frets and fears . . . effeminate in manner, drinks considerably, smokes cigarettes in chains, and he often loses his audience with overblown arguments." Nevertheless, concluded the news weekly, no other American writer had captured "with such poignancy and abrasiveness the dark realities of the racial ferment in North and South." Without so much as mentioning the anniversaries of the Civil War and Emancipation, *Time*'s writers nonetheless picked up on Baldwin's central theme of a stunted, unfulfilled American history. They quoted one of Baldwin's speeches: "When I was going to school I began to be bugged by the teaching of American history, because it seemed that history had been taught without cognizance of my presence. It is my responsibility now to give you as true a version of your history as I can." And *Time* also observed Baldwin's penchant, in every speech, for personifying "the Negro," using a litany of first-person pronouns. "I hoed a lot of cotton, I laid a lot of track, I dammed a lot of rivers, you wouldn't have had this country if it hadn't been for me" was the standard expression. In print, and now on the stump, Baldwin had made himself the symbolic representative of a history of oppression and endurance for nearly a decade. Without doubt, as Irving Howe suggested, Baldwin sometimes overdid the "confessional stance," the self-identification with the "Negro problem"; but rhetorically it probably worked in churches and university fieldhouses better than it did in print.[62] The eloquence and personal storytelling flowing from his small body, even if sometimes a bit disjointed and overwrought, could move an audience to new awareness without intimidation.

As America's racial mythbuster, Baldwin performed to the limits of his energy. One of his friendliest critics characterized a Baldwin appearance in the early Sixties as "courageous" but also as "performative flamboyance." In August he was in Washington, D.C., for the iconic March on Washington, where organizers at first invited him to be one of the speakers on the steps of the Lincoln Memorial— and then apparently uninvited him, because of his homosexuality. He attended anyway, and marched with a group of celebrities that included Marlon Brando, Sidney Poitier, Harry Belafonte, Charlton Heston, Joan Baez, and others. With them, Baldwin was moved by Martin Luther King's use of the Emancipation anniversary, the opening part of the "I Have a Dream" speech so often forgotten in endless recitals of the speech's more famous refrain. King announced that they had gathered on the Mall to stand in the "shadow of the Great Emancipator" and tell the nation that the "promissory note" signed in the Declaration of Independence had come back labeled "insufficient funds" in the "bank of American justice"—and in these words, Baldwin heard the master orator of the twentieth century capture his own theme about history and memory as never before. Baldwin later remembered the scene: "Martin finished with one hand raised: 'Free at last, free at last, praise God Almighty I'm free at last!'" It is interesting that Baldwin remembered King's "we" as an "I." But then the recollection is for all time: "That day, for a moment, it almost seemed that we stood on a height, and could see our inheritance; perhaps we could make the kingdom real, perhaps the beloved community would not forever remain that dream one dreamed in agony." As Baldwin put an ending on his memory of August 28, 1963, saying that as of that moment "no one could any longer doubt that their [African Americans'] suffering was real," it was as though he were declaring that if anyone wished to appropriate King's transcendent historical moment in Lincoln's long shadow, they had better have a very good cause.[63] Seeing one's inheritance, even glimpses of it, is no trifling matter.

On the evening of the March on Washington, as the throngs boarded buses and embarked for homes all over the United States, Baldwin joined Brando, Poitier, Belafonte, Heston, and the activist and film director Joseph Mankiewicz on a live television "Civil Rights Roundtable" interview in Washington. All the guests spoke in solemn, inspirational tones about the day's events and experiences. The march had been both grave and magnificent; they described it as an unprecedented and potentially life-changing marker in American history. Mankiewicz and Heston addressed the need for white Americans to awaken to the cause of Negro suffering and equality—especially Mankiewicz, who declared that personal change in the hearts of whites was the most dire need in the land. Heston saw the day as an affirmation of American principles and patriotism. Brando universalized the dilemma, saying that "hatred . . . fear and anguish" were enduring elements of the "human heart." Poitier sustained the conversation on a high plane, but drew upon his own career and immigration to describe the "urgency" that black Americans felt about their "survival." Belafonte all but took over the room, and in his mellifluous voice announced that after "one hundred years" black people truly meant the slogan "Freedom now!" and that there could be no more "compromise" on equality. It was well past time, said the singer, for "generations of black Americans trying to appeal to the conscience of white supremacy." Baldwin held back until called upon. He addressed King's use of the "dream" metaphor, meant to "free Americans" of all backgrounds. He said the day's events had shown that perhaps it was blacks who had "the most faith in this country." Then, repeatedly referring to the Emancipation centennial, Baldwin took great hope from the day, "the first time in one hundred years the nation showed some signs of really dealing with this problem . . . after one hundred years of pretending it does not exist."[64] Watching a video of that interview today makes the 1963 Centennial, like many pivotal moments in history, seem both oddly remote and disturbingly current. It also makes one realize how utterly irrelevant Civil War Centennial coins or commemorative editions of newspapers and books about the Blue and the Gray appear in retrospect when coupled with that transcendent day at the Lincoln Memorial. We all choose how to see our inheritance or to use a voice from the mountaintop.

Anniversaries can seem so fleeting and can be so easily exploited for commercial or ideological purposes. The March on Washington in August 1963, with King's refrain of the interracial "dream" as soundtrack or mere visual image, has become so iconic that to new generations it may have lost meaning altogether. The day was, in part, a massive lobbying effort for a new Emancipation Proclamation—which indeed within a year emerged as the 1964 Civil Rights Act from a Congress that could never have conceived of such a series of transformative laws even two years earlier. But that day also, at its core, was a powerful and eloquent expression of how national anniversaries can be used to nudge history in new directions. The March was a friendly and peaceful dagger in the heart of the nation's understanding of the never-ending Civil War. King's "Dream" speech is the Gettysburg Address of the twentieth century. But the "dream" metaphor and refrain is only the last of several King employed: "with this faith," "we are not satisfied," and "let freedom ring" are three he repeated many times, making the "dream" the softest of the metaphors. But in the opening of the speech, King declared four times that "one hundred years later" the "Negro still is not free." "One hundred years later!" As Baldwin acknowledged, the "Dream" speech was a young black preacher's magnificent declaration of the deepest meaning of the Civil War Centennial, and thereby of America's purpose. On that day, the artist as minister of pronouncements on civil rights heard the ultimate pronouncement—and for that day at least, it made even him a believer.

. . .

In the spring and summer of 1964, Baldwin's play *Blues for Mr. Charlie*, directed by Burgess Meredith and starring Pat Hingle, Al Freeman, Jr., Diana Sands, and Rip Torn, ran on Broadway with mixed reviews. The play drove Baldwin nearly to exhaustion and breakdown; its subjects were the roots of racism and violence found in America generally, and of black hatred for white people in the South in particular. Drawn in part from Baldwin's own despair over the murder of Medgar Evers in Mississippi on June 12, 1963, *Blues* received some accolades for the passion and brilliance of the acting, but not for its awkward pacing and structure, or its portrayal (many said "stereotypes") of Southern whites. The drama was as raw a creation of racial attitudes and language on stage as Broadway had ever seen. The *New York Times* review segued from praising the "thunderous battle cry" for black dignity and equality to calling the Southern whites mere "caricatures." *Time* magazine said the performance was "a hard play for a white man to take. Brutally, sometimes eloquently, it tells every white man how much every Negro hates him." What may have worked as a kind of social "preachment" did not work so well as art. Audiences dwindled, receipts fell, the play steadily lost money and finally failed, with Baldwin in great anger and proclaiming, "I'm not concerned with the success or failure of the play. I just want to shock the people and make them think." A hastily arranged London opening of the play late that year was an even more unqualified disaster. The vulnerabilities and risks unique to the theater came with psychological costs for Baldwin as a person and an artist.[65]

But he hardly rested his slight body and giant ambition, nor would publicity agents allow him much time for writing. On February 18, 1965, Baldwin debated William F. Buckley, the conservative founder of the *National Review*, at the Cambridge University Union in England. The two men debated the proposition "The American Dream Is at the Expense of the American Negro," before an audience of more than seven hundred students in the hall and hundreds more in adjoining rooms watching on closed-circuit television.[66] Back in America, by 1965 the tenor of civic discourse had worsened; a radical new left had emerged, both white and black; the Vietnam War was beginning to divide people as no foreign policy question ever had; white activists were rejected by black militants; and the voting-rights campaign in the South seemed in stalemate. The Civil Rights Movement was a decade old, and its "rights phase" showed signs of fraying in the face of deep impatience with nonviolence and legal action as a strategy. "Black Power!" could already be heard as an alternative rallying cry to "Freedom Now!" among the young leaders of SNCC. The many murders of civil rights workers made peaceful resolutions to America's racial crisis seem elusive at best. Unprecedented urban riots would break out later that year and rage through the summer of 1968; violence and fear, more than interracialism and redemptive hope, seemed to characterize the prevailing debates. "One hundred years later" now seemed a hollow, embittered refrain. A revolution had been unleashed in America, but its direction and results seemed increasingly beyond anyone's control.

At a podium in the middle of the packed room, Baldwin, with no college degrees but now a celebrity to the predominantly white British students at ancient Cambridge, opened his remarks by saying, "I find myself, not for the first time, in the position of a kind of Jeremiah." Then he tried to do the prophet's work—calling for justice for the poor and oppressed by naming the sins of the oppressor; dragging his auditors through the psychological traumas caused by racism and poverty; puncturing the piety and irony of mainstream American mythology and patriotism; and finally, demanding that whites face their past before they could hope for redemption. Baldwin gave the students a brief course in the dangers of black self-hatred. From earliest youth, he said, a black person was told, "You're a worthless human being." "From the moment you are born, every stick and stone, every face, is white. . . . It comes as a shock around age five, six, or seven to discover that the flag to which you have pledged allegiance, along with everybody else, has not pledged allegiance to you." In a language of popular culture the young British students would immediately grasp, he pushed the point: "It comes as a great shock to see Gary Cooper killing off Indians and, although you are rooting for Gary Cooper, [to realize] that the Indians are you. . . . It comes as a great shock to discover that the country which is your birthplace and to which you owe your life and identity has not, in its whole system of reality, evolved any place for you." Then, as so often before, the small man in the black suit became the "I" representing "the Negro": "I picked the cotton, I carried it to market, I built the railroads under someone else's whip for nothing."[67] Baldwin gave a powerful performance.

Buckley, a product of American aristocratic privilege and Ivy League education, supporter of the recently disastrous Barry Goldwater campaign for the presidency, staunch anticommunist, and self-styled defender of social order above all else, was, as always, eloquent, but he had no chance of winning this contest. He tried to be conciliatory but came across as sarcastic, while making Baldwin himself the issue. The writer, said the conservative, had been treated by the American public with the "kind of satisfaction that a posturing hero gets for his flagellations of our civilization." Buckley did not believe in civil disobedience; no cause, however just, had a right to overthrow a "system" that would ultimately, in his view, serve the ends of black equality over time. "You cannot go to any university in the United States," claimed Buckley, "in which practically every other problem in public policy is not preempted by the primary concern for the Negro. I challenge you to name me another civilization in the history of the world in which the problems of the minority . . . are as much a subject of concern as in the United States." Such an argument about "concern" tended to demonstrate Buckley's moral bankruptcy when it came to any solutions to America's racial crisis. Patience, faith in the constitutional system, and in "Judeo-Christian" principles could hardly answer the sense of urgency emanating from African American communities and from their young leaders. Buckley also saw Baldwin as essentially long-winded and dangerous. Baldwin's "brooding moroseness" was all too "darkly attractive," Buckley later wrote, to "young Englishmen with large appetites to deplore the United States." In print, he eventually dismissed Baldwin as a voice of "swollen irrationalities" and the leader of a "coterie of America-haters."[68] Unfortunately, as the terrible violence of the later Sixties unfolded, Baldwin would appear to welcome such reactions more than he actually countered them.

As the years of Centennial consciousness about the Civil War and Emancipation waned, Baldwin did attract one further important white admirer-critic: Robert Penn Warren. In 1964, Warren traveled the country conducting extensive interviews with a large number of black leaders of all persuasions and fields. He tape-recorded hundreds of hours of conversation about every aspect of strategy and tactics in the Civil Rights Movement, about the phases and place of the Movement in American and world history, about the racial crisis in presidential politics, about the nature of black leadership, about integration and separatism, about the personal backgrounds and psychological standing of his subjects, and many more topics. The book Warren produced, *Who Speaks for the Negro?* (1965), is composed of short biographies of his many interviewees woven into 444 pages of oral history—much of it, though not all, verbatim transcript. Despite its chatty, unconventional structure, *Who Speaks for the Negro?* is a neglected classic of the civil rights era and an underappreciated goldmine of African American thought about the meaning of what Warren called the "Negro Revolution" while it was in midcourse. It is also one white Southern writer's take on what white American readers might wish to know about the inside worlds of many of the black figures they encountered in the press almost daily. He did not intend the book as a "history," said Warren, "or an anthropological study, or a *Who's Who.*" He merely wanted "to find out what he could find out" about "one of the dramatic events of the American story." Ever the poet-historian in search of the story, Warren wanted to "make my reader see, hear, and feel as immediately as possible what I saw, heard, and felt."[69]

Warren conducted interviews with virtually every major male "leader" of the Civil Rights Movement: King, Evers, James Farmer, Whitney Young, Roy Wilkins, Adam Clayton Powell, Stokely Carmichael, Robert Moses, Aaron Henry, and Malcolm X, to name only those with whom he seems to have managed the longest interviews. Warren may have spent more time interviewing Baldwin than he did anyone else; he certainly had a deep fascination for the black writer's role in the story, and Baldwin had shown a certain respect for the Kentuckian's work as well. Warren would sometimes use a quote from "Nobody Knows My Name" or some other Baldwin essay or speech to prompt whomever he was interviewing.[70] Of all the journalists, television hosts, and intellectuals who interviewed Baldwin, at least at the peak of his public fame, few captured the writer's persona and significance better than Warren.

That the authors of *The Legacy of the Civil War* and *The Fire Next Time* would sit down to talk about race relations and history is not surprising. Warren was deeply intrigued by Baldwin as both an artist and a phenomenon. He weaves Baldwin in and out of his text, but he introduces him with an astute observation: "James Baldwin has often been called a 'voice'—the voice of a generation, the voice of a revolution, the voice of an age, the voice of conscience, the voice of the New Negro, the voice of this and the voice of that. He has not been called the one thing he really, specifically, and strictly is: the voice of himself." Warren then explores the many versions of that "self," sometimes quoting at length from previous published interviews, as well as from Baldwin's extensive autobiographical writing. In an earlier interview in 1963, Baldwin had tried to describe the many parts of his identity: "Lots of people, some of them are unmentionable. There's a man. There's a woman, too. There are lots of people here." But Warren suggested that at this stage in Baldwin's life and fame, he tended not to mention the former "boy preacher" who, though "he may have long since left the church, . . . smuggled out the Gift of Tongues."[71]

The two writers from such different backgrounds and generations began by discussing the character of the "Negro revolution" in historical perspective. Baldwin compared America's crisis to the Algerian revolution and argued that, to succeed, the United States needed to undergo the "reestablishment of a union." Then, Warren was struck by how Baldwin's wide-ranging discussion of history quickly glided, whether prodded or not, into a focus on his "personal drama" and "interior life." Warren delivered as illuminating a description of Baldwin during an interview as one will ever find: "Even as Baldwin, sitting there before me, enters upon the words which, suddenly, have that inner vibrance, his eyes widen slightly, a glint comes in them, he sits up in his chair, and the nerves, you are sure, tighten, and there is the acceleration of pulse beat and respiration. He is not looking at you now, or talking at you, at all: his eyes are fixed on something over yonder, across the room. He is talking of the change that would have to come over American life." And on cue, Baldwin pours forth the following into Warren's tape recorder: "In order to accommodate me, in order to overcome so many centuries of cruelty and bad faith and genocide and fear—simple fear—all the American institutions and all the American values, public and private, will have to change!" Warren had, after all, asked about "revolution." Warren witnessed and described Baldwin's sensibilities, whether about history or about himself (the two were rarely disconnected), with a keen and respectful if wary eye. Baldwin's analysis, he found, often devolved into "apocalyptic intensity," that old Yankee abolitionist trait both he and Edmund Wilson had decried in their Civil War writings.[72] It was as though Warren sat with a latter-day but much more literary Nat Turner–Frederick Douglass in front of him, and it may have been a much more intellectually stimulating experience than he (the white

writer) had ever imagined. In their exchanges flowed enough variet-
ies of Civil War legacies to fill a day-long Centennial symposium, had
any commission ever thought to plan such a public encounter.

But Warren also found Baldwin disturbing, perhaps even tragic.
He wrote both sardonically and respectfully about Baldwin; he had
read and studied him, admired much of his lyrical writing in essays,
but also saw how contradictory, unspecific, and mythical he could
be even as he sought to destroy older myths. Warren chided Baldwin for his "strong ambivalence" about white liberals, suggesting
that the black spokesman could not in the end have it both ways—
demanding repentance and redemption but rejecting the redeemed.
He also boldly maintained that Baldwin's arguments about the dif-
ferences between white and black sexuality too often took the form
of hyperbole and mere confrontation; recurring declarations that in
North and South, whites merely "castrated" the Negro differently had
stopped too many good conversations. Baldwin's tendency to sidestep analysis of a problem and launch into a "general . . . shadowy
depth" where the "emotion coils" (as Warren put it) earned him many
black critics as well. Warren quoted the Southern activist Wyatt Tee
Walker, saying that Baldwin "can speak for James Baldwin and what
he feels, but that does not make him the architect of expression for
the Negro community." But as critic and listener, Warren nevertheless found the deeply personalized rhetoric to be "the source of Baldwin's power." "Whatever is vague, blurred, or self-contradictory in
his utterances," Warren astutely observed, "somehow testifies to the
magisterial authenticity of the utterance—it is the dramatic image of
a man struggling to make sense of the relation of personal tensions
to the tensions of the race issue." The race issue, Warren maintained,
did "permeate all things" in 1964. More than any other voice, Baldwin
brought a "frightening—and fascinating—immediacy" to this most
American story. "It is *his* story we finally listen to," Warren concluded, "in all its complexity of precise and shocking image, and shadowy

allusiveness."[73] Warren seems to have found Baldwin at times exasperating, as many did, but in the end paid him the ultimate writer's tribute to a writer: the "voice" was real and unique.

The interviews between the white Southern expatriate Yale professor and the busy, chain-smoking, suspicious Baldwin were undoubtedly testy. Some of Jimmy's answers were monosyllabic and brief, some florid and revealing. But the two writers shared drinks and a long lunch at a midtown Manhattan restaurant, from which Warren recorded two telling episodes. A black waiter approached their table and "asked if he [Baldwin] were James Baldwin, and receiving the answer, stood and stared reverentially for a full minute." Then, after lunch, "walking up Fifth Avenue," writes Warren, "we encountered a young woman, white and well-dressed, who stopped, stock-still, right in the middle of the crowd, blocking us, and stared into his face and burst out: 'Oh—You're James Baldwin—oh, thank you, thank you!'" To Warren, these two people represented the "different worlds" Baldwin had reached with his pen, and the "promise of redemption" in his voice.[74]

Like many others, Warren noticed how debilitating fame and the constant demands of being "the voice" had been for Baldwin. It was easy to see that Baldwin had become an artist to whom stardom and the desperate need for affection had not been kind. Before they parted, Baldwin said to Warren: "I've got to get away from here. I've been associating with all these civil rights people, the kind of people you wouldn't ordinarily see. I've got to get off somewhere and be by myself and do some work." A central theme of all Baldwin biography is how the thirteen years from 1957 to 1970, during which he threw himself into public activism and the bright lights of media fame, all but destroyed him as an artist. For Baldwin, according to James Campbell, "fame shut him up in a kind of cage," and furthermore made him and parts of his family the object of extensive FBI surveillance and harassment. Even when he fled into relative hiding to try to write, Baldwin rarely turned down an interview. His drinking became so bad that it too often led to bizarre and belligerent screaming episodes in restaurants and bars that would baffle or outrage reporters and new acquaintances. The pressures of the civil rights campaign may have destroyed Baldwin's voice and his wits; but a drunken literary celebrity is still a drunk. Caryl Phillips, who as a young writer spent considerable time with Baldwin at his retreat in St. Paul de Vence, France, before the elder writer died there in 1987, captured this story of decline succinctly and poignantly. The "monster called fame" had often forced Baldwin into hiding so that he could finish books and essays, writes Phillips, but it "was a monster he had chased down and fed." To his lasting detriment, Baldwin craved more than he hated the glitter and attention of his stardom. In a 1965 interview, Baldwin told a British audience on the BBC that "the great terror of public speaking is that you begin to listen to yourself. By and by, since you are always telling people what to think, you begin to forget what you do think. . . . The moment that happens . . . it's over."[75]

By 1973, *Time* magazine had declared Baldwin "passé." That same year, the FBI closed its extensive file on Baldwin. The times had indeed changed markedly in America. The assassination of Martin Luther King, Jr., in 1968 had hollowed out Baldwin's heart for a time; he also fell into and out of favor with the Black Power Movement, both its political and its artistic impulses. Too often he tried to be a voice that would gain radical black favor, but the moment passed him by, since he could never quite give up his quest for "redemptive love." Baldwin's efforts at fiction in the Seventies were, as Phillips has carefully assayed, failures of structure and characterization, and sometimes "padded with irrelevant autobiographical asides." Baldwin could still fire off a short essay like a dart at the heart of some issue or experience, and he could still, on occasion, draw powerfully from his autobiographical well, as he did in *No Name in the Street* in 1972. But his novelistic art had "atrophied" in a painful decline from what Phillips remembers as the early Baldwin who wrote in "gracefully lilting sentences," with "mutable words and elliptical phrases" and a unique "self-questioning manner," mixing "doubt" and "certitude" in his trademark use of paradox.[76]

At the peak of his lyrical powers as a writer, at least as early as 1959, Baldwin planned to write a "slave novel," originally titled *Talking at the Gates,* and set on Emancipation Day. In a proposal to the Ford Foundation, which gave Baldwin a generous grant, it is clear the subject fired his imagination; he intended to probe the deep blood ties of whites and blacks born of the slavery experience, as well as the long-term collective denial that had produced what he saw as the racial nightmare of modern America. As early as 1960, moreover, Baldwin also imagined a film epic, beginning with African "slaves boarding the good ship *Jesus:* a white ship, on a dark sea, with master as white as the sails of their ship, and slaves as black as the ocean. There would be one intransigent slave, an eternal figure, destined to appear, and to be put to death, in every generation." We can only guess at where Baldwin's imagination might have gone with this project. He talked about it for many years, but apparently never really wrote any of it. The idea seemed fraught with potential melodrama, but it is intriguing to imagine how a talented filmmaker might have handled the later "intransigent" figure, who, "during the Reconstruction . . . would be murdered upon leaving Congress . . . would be a returning soldier during the First World War, and be burned alive; and then, during the Depression, he would become a jazz musician, and go mad."[77] This tragic and apocalyptic imagination might have turned American slavery into some version of a radical expressionist film. The culture of the Centennial era desperately needed it, but would likely have rejected it, even if it had been good art.

Baldwin wrote more poetry during the third and final "act" of his career (1970–1987). In a long heart-breaking poem, "Inventory / On Being 52," written in 1976, Baldwin imagines himself on a "journey to the palace of wisdom." It is a "discouraging" journey, and much "farther" than he had ever believed it would be, and at each turn he feels so ill-equipped:

I lack certain indispensable aptitudes.
Furthermore, it appears
that I packed the wrong things.
I thought I packed what was necessary,
or what little I had:
But there is always something one overlooks,
something one was not told,
or did not hear.
Furthermore,
some time ago, I seem to have made an error in judgment,
turned this way instead of that,
and, now, I cannot radio my position.
(I am not sure that my radio is working.
No voice has answered me for a long time now.)[78]

The full poem merits a careful reading; it is James Baldwin telling himself, and us, that he feared the "voice" was gone.

In 1984, Baldwin assembled his collected nonfiction—as though he knew that was his best work—in a large volume he entitled *The Price of the Ticket.* Phillips remembered the moment Jimmy told him the title, and, with time, came to understand how he had "purchased" that ticket to fame by "mortgaging his life as a writer."[79] Who is to say whether the price was worth it? What we do know is that James Baldwin—artist, orator, frenetic critic of the country he tried to love—gave America a different way of thinking about its history and its soul at a time when it sorely needed it. The Civil War Centennial, in the deeper scheme of history, was really the era of the Civil Rights Revolution. It was the new founding that Baldwin constantly struggled to imagine and describe. Baldwin's work in the era of the Fifties and Sixties tells us that perhaps the United States, and its history, needed to be loved and hated nearly to death in order to be resurrected to a new life, not unlike the way it had been reborn a century before.

By the 1960s, Baldwin and other writers who tried to provide the country with an alternative story to the mainstream impulses of the

Civil War Centennial were surrounded by an emerging and vibrant scholarship that would, within the decade, begin to revolutionize American and African American history. Led by John Hope Franklin, Rayford Logan, Benjamin Quarles, Saunders Redding, Kenneth Stampp, Leon Litwack, Nathan Huggins, John Blassingame, Sterling Stuckey, and so many others, the story of slavery, the Civil War, and Reconstruction underwent a revision like no other; Baldwin's constant demands for a new "history" were hardly unheeded by scholars.[80] But popular memory always lags far behind scholarship, and all revolutions can be turned around—as the new historiography of Reconstruction poignantly demonstrated, and as our political culture in the early twenty-first century reminds us, election after election.

. . .

On February 21, 1965, three days after Baldwin debated Buckley in England, Malcolm X was assassinated at the Apollo Theater in Harlem. Two weeks after that, six hundred civil rights marchers were brutally beaten by sheriff's deputies and state police on the Edmund Pettis Bridge in Selma, Alabama; the incident came to be known as "Bloody Sunday," one of the most important markers in the Movement's history. If anything, now, *The Fire Next Time* seemed a bit too prophetic. By late March, Baldwin was in Selma to participate in the voter registration drive and ultimately in the famous march from Selma to Montgomery, March 25–29. Baldwin joined the throng as it swelled along the highways, 25,000 strong from all over America, and finally reached the old capital of the Confederacy.

If we wish to see just what was at stake in the clashing versions of the history and memory of the Civil War era, with all their resonances in the Civil Rights era, a small remembrance in one of Baldwin's 1965 essays tells the tale. The "voice" was powerfully alive in that essay—"Unnameable Objects, Unspeakable Crimes"—which Baldwin published in *Ebony* magazine in August 1965. Baldwin charted the ways whites and blacks had forged segregated and deeply suspicious historical memories. Drawing on Cold War imagery, he argued that Americans had built a "color curtain" in their lives and in their historical consciousness which "may prove to be more deadly . . . than that iron curtain of which we speak so much." Baldwin used a refrain about "distance" between whites and blacks, between whites and themselves, and between the stories within which people claimed to be living. As the celebratory marchers arrived in the center of Montgomery, Baldwin noticed that the "Confederate flag was flying from the capitol dome" and that the federalized Alabama National Guard ordered to protect the marchers "wore Confederate flags on their jackets." All along the road, wrote Baldwin, older "black men and women, who have endured unspeakable oppression for so long, waved and cheered and wept." In the white section of town, Baldwin saw businessmen "on balconies, jeering," their "maids in back doors, silent." A "beige-colored woman" standing on the street, a bit nervous, suddenly joined the marchers.[81]

With a small American flag in his hand, Baldwin marched next to Harry Belafonte, his fellow Harlem-born comrade, who also happened to be a U.S. Navy veteran of World War II. White secretaries in upstairs office windows kept extending "thumbs-down" signs to the marchers, until, suddenly, many of them saw the stunningly handsome "reigning matinee idol," Belafonte, in the crowd. When they saw that "beautiful cat," said Baldwin, these women demonstrated that America was the "most desperately schizophrenic of republics." Baldwin's storytelling prose, and his insight, were never in better form. This was vintage Baldwin—race, sex, and his country, all on extraordinary display and subject to his scorching pen. Those young women in the windows, Baldwin declared, "could only . . . look forward to an alliance . . . with one of the jeering businessmen." And they were "female, a word, which, in the context of the color curtain, has suffered the same fate as the word 'male.'" Baldwin did not miss this chance. "When those girls saw Harry Belafonte," he wrote, "a collision occurred in them so visible as to be at once hilarious and unutterably sad. At one moment, the thumbs were down, they were barricaded within their skins, at the next moment, those down-turned thumbs flew to their mouths . . . their faces changed, and exactly like bobby-soxers, they oohed and aahed and moaned. God knows what was happening in the minds and hearts of those girls. Perhaps they would like to be free."[82]

Out of imagery that only Baldwin might have seen, in a world-historical moment, amid the joy and solemnity of the spectacular Selma march, he made art out of all the real people around him, "barricaded in their skins." On the eve of the centennial of the surrender at Appomattox, in the city where the Confederacy was born, Baldwin tried to kill that old story, asking everyone to see into a new history as they never had before. After all, he too just wanted to be loved, and just wanted to be free.

"The Wisdom of Tragedy"

Ralph Ellison Had a Dream

AFTER his magnificent novel *Invisible Man* was published in 1952, Ralph Ellison became a powerful and prolific essayist. His essays examined the meaning of race and identity in American society and culture with unique insight and imagination. Ellison possessed a profound sense of history, but he only rarely addressed the Civil War specifically as an enduring marker in the nation's past.

In the summer of 1953, while at a symposium held in Harvard University's Memorial Hall, which is physically one of the largest Civil War monuments in the United States, Ellison experienced what Arnold Rampersad calls an "epiphany that overwhelmed him." As he wandered through the majestic hallway outside Sanders Theater, "my attention was drawn upward," Ellison later remembered, "and I was aware of the marble walls, somber and carved with names." Until then, when he was forty, the Civil War had never fully captured Ellison's fertile imagination. But suddenly, looking up at the names of the New England Harvard men, each of whom had given his life on the battlefields of 1861–1865, "a tourist's curiosity flamed into something harrowing" for Ellison, as Rampersad says. "I knew its significance almost without knowing," Ellison recollected, "and the shock of recognition filled me with a kind of anguish. Something within me cried out 'No!' against that painful knowledge, for I knew that I stood in the presence of Harvard men who had given their young lives to set me free." As the author reflected on his 1953 revelation, he admitted to being "ignorant of their sacrifice," and "I was ashamed of my ignorance." Not only had he, the black Oklahoman who had grown up poor and dropped out of Tuskegee Institute, "repressed" this story to which he now felt emotionally drawn, but the whole nation had also forgotten "the details of the shameful abandonment of those goals for which they had given up their lives." As Ellison later reflected on this "betrayal of ideal and memory," he did so in part by recalling the language and arguments in Abraham Lincoln's Gettysburg Address.[1] It would not be the only time he appealed to Lincoln's elegiac masterpiece, or imagined in his art the shocks and recognitions that lay waiting in Civil War memory.

In June 1965, Ellison published an essay-story in the *Nation*, entitled "Tell It Like It Is, Baby." It suggests a fitting and provocative ending for this examination of literary and historical meditations on the Civil War during its Centennial years. Ellison apparently began writing the piece in 1956 while living in Rome, Italy, on a writing fellowship at the American Academy. It was inspired by a letter from an old childhood friend from Oklahoma who wrote to Ellison wondering if he had "read about those cracker senators cussing out the Supreme Court and all that mess" (a reference to Southern white resistance to the desegregation decision in *Brown v. Board* in 1954). The friend, "Virgil B.," wanted his "home-boy gone intellectual" to "tell a man how it is." Ellison found this challenge deeply "unsettling," he wrote, as he discovered "that there lay deeply within me a great deal of the horror generated by the Civil War and the tragic incident which marked the reversal of the North's 'victory,' and which foreshadowed the tenor of the ninety years to follow." Ellison then described a dream he had had one night in Rome, falling asleep after reading a book about tragedy and literature, and contemplating desegregation and the emergence of the Civil Rights Movement back home. The piece languished for nine years; he finally found the inspiration to finish it in 1965, the year of the Selma march, the Voting Rights Act, and the end of the Civil War Centennial.[2]

"Tell It Like It Is, Baby" is a startling allegory about the meaning and memory of Emancipation and the Civil War. Ellison begins with some musings about how racial "inequalities" in America seem to persist in an "atmosphere of dream-like irrationality"; he observes how competing "myth-image[s]" of Southerners and Northerners, whites and blacks, infest the American imagination like a "whirling nightmare." Then, from the "Roman dark," flows Ellison's terrifying remembrance of one of his own nightmares, which was like "a state of *civil war*, an impersonal and dreamlike chaos."[3]

The dream begins with misty images of a young man walking along a street in Oklahoma City, where Ellison was born and raised. He is "filled with expectation" because he anticipates seeing his father; just as he notices a "tall, familiar man," he sees that the figure is a stranger, who turns away. In the dream, Ellison wanders into the center of the city, into the streetcar terminal with its noises and smells, and then out into the public square, dominated by "a tall, equestrian statue . . . the rider poised in full gallop . . . high in his stirrups flourishing a broad military hat with plume." From this image of the unnamed Confederate monument, the protagonist suddenly travels back in time and finds himself among a hostile crowd, "as though a book of 19th-century photographs had erupted into vivid life." He is in the streets of Washington, "flags and bunting" wave from buildings, and he is swept up by the "crowd moving with sweating excitement," as they surge to see "a sheet-covered form being removed on a litter."[4] As readers, we quickly realize that Ellison is mixing a recollection of his own father's death when the writer was but three years old, a first memory, with a haunted, increasingly horrifying remembrance of the death of Abraham Lincoln.

What Ellison witnesses next, in the dream, is a hideous reversal of the history of Lincoln's funeral. He finds himself reverted to childhood as a barefoot "young slave" in a tunic, forced into the mob that carries Lincoln's body not to a noble and majestic burial, but to eternal desecration and defilement. Trapped, the boy "could not cry" and "could not scream," as he hears shouts of *"Sic semper tyrannis!"* He has "fallen out of time into chaos," Ellison writes, as "history book descriptions of the event flickered through my mind in visual counterpoint . . . but nothing was going as it was written." There was "no escort of grieving high dignitaries," nor any "weeping, recently freed slaves forming an anguished second line." In this "carnival," the mob shouts, "We've caught the old coon at last . . . COON! COON! COON!"[5]

As the story continues, the mob becomes deranged in its fury. The desecrators begin to cut away parts of Lincoln's clothing; they "hacked" at his coat with "pieces of broken bottle," ripping away souvenir slices of his necktie while "squawking like carrion crows." The "President's stovepipe hat" is thrown around among the feverish crowd. "A man grabbed it as it fell and, turning on his toes like a ballet dancer, jammed it on the head of a floozy, cotton-topped blonde, who wiggling wobbly . . . cutting a clumsy cakewalk . . . lurched . . . with a suggestion of bump and grind." Soon, "four ragged Negro men[,] . . . kicked and pummeled as they stumbled along," are forced to carry the litter containing the "bony railsplitter's" half-naked body. The macabre parade turns into an ugly minstrel show, as "a short, fat man wearing a long, gray coat, and who resembled Edmund Wilson, turned from drinking beer from a tin bucket," throws back a final draught, and "jammed the 'growler' on the Great Emancipator's head, clamping the wire handle beneath the bearded chin." As the throng reaches its destination, the Washington Monument, a hooligan pushes "the stem of a corncob pipe between the once so eloquent lips, twisting the bowl so that its contents spilled upon the shrunken chest."[6]

Ellison, the young slave boy in the dream, is compelled to stay and watch this horror show, "forced to the front of the crowd" by an "invisible hand." In sheer terror, he then sees "a man wearing a voluminous opera cape, and who looked oddly like Mr. Justice Holmes," use his boot, "flipping the corpse into a grotesque attitude." The Holmes-like figure opens his cape and sticks his "long finger through a series of bullet holes" as the frenzied mob moves closer, to kick Lincoln's body into "fantastic positions . . . twisting it in the cordwood postures of Dachau, shouting and cursing all the while." The slave boy desperately wants the nightmare to end, but "no tears would flow to bring relief."[7] This prolonged destruction of American freedom is beyond grief, beyond understanding. The story seems like the bleakest of tragedies, with no resolution and no exit—not even tears to assuage the agony.

Although Ellison's readers may wish for relief, the story and the unbearable tension only worsen. The author refuses to believe Lincoln is dead, imagining the "desecration" as the Emancipator's "tragic duty of keeping the country unified even through an act of fratricidal war," a terrible playing-out of his "fated role." Then Ellison remembers the dream in "accelerated tempo": the "corpse rebelled," swelling to a "state of putrefaction," and Lincoln's "underwear" comes to resemble "inner tubes that form the body of the figure in the Michelin trademark." The mob continues to claw at Lincoln's bloated limbs as Ellison lets the dream mercifully end in a scene of apocalyptic horror. The slave boy is pinned against the wall of the Monument, as "slime-drenched birds burst up from the earth on swift metallic wings and attacked the onlookers with feet of fire." The four Negro men reappear, carrying a black box and holding gleaming shovels. The entire scene, says Ellison, now appears as if on a "movie screen"; he stands with the other blacks peering down into a "great hole" in the ground, where he sees "a multitude, some black faces among them, sitting at table making a ghoulish meal of some frightful thing that a white sheet hid from view."[8]

Ellison awakes in a "cold sweat." He hears a "nightingale singing" and the sound of the "lonely play of the fountain" in a Roman piazza beneath his window. In the voice of the essayist of 1965, Ellison recollects that he tried "exorcizing the dream" by "desperately" reciting the words of the Gettysburg Address. He once memorized the lines at "Frederick Douglass" high school in Oklahoma City, writes Ellison, and they have been "profoundly implicated both in my life and in the failure of my promised freedom." But the "words had hidden themselves, become mute before the vivid mist of nightmare." Stunningly, Ellison recollects the scene in the 1935 movie *Ruggles of Red Gap,* in which Charles Laughton, playing the English butler-servant to a vulgar American nouveau riche family of oil barons during the Gilded Age, announces to his employer that he has decided to make a life of his own in the American land of opportunity. In a Western bar full of ignorant bumpkins who cannot fathom any answers to the question "What did Lincoln say at Gettysburg?" Ruggles (Laughton) recites the complete Address to a roomful of rapt drunks and American philistines.[9] Ellison's reference to that Depression-era film, which delivered a savage parody of Gilded Age greed and materialism, makes all the more interesting the presence of Edmund Wilson and Oliver Wendell Holmes, Jr., in the dream. It was precisely this Gilded Age materialism that Wilson saw as the principal legacy of the Civil War, and that Holmes, according to Wilson, most resisted with his Puritan work ethic. Undoubtedly, Ellison had only recently read *Patriotic Gore* before writing "Tell It Like It Is, Baby." He is neither the first nor the last American writer to harbor ambivalence about Edmund Wilson, nor is he perhaps the only one to have encountered the critic in his dreams.

As Ellison ends his story, he does not allow this brilliant piece of art merely to speak for itself; he offers some interpretation of his own dream. "I could not ignore the fact that no one tried to stop the mob," Ellison says, "nor that I myself was a trapped and impotent observer—in fact, most infantile, my mind became an incongruous scene for historical horrors personalized." He further suggests that his dream simply fits a "pattern of classical tragedy: the hero-father murdered (for Lincoln is a kind of father of 20th century America), his life evilly sacrificed and the fruits of his neglected labors withering some ninety years in the fields." In the end, Ellison reaches for understanding through the "insights made available in the wisdom of tragedy." He confesses "defeat" in his effort to know the full personal meaning of his dream, but he is quite certain about the social and historical meanings. The deepest legacy of the Civil War, for ninety dark years, had been the betrayal of the promises of Emancipation for blacks and of the expansion of liberty and equality for all Americans. The best approach to understanding that dark time, and whether a brighter era might be dawning, must be one chastened and informed by a sense of tragedy. But the country, in its favored and official memories, has ceased trying to find the deepest meanings in the Civil War era. "The last true note of tragedy was sounded (and quickly muffled) in our land," Ellison concludes, "when the North buried Lincoln and the South buried Lee, and between them cast the better part, both of our tragic sense—except perhaps the Negroes'—and our capacity for tragic heroism into the grave. The sheet-covered figure in my dream might well have been General Robert E. Lee."[10]

Ellison may not have written as often or as explicitly about the Civil War as the other four writers analyzed in this book. But like them, he demonstrated that true notes of tragedy, though almost buried in the recesses of American memory in the 1860s, had sprung to life again one hundred years later. If we look closely, the "corpses" of the Civil War still "rebel," our "tears" bring only partial "relief," and we forever yearn to awake.

Notes

Acknowledgments

Index

Notes

Prologue

1. Martin Luther King, Jr., "I Have a Dream," in James M. Washington, ed., *A Testament of Hope: The Essential Writings of Martin Luther King, Jr.* (San Francisco: Harper San Francisco, 1991), 217–220.

2. On the Union and the North's "victorious cause," see John R. Neff, *Honoring the Civil War Dead: Commemoration and the Problem of Reconciliation* (Lawrence: University of Kansas Press, 2005); and Gary Gallagher, *The Union War* (Cambridge, Mass.: Harvard University Press, 2011). On the range and development of Civil War scholarship over time, from the 1950s through the early twenty-first century, see Thomas J. Pressley, *Americans Interpret Their Civil War* (Princeton: Princeton University Press, 1954); Robert P. Swierenga, ed., *Beyond the Civil War Synthesis: Political Essays of the Civil War Era* (Westport, Conn.: Greenwood Press, 1975); James M. McPherson and William J. Cooper, eds., *Writing the Civil War: The Quest to Understand* (Columbia: University of South Carolina Press, 1998); and Edward L. Ayers, *What Caused the Civil War? Reflections on the South and Southern History* (New York: Norton, 2005). For a thorough discussion of the revolutions in the study of race and African American history in this period, see August Meier and Elliott Rudwick, *Black History and the Historical Profession, 1915–1980* (Urbana: University of Illinois Press, 1986), chs. 2–3.

3. Paul Fussell, *The Great War and Modern Memory* (London: Oxford University Press, 1975), 6, 8, 74, 36–74. Elsewhere, I have developed at length the theme of Civil War reconciliation through "the Blue and the Gray" at the expense of the issues of race and the lives of the former slaves; see David W. Blight, *Race and Reunion: The Civil War in American Memory* (Cambridge, Mass.: Harvard University Press, 2001). On Fussell's stress on irony in the work of British writers, while the French largely avoided the use of irony, see Jay Winter, *Remembering War: The Great War between Memory and History in the Twentieth Century* (New Haven: Yale University Press, 2006), 118–134.

4. Fussell, *The Great War and Modern Memory,* 69–70.

5. Conwell's letters from his tour are published in Joseph C. Carter, ed., *Magnolia Journey: A Union Veteran Revisits the Former Confederate States* (Tuscaloosa: University of Alabama Press, 1974), 3, 7, 22–23, 59–60, 76–78. For further discussion of Conwell's tour, see Blight, *Race and Reunion*, 154–156.

6. Fussell, *The Great War and Modern Memory*, 70–71.

7. The list of potential authors for such a longer book is extensive. Among white, distinctly Southern popular writers, Douglas Southall Freeman, Clifford Dowdey, and Shelby Foote might have been selected. Certainly William Faulkner hovers over or behind my four authors, especially Warren and Baldwin, but the Squire of Oxford died in 1962, his most powerful writing long behind him. Had this book been primarily about the historiographic revolutions of the 1950s and 1960s regarding slavery, race, and the Civil War, a large number of academically trained historians could have populated a much longer book. Although they did not have nearly the public impact that my four selections did, these historians launched a fundamental and lasting revision of the Civil War era. That list, though hardly complete and representing at least two generations, might have included Herbert Aptheker, Lerone Bennett, Richard Current, Carl Degler, David Donald, Richard Hofstadter, John Hope Franklin, Leon Litwack, Rayford Logan, James McPherson, August Meier, Allan Nevins, David Potter, Benjamin Quarles, James I. (Bud) Robertson, Willie Lee Rose, Arthur M. Schlesinger, Jr., Kenneth Stampp, Bell Wiley, T. Harry Williams, and C. Vann Woodward. Among novelists, essayists, and journalists, one might certainly also have considered Ralph Ellison, Howard Fast, McKinley Kantor, Margaret Leech, Flannery O'Connor, J. Saunders Redding, J. A. Rogers, Carl Sandburg, Margaret Walker, and numerous others. Some new variation of Edmund Wilson's *Patriotic Gore* for the 1950s and 1960s could and should be written. Such a work could become encyclopedic, and might extend well beyond Wilson's eight hundred pages; it would have to find a delicate balance between scholarly and popular writers for a period awash in publishing about the Civil War era.

8. Robert Penn Warren, *The Legacy of the Civil War* (Cambridge, Mass.: Harvard University Press, 1983; orig. pub. 1961), 3. On the idea of the "war story" as a central thread of American historical self-understanding in the Cold War era, see Tom Engelhardt, *The End of Victory Culture:*

Cold War America and the Disillusioning of a Generation (Amherst: University of Massachusetts Press, 1995), 3–65.

9. See Jon Wiener, "Civil War, Cold War, Civil Rights: The Civil War Centennial in Context, 1960–1965," in Alice Fahs and Joan Waugh, eds., *The Memory of the Civil War in American Culture* (Chapel Hill: University of North Carolina Press, 2004), 237–257; and Robert J. Cook, *Troubled Commemoration: The American Civil War Centennial, 1961–1965* (Baton Rouge: Louisiana State University Press, 2007).

10. Cook, *Troubled Commemoration*, 15–49; *New York Times*, May 21 and June 9, 1957; *Washington Post*, January 30, 1957; *Hartford Courant*, May 21, 1957.

11. *New York Times*, February 12, 13, 16, 18, 1961; Cook, *Troubled Commemoration*, 79–84.

12. Wiener, "Civil War, Cold War, Civil Rights," 238–241; Cook, *Troubled Commemoration*, 88–119. For highly critical reactions to the Charleston controversy in the black press, see *Atlanta Daily World*, March 23, 25, 26, and April 2, 13, 1961; *Baltimore Afro-American*, April 15, 1961. The *Afro-American* editors concluded: "Substitute segregation for slavery and solution of that issue remains as important today as it was a century ago. Unless the centennial is designed to re-echo Lincoln's great and thrilling pronouncement that this nation is 'conceived in liberty and dedicated to the proposition that all men are created equal' it will completely lack any real meaning and should be called off."

13. Cook, *Troubled Commemoration*, 126–131; Wiener, "Civil War, Cold War, Civil Rights," 241–243 (italics in original).

14. See Raymond Arsenault, *Freedom Riders: 1961 and the Struggle for Racial Justice* (New York: Oxford University Press, 2005).

15. *Holiday*, July 1961; *New York Herald-Tribune*, July 22, 1961; *New York Times*, July 29, 1961; J. A. Rogers, "History Shows" series, *Pittsburgh Courier*, November 4, January 13, 19, 26, February 3, July 20, 1963. And see Cook, *Troubled Commemoration*, 125–131.

16. Allan Nevins, "The Glorious and the Terrible," *Saturday Review*, September 2, 1961, 48; Nevins policy paper quoted in Cook, *Troubled Commemoration*, 147, and see 120–148.

17. For the quotation (which is by Karl Betts) and on the American Negro Emancipation Centennial Authority, see Cook, *Troubled Commemoration*, 150, 165, 183–184.

18. See ibid., 181–188.

19. On the Robertson compromise, see ibid., 151–153.

20. On the September 22 ceremony and boycott, see *New York Times,* September 18, 23, 1962. J. A. Rogers kept up a drumbeat about Emancipation and a critique of the CWCC's September 22 ceremony. See *Pittsburgh Courier,* October 6, November 3, 1962, January 19, 26, 1963. See Cook, *Troubled Commemoration,* 170–176; and Wiener, "Civil War, Cold War, Civil Rights," 248–250. For a celebratory report about the September 22 event, see *The Civil War Centennial: A Report to Congress* (Washington, D.C.: U.S. Civil War Centennial Commission, 1968), 17–19, copy in Huntington Library, San Marino, Calif.

21. Kennedy and Stevenson are quoted in Cook, *Troubled Commemoration,* 176–177.

22. James Baldwin, *The Fire Next Time* (New York: Dell, 1963), 118 (the italics are Baldwin's).

23. *Atlanta Daily World,* February 23, 1960; *Norfolk Journal and Guide,* April 29, 1961; Dorothy Sterling quoted in *Norfolk Journal and Guide,* March 11, 1961; *Pittsburgh Courier,* March 25, 1961; Charles Wesley quoted in *Baltimore Afro-American,* November 25, 1961. Had the CWCC leadership employed staff members to read the black press on a regular basis, they might have conceived somewhat different and more racially inclusive events.

24. *Baltimore Afro-American,* March 25 and May 27, 1961; *New York Amsterdam News,* March 25, 1961.

25. See, for example, the *Negro History Bulletin* for January 1963, which published, among other things, a plan by which local organizations could organize their own Emancipation commemorations, a profile of black historian Benjamin Quarles, letters to the editor criticizing the CWCC and speeches by Bell Wiley, and stories about African American history.

26. George Bancroft, *History of the United States of America, from the Discovery of the Continent* (New York: D. Appleton, 1885), 5, 207.

27. "Counterstatement" is a quote from F. O. Matthiessen, *American Renaissance* (New York: Oxford University Press, 1941), 179. See the essays in C. Vann Woodward, *The Burden of Southern History* (Baton Rouge: Louisiana State University Press, 1960).

28. There are many exceptions to this pattern. In an earlier work, I tried to write, through the evidence, with a sense of tragedy in mind; see David

W. Blight, *Race and Reunion: The Civil War in American Memory* (Cambridge, Mass.: Harvard University Press, 2001). Other examples abound, but on this topic of Civil War and Southern memory, see especially Drew Gilpin Faust, *This Republic of Suffering: Death and the American Civil War* (New York: Knopf, 2008); and Fitzhugh W. Brundage, *The Southern Past: A Clash of Race and Memory* (Cambridge, Mass.: Harvard University Press, 2005). On the war as a problem for "just war" consideration, see especially Harry S. Stout, *Upon the Altar of the Nation: A Moral History of the Civil War* (New York: Penguin, 2007).

29. Raymond Williams, *Modern Tragedy* (Stanford: Stanford University Press, 1966), 18; Richard B. Sewall, *The Vision of Tragedy* (New Haven: Yale University Press, 1980), ix, 3–4; Terry Eagleton, *Sweet Violence: The Idea of the Tragic* (Malden, Mass.: Blackwell, 2003); Geoffrey Brereton, *Principles of Tragedy: A Rational Examination of the Tragic Concept in Life and Literature* (Coral Gables, Fla.: University of Miami Press, 1968), 21–47; T. R. Henn, *The Harvest of Tragedy* (London: Methuen, 1956), 1–7; D. D. Raphael, "Why Does Tragedy Please?" in Raphael, *The Paradox of Tragedy* (Bloomington: Indiana University Press, 1960), 13–36.

30. Sewall, *Vision of Tragedy,* 92; Melville is quoted in Matthiessen, *American Renaissance,* 436. See also Oscar Mandel, *A Definition of Tragedy* (New York: New York University Press, 1961), 3–22, 162–168.

31. Matthiessen, *American Renaissance,* 441–442.

32. Warren, *The Legacy of the Civil War,* 102.

33. Ralph Ellison, "Tell It Like It Is, Baby," *Nation,* June 1965, 136.

1. "Gods and Devils Aplenty"

1. Joseph Blotner, *Robert Penn Warren: A Biography* (New York: Random House, 1997), 11–15.

2. Transcript of interview with Dick Cavett, 1978; and transcript of interview with L. G. Bridson, taped for the BBC at the Algonquin Hotel, New York, April 1961; both in Robert Penn Warren Papers, Beinecke Library, Yale University, box 239, folders 4626, 4627. Blotner, *Warren,* 12; interview with John Baker, spring 1977, in Floyd C. Watkins, John T. Hiers, and Mary Louise Weaks, eds., *Talking with Robert Penn Warren* (Athens: University of Georgia Press, 1990), 248–249.

3. Robert Penn Warren, *Jefferson Davis Gets His Citizenship Back* (Lexington: University of Kentucky Press, 1980), 5–9; originally published in the *New Yorker.*

4. Ibid., 4, 6, 9; interview with Peter Stitt, published in *Sewanee Review* (Summer 1977), 467–477, Warren Papers, box 239, folder 4650; interview with Richard B. Sale, March 4, 1969, in Watkins et al., *Talking*, 124.

5. Robert Penn Warren, *Segregation: The Inner Conflict in the South* (New York: Random House, 1956), 5.

6. Stitt interview, 1977, Warren Papers; interview with Marshall Walker, September 11, 1969, in Watkins et al., *Talking*, 149; Warren, *Jefferson Davis*, 10.

7. Warren, *Jefferson Davis*, 10–11; Bridson interview, 1961, Warren Papers.

8. Warren, *Jefferson Davis*, 20–21.

9. Blotner, *Warren*, 16–19; Robert Penn Warren, "Rebuke of the Rocks" and "History among the Rocks," in Warren, *The Collected Poems*, ed. John Burt (Baton Rouge: Louisiana State University Press, 1998), 35–37.

10. Blotner, *Warren*, 29–30, 40–43.

11. Ibid., 44–58; Paul K. Conkin, *The Southern Agrarians* (Knoxville: University of Tennessee Press, 1988), 57–61.

12. Blotner, *Warren*, 61–108; Robert Penn Warren, *John Brown: The Making of a Martyr* (New York: Payson and Clarke, 1929), 424, 428–434.

13. Conkin, *Southern Agrarians*, 32–56.

14. Robert Penn Warren, "The Briar Patch," in Twelve Southerners, *I'll Take My Stand: The South and the Agrarian Tradition* (New York: Harper and Brothers, 1962; orig. pub. 1930), 246–264. On the conception of the book and Warren's invitation from Ransom and Davidson, see Blotner, *Warren*, 105–106; and Conkin, *Southern Agrarians*, 57–88. On Warren's writing as an Agrarian, see Leonard Casper, *Robert Penn Warren: The Dark and Bloody Ground* (Seattle: University of Washington Press, 1960), 24–32.

15. Robert Penn Warren, *Night Rider* (Boston: Houghton Mifflin, 1939). On *Night Rider*, see John Burt, *Robert Penn Warren and American Idealism* (New Haven: Yale University Press, 1988), 127–140; and Blotner, *Warren*, 169–175.

16. Concerning Warren's views on history, and the notion that "history is blind," which Jack Burden says a number of times in *All the King's Men*, see L. Hugh Moore, Jr., *Robert Penn Warren and History: "The Big Myth*

We Live" (Paris: Mouton, 1970), 70–104. And on Warren's many uses of history in various genres, see Jonathan S. Cullick, *Making History: The Biographical Narratives of Robert Penn Warren* (Baton Rouge: Louisiana State University Press, 2000).

17. Robert Penn Warren, *All the King's Men* (New York: Harcourt, 2001; orig. pub. 1946), 247–250.

18. Ibid., 223–229, 268, 320.

19. Ibid., 247–249, 253–257, 259–260.

20. Ibid., 260–264.

21. Ibid., 266. On the "spider web" theory of history, see Beekman W. Cottrell, "Cass Mastern and the Awful Responsibility of Time," in Robert H. Chambers, ed., *Twentieth-Century Interpretations of "All the King's Men": A Collection of Critical Essays* (Englewood Cliffs, N.J.: Prentice-Hall, 1977), 116–125.

22. Burt, *Warren and American Idealism,* 168–169; Warren, *All the King's Men,* 319.

23. Robert Penn Warren, *Wilderness: A Tale of the Civil War* (New York: Random House, 1961), 42–44, 71. On the roots of the book in classical Greek and Roman mythology and for an admiring critique, see L. Hugh Moore, Jr., "Wilderness: The 'Little Myth,'" in Moore, *Robert Penn Warren and History,* 142–182.

24. Warren, *Wilderness,* 96–97; Leonard Casper, "Trial by Wilderness: Warren's Exemplum," in Richard Gray, ed., *Robert Penn Warren: A Collection of Critical Essays* (Englewood Cliffs, N.J.: Prentice-Hall, 1980), 99.

25. Warren, *Wilderness,* 187, 212–215.

26. Ibid., 221–222, 227–232.

27. Ibid., 287–310.

28. Ibid., 73, 77. On Warren's characters and their search for self-knowledge, see especially Cleanth Brooks, "Experience Redeemed in Knowledge," in Gray, ed., *Robert Penn Warren: A Collection of Critical Essays,* 17–31.

29. Robert Penn Warren, "The Sense of the Past," edited transcript of unpublished essay, Warren Papers, box 235, folder 4507, later published as "The Use of the Past," in Warren, *A Time to Hear and Answer: Essays for the Bicentennial Season* (Tuscaloosa: University of Alabama Press, 1977).

30. Robert Penn Warren, "Irony with a Center: Katherine Anne Porter," in Warren, *Selected Essays* (New York: Random House, 1951), 142–143.

31. Stitt interview, 1977, Warren Papers; Robert Penn Warren, *Homage to*

Theodore Dreiser (New York: Ransom House, 1971), 116, 129, 138; Warren, "The Sense of the Past," Warren Papers; Warren, "Shoes in Rain Jungle," in Warren, *Collected Poems*, 198.

32. Stitt interview, 1977, Warren Papers; Warren, "Melville the Poet," in Warren, *Selected Essays*, 190.

33. Andrew Delbanco, *Melville: His World and Work* (New York: Knopf, 2005), 268n375.

34. "Introduction," in Herman Melville, *Selected Poems of Herman Melville: A Reader's Edition*, ed. Robert Penn Warren (New York: Random House, 1967), 8–9. Warren declares that he called the book a "reader's edition" because he is himself the reader, delivering the Melville he most appreciates. "The book may be regarded," he says, "as a log of my own long reading of Melville's poetry" (vii).

35. Ibid., 11–12, 23.

36. Ibid., 15, 18; Herman Melville, *Selected Poems of Herman Melville*, ed. Hennig Cohen (Garden City, N.Y.: Doubleday, 1964), 9–10.

37. Melville, *Selected Poems*, ed. Cohen, 50–51.

38. Melville, *Selected Poems*, ed. Warren, 20–22, 27; Melville, *Selected Poems*, ed. Cohen, 57.

39. Melville, *Selected Poems*, ed. Warren, 26–27; Robert Penn Warren, *The Legacy of the Civil War* (Cambridge, Mass.: Harvard University Press, 1961), 109.

40. Casper, "Trial by Wilderness," 102.

41. Robert Penn Warren, *Brother to Dragons: A Tale in Verse and Voices* (New York: Random House, 1953), xiii.

42. Warren, *Legacy*, 100, 102.

43. Ibid., 3–4.

44. Ibid., 101–102.

45. Warren to Cleanth Brooks, July 21, 1960, in Robert Penn Warren, *Selected Letters*, ed. Randy Hendricks and James A. Perkins (Baton Rouge: Louisiana State University Press, 2008), 4:295; Warren to Jerry Korn, September 25, 1960, Warren Papers, box 154, folder 2812. Warren considered other titles for his book, including *The Civil War and the American Imagination* and *The Meaning of the Civil War*, titles that tell us much about what he sought to accomplish. See the various drafts of *Legacy*, including research notes, in Warren Papers, box 154, folders 2810, 2811.

46. Warren, *Legacy*, 76, 80–82. See David W. Blight, "Homer with a Camera: Our Iliad without the Aftermath," in *Reviews in American History* (June 1997). Burns has stated that Warren's *Legacy* was a major influence on him while he was making the documentary series.

47. Warren, *Legacy*, 82–84, 90. On Warren's heroes as "fallen," see also John Burt, "Robert Penn Warren's *The Legacy of the Civil War* and the Meaning of Pragmatism," *American Literary History* (September 2007), 966, 974.

48. Warren, *Legacy*, 93–95.

49. Ibid., 98–100.

50. Ibid., 71.

51. Ibid., 53.

52. On the Lost Cause tradition treated as a racial ideology in particular, see David W. Blight, *Race and Reunion: The Civil War in American Memory* (Cambridge, Mass.: Harvard University Press, 2001), 255–299, and for numerous other definitions, 452n7. On the Lost Cause as a cultural movement among ex-Confederates, see Gaines M. Foster, *Ghost of the Confederacy: Defeat, the Lost Cause, and the Emergence of the New South, 1865–1913* (New York: Oxford University Press, 1987).

53. Warren, *Legacy*, 54–55.

54. Ibid., 57–58. Warren was deeply influenced by the writings of Reinhold Niebuhr and C. Vann Woodward on the nature of American history, as well as on theology. He probably drew on Niebuhr's and Woodward's musings about original sin, the burdens of the past, and the quest in America for a history that could float innocently above the real tragedy at its core. See Reinhold Niebuhr, *The Irony of American History* (New York: Scribner's, 1952); and C. Vann Woodward, *The Burden of Southern History* (New York: New American Library, 1968; orig. pub. 1960). Niebuhr's influence on Warren is mentioned in Burt, "Robert Penn Warren's *The Legacy of the Civil War* and the Meaning of Pragmatism," 966. I am skeptical of Burt's claim that what Warren saw as the "Great Alibi" "has passed from the scene" since the 1970s (981). The neo-Confederate movement has demonstrated extraordinary resiliency among whites, and not only in the South.

55. Warren, *Legacy*, 59.

56. Ibid., 60–63.

57. Ibid., 60.

58. Warren to Charles H. Foster, March 19, 1962, in Warren, *Selected Letters*, 4:334–335.

59. Warren, *Legacy*, 20–27; David Donald, "Toward a Reconsideration of Abolitionists," in Donald, *Lincoln Reconsidered* (New York: Vintage, 1961), 19–36; Stanley M. Elkins, *Slavery: A Problem in American Institutional and Intellectual Life* (New York: Grosset and Dunlap, 1963; orig. pub. 1959), 140–222. On Warren's "higher law" and "legalism," see also Burt, "Robert Penn Warren's *The Legacy of the Civil War* and the Meaning of Pragmatism," 975–980.

60. Warren, *Legacy*, 22–23, 29, 32.

61. Ibid., 34–36, 39. Fragments of outlines and notes survive from Warren's writing process for *Legacy*. Especially on the questions of abstractions and absolutes, on the South as a "closed society," and on James's "pragmatism," one can see Warren making lists of the points he would convert into prose. See Warren Papers, box 154, folder 2808.

62. Warren, *Legacy*, 16–18. The literature on pragmatism is vast, but for an understanding of Warren's use of the concept, see H. S. Thayer, ed., *Pragmatism: The Classic Writings* (Indianapolis: Hackett, 1982), 11–23; and Burt, "Robert Penn Warren's *The Legacy of the Civil War* and the Meaning of Pragmatism." For a succinct explanation of James's development of pragmatism, see Jacques Barzun, *A Stroll with William James* (Chicago: University of Chicago Press, 1983), 83–108.

63. William James, "What Pragmatism Means" (1907), in James, *Pragmatism*, ed. Bruce Kuklick (Indianapolis: Hackett, 1981), 37–38; Warren, *Legacy*, 17.

64. Robert Penn Warren, introduction to 1953 edition of *All the King's Men*, in Chambers, ed., *Twentieth-Century Interpretations of "All the King's Men,"* 97.

65. Warren, *Legacy*, 19, 43–45.

66. Ibid., 45.

67. Woodward to Warren, September 4, 1960, Warren Papers, box 82, folder 1609.

68. Reviews of Warren's *Legacy of the Civil War*: Richard L. Tobin, "U.S. History's Great Single Event," *New Yorker*, July 8, 1961, copy in Warren Papers, box 155, folder 2821; Richard Harwell, "1861–1865: Perspective

and Participation," labeled only "magazine," n.d., ibid.; and Alfred Kazin, review in the *Reporter*, n.d., ibid.

69. Reviews of Warren's *Legacy of the Civil War:* Richard Weaver, "An Altered Stand," *National Review*, June 17, 1961; Truman Nelson, "History Stood on Its Head," *National Guardian*, May 8, 1961; Peter d'A. Jones, review in the *New Republic*, May 5, 1961. Copies of all of these are in the Warren Papers, box 155, folder 2821.

70. Warren to editor of the *New Republic*, June 5, 1961, in Warren, *Selected Letters*, 4:314–315.

71. Warren, *Legacy*, 107–108. On the various forms and literary-philosophical roots of tragedy, see Terry Eagleton, *Sweet Violence: The Idea of the Tragic* (London: Blackwell, 2003).

72. Warren, *Legacy*, 103.

73. Warren, "Truth," in Warren, *Collected Poems*, 415.

2. A Formula for Enjoying the War

1. Bruce Catton to Sterling North, November 17, 1954, Bruce Catton Papers, American Heritage Center, University of Wyoming, Laramie, box 2, folder 1; Bruce Catton, *Waiting for the Morning Train: An American Boyhood* (Garden City, N.Y.: Doubleday, 1972), 39–40. Catton was born in Petoskey, Michigan, on October 9, 1899. His mother was the former Adella Patten. See Ethel Rowan Fasquelle, "Mrs. Fasquelle Writes of Noted Authors Who Lived in This Area," *Petoskey News* (Mich.), May 4, 1956, clipping held in Catton Papers, Wyoming, box 1, folder 1.

2. Catton, *Waiting for the Morning Train*, 40–41.

3. Ibid., 191–192. The connection between Catton's deep interest in the Civil War and the influence of the veterans in Benzonia is confirmed in numerous interviews with Catton and articles about his life. Two examples are James H. Bready, "After Appomattox, for This Novelist, Come Further Projects in History," from an unidentified Maryland newspaper, Bruce Catton Papers, The Citadel Archives and Museum, Charleston, S.C., box 28, folder 6; and interview with Bill Moyers, *Bill Moyers Journal*, WNET, transcript, p. 6, Catton Papers, Wyoming, box 3, miscellaneous folder.

4. Catton, *Waiting for the Morning Train*, 189–192.

5. Ibid., 214–216.

6. Ibid., 216–220.

7. Brief Catton biography, American Heritage Publishing Company, 1965, Catton Papers, Wyoming, box 5; Catton obituary, *Washington Post*, August 29, 1978, Bruce Catton Biographical File, American Heritage Center, University of Wyoming, Laramie; Catton, speech at Oberlin College Alumni dinner, New York, December 11, 1956, and Catton to Henry Ladd Smith, August 9, 1955, Catton Papers, Wyoming, box 1, speeches folder, and box 2, folder 2. Smith had invited Catton to take a visiting professorship in history at the University of Washington in Seattle, but the author declined, saying he had no "A.B. degree" and "no teaching experience."

8. Mordecai Lee, "Origins of the Epithet 'Government by Public Relations': Revisiting Bruce Catton's *War Lords of Washington*, 1948," *Public Relations Review*, July 14, 2009, 388–394.

9. Bruce Catton, *The War Lords of Washington* (New York: Harcourt, Brace, 1948), 307, 311.

10. Ibid., 51, 123; Lee, "Origins of the Epithet 'Government by Public Relations,'" 390.

11. Catton, *War Lords*, 308, 311. On Catton's left-leaning, populist rhetoric, see Roy Rosenzweig, "Marketing the Past: American Heritage and Popular History in the United States," in S. P. Benson, Stephen Brier, and Roy Rosenzweig, eds., *Presenting the Past: Essays on History and the Public* (Philadelphia: Temple University Press, 1986), 31.

12. Lee, "Origins of the Epithet 'Government by Public Relations,'" 391; Marvin H. Bernstein, review of *War Lords of Washington*, in *Public Opinion Quarterly* (Summer 1949), 341–343; Horace M. Gray, review of *War Lords of Washington*, in *Annals of the American Academy of Political and Social Sciences* (January 1949), 184–185; Leo Tolstoy, *War and Peace* (New York: Signet Classic, 1968), 1429, 732. Reviewers sometimes compared Catton to Tolstoy, but his readers did so often. For a striking example, see Jason Epstein to Catton, December 10, 1953, Catton Papers, Citadel, box 28, file 3. Epstein was one of Catton's editors at Doubleday. He saw in Catton's writing what he admired in Tolstoy's: work that "begins and ends in the imagination" and in the "historian's poetic instinct."

13. In response to a 1957 fan letter from a graduate student at Claremont Graduate School in California who asked about how *War Lords* related

to the present, Catton wrote that his "experience in Washington during World War II was invaluable to me, in that it enabled me to understand many things about the Civil War which had previously been very puzzling. . . . I learned a great deal about how government works in times of crisis." Catton to Brian A. Shannon, February 8, 1957, Catton Papers, Wyoming, box 2, folder 4.

14. Bruce Catton, *Mr. Lincoln's Army* (Garden City, N.Y.: Doubleday, 1951); *Glory Road* (Garden City, N.Y.: Doubleday, 1952); *A Stillness at Appomattox* (Garden City, N.Y.: Doubleday, 1954). All three books bore the group title "The Army of the Potomac," and hence they have become known as the "Army of the Potomac" Trilogy, the first of two trilogies Catton would write. Bruce Catton, *Ulysses S. Grant and the American Military Tradition* (Boston: Little, Brown, 1954); Lloyd Lewis, *Captain Sam Grant* (Boston: Little, Brown, 1950); Oscar Handlin to Catton, May 3, 1951, and Handlin to Catton, September 11, 1953, Catton Papers, Citadel, box 28, folder 1. The second letter contains Handlin's editing of the Catton manuscript. "The Civil War was a triumph," Handlin argued, "but one that was combined with a bloody disaster. All that happened to Grant was in a sense a model of what was happening to the nation." Others would likewise describe Catton's tone as "too triumphal."

15. Catton, *Mr. Lincoln's Army*, 14. On the automobile and Civil War tourism, see Jim Weeks, *Gettysburg: Memory, Market, and an American Shrine* (Princeton: Princeton University Press, 2003); and the anonymous article "Great Revival: In Song and in Story, the U.S. Lives Its Civil War Again," *Life*, September 12, 1955, 161–167.

16. Catton, *Glory Road*, 336–337.

17. Catton, *Stillness*, 1–10.

18. Ibid., 253.

19. Harry Elkins to Catton, March 31, 1952; Lawrence Stallings to Catton, June 10, 1960; Carl Hillyer Bissell to Catton, November 12, 1956; Homer T. Bone to Catton, April 20, 1954; all in Catton Papers, Citadel, box 28, folders 3 and 5, and box 29, folder 3. Rosser Reeves to Catton, January 18, 1955, Catton Papers, Wyoming, box 2, folder 2.

20. Bruce Catton, *Terrible Swift Sword* (New York: Doubleday, 1963), 387; Jay Monaghan, unpublished review of *A Stillness at Appomattox*, Catton Papers, Citadel, box 28, folder 3.

21. Ken McCormick to Catton, December 5, 1960; Paul Bennyhoff to Cat-

ton, March 19, 1957; William A. Keim to Catton, January 13, 1954; Catton to Mary Griffith, editor for the *Bookman,* April 25, 1957; all in Catton Papers, Citadel, box 28, folders 3 and 5–6. Bruce Catton, *This Hallowed Ground: The Story of the Union Side in the Civil War* (Garden City, N.Y.: Doubleday, 1956). *Hallowed Ground* narrates the entire story of the war, from immediate pre-war political events to the aftermath; it brings the slavery question more into play than does any previous Catton volume.

22. Ellery Queen (Manfred B. Lee) to Catton, February 9, 1954, Catton Papers, Citadel, box 28, folder 5; Catton, speech at Kansas State University, Manhattan, Kansas, October 11, 1957, Catton Papers, Wyoming, box 1, speeches file.

23. Donald Y. Yonker to Catton, January 20, 1957, Catton Papers, Citadel, box 28, folder 6. On the growing success of *American Heritage* during the Centennial, see "History Takes on New Sparkle," *Christian Science Monitor,* May 6, 1962. See the series of letters from Nevins to Catton, June and July 1954, offering Catton the role of editor at *American Heritage;* also Nevins to Catton, August 2 and 22, September 2, 1954; Nevins to Catton, August 7, 1955; all in Catton Papers, Wyoming, box 2, folders 1–2. On Catton reading Nevins's manuscripts for *Ordeal,* see Catton to Nevins, May 4, 1960, Catton Papers, Wyoming, box 3, folder 7. The two historians gave each other detailed critiques, but Catton did admit that he was "left wondering just what room is left for my own Civil War history." Catton sold much more widely than Nevins.

24. Benjamin P. Thomas to Doubleday editors, November 28, 1953, Catton Papers, Citadel, box 29. T. Harry Williams to Catton, February 6, 1960; David Donald to Catton, June 19, July 3 and 11, 1958; Catton to Donald, July 7 and 14, 1958; Russell Nye to Catton, April 2, 1959; Carl Sandburg to Catton, March 5, 1955, December 14, 1956. All in Catton Papers, Wyoming, box 3, folders 5–6, box 9, folders for 1955, 1956, and 1960.

25. Catton, speech at the Illinois Historical Society, Galesburg, Illinois, October 4, 1958, copy in Catton Papers, Wyoming, box 1, speeches file; Catton, "A Newspaperman Is a Historian," *Christian Science Monitor,* February 4, 1954, 13.

26. Ralph Newman, "Everette Beach 'Pete' Long, 1919–1981," a eulogy, *Chicago Civil War Roundtable Bulletin,* n.d., E. B. Long Papers, American Heritage Center, University of Wyoming, biographical file. At first, Doubleday may have paid Long in $1,500-per-month installments directly

to Catton's personal account. Beginning in October 1955 and ending in February 1960, Long was paid full-time, at what appears to have been a salary of $18,000 per year. In 1961 his pay and work were reduced to half-time, although Doubleday put him back on full-time for three months in 1964 to "work on Mr. Catton's manuscripts, proofs, maps, footnotes, bibliography and processing of the Doubleday set of the notes." Walter I. Bradbury to Catton, August 3, 1956; Sam Vaughn to E. B. Long, February 2, 1960; "Annual Report on Research for Centennial History, January 1, 1964, through December 31, 1964," Catton Papers, Wyoming, box 9, folders for 1956 and 1960, box 6, reports folder.

27. The Catton Papers both at the Citadel and at the University of Wyoming contain almost countless examples of Long's "Reports." For one of the travel itineraries, see "Itinerary of Gulf Coast Trip," 1958, Catton Papers, Wyoming, box 9. For many of the best examples of the research reports, see Catton Papers, Wyoming, boxes 6, 9, and 19; and Catton Papers, Citadel, box 24, files 1–3. For examples of the way Catton continued to do research himself and of the way he and Long worked via correspondence and occasional meetings, see Catton to Long, January 22 and 29, 1959, Catton Papers, box 3, folder 6.

28. Long's note cards and Catton's index cards, Catton Papers, box 24, files 5–6.

29. Catton to Miss Susan Kohlus, May 4, 1960, Catton Papers, Wyoming, box 3, folder 7; Catton to Walter Bradbury, December 20, 1950; and Catton to Walter Bradbury, December 29, 1951. All in Catton Papers, Citadel, box 28, folder 3.

30. E. B. Long, "Research Report for Centennial History, September 1–October 31, 1964"; E. B. Long, "Report on Assets and Progress of Centennial History of the Civil War, To Be Written by Bruce Catton and Published by Doubleday and Company, as of December 31, 1959," Catton Papers, Wyoming, box 9, 1960 folder; E. B. Long, "The Centennial History of the Civil War and Table of Contents," March 1965, Catton Papers, Citadel, attached to Finding Aid. On Doubleday's marketing of the Centennial series, see James Parton to Catton et al., March 28, 1960 (Parton was publisher of *American Heritage*); Sam Vaughn to Catton, March 2, 1960, including ten-page marketing plan; Sam Vaughn to Catton, February 8, 1960 (a plan for selling paperback rights to Pocket Books); and Sam Vaughn to Catton and Long, internal memorandum on layout and

marketing, "The Master Historian Begins His Magnum Work," 1961, Catton Papers, Wyoming, boxes 9 and 19.

31. Avery Craven, "Lincoln and Davis as Carriers of National Tragedy," *Chicago Tribune*, June 23, 1963.

32. Paul Angle, review of *The Coming Fury*, in *Chicago Tribune*, October 29, 1961; Roy F. Nichols, review of *This Hallowed Ground*, in *American Historical Review* (October 1957), 143–144.

33. Charles Poore, review of Edmund Wilson's *Patriotic Gore*, in *New York Times*, April 26, 1962. On the way Americans over time come to "love" the Civil War, see Drew Gilpin Faust, "'We Should Grow Too Fond of It': Why We Love the Civil War," *Civil War History* 50 (2004), 368–383.

34. Orville Prescott, "Books of the Times," *New York Times*, October 20, 1961, and May 24, 1963; Charles Poore, "Books of the Times," *New York Times*, June 30, 1960, and November 30, 1965; Henry Patrick, "Reading for Pleasure," *Wall Street Journal*, October 31, 1961.

35. Bruce Catton, *America Goes to War* (New York: Hill and Wang, 1961; orig. pub. 1958), 11–12; Earl Schenk Miers, "A Bookshelf of Battles and Leaders," *New York Times*, December 3, 1961.

36. Untitled draft of paper or speech on Civil War "buffs," with penciled corrections, n.d.; speech to Chicago Civil War Roundtable, delivered in Fort Wayne, Indiana, April 12, 1957, Catton Papers, Wyoming, box 1, speeches file.

37. Speech at Union College, Schenectady, New York, December 4, 1956, untitled, Catton Papers, Wyoming, box 1, speeches file. In the Union College speech, Catton calls American history "literally unique"—about as explicit an endorsement of American exceptionalism as one can make.

38. Kay Dixon to Catton, January 17, 1957; Muriel Brown to Catton, June 8, 1954; Harold Duane Jacobs to Catton, December 8, 1953; Curtis Dawes to Catton, May 18, 1954; and Theodore Clapp to Catton, February 3, 1954. All in Catton Papers, Citadel, box 28, folders 5–6.

39. Homer T. Bone to Catton, April 20, 1954; Clarence D. Foster to Catton, July 21, 1954, Catton Papers, Citadel, box 28, folder 5.

40. Robert J. Cook, *Troubled Commemoration: The American Civil War Centennial, 1961–1965* (Baton Rouge: Louisiana State University Press, 2007), 19–21, 216–217, 252–258.

41. O. Preston Chaney to Catton, May 31, 1954; Clifford Dowdey to Catton, August 18, 1957, and Catton to Dowdey, August 20, 1957, Catton Papers,

Citadel, box 28, folder 3; William Phillip Simms to Catton, October 28, 1956; Clifford Dowdey to Catton, November 21, 1954. All in Catton Papers, Wyoming, Box 2, folders 1 and 3.

42. Catton to William Coughlin, March 31, 1961; Catton to Hugh A. McCloskey, October 4, 1955. Both in Catton Papers, Wyoming, box 2, folders 2 and 8.

43. Bruce Catton, *The Coming Fury* (Garden City, N.Y.: Doubleday, 1961), 68–69. Catton argued variations of the "needless war" thesis in many public forums. See Bruce Catton, "U.S. Civil War: Rigidity's Toll, the Needless War—Democracy Fails a Test," *Christian Science Monitor*, January 6, 1961, 11.

44. Catton, *Coming Fury*, 85, 78–79. For a typical letter responding to a reader about the war's causes, see Catton to Edgar F. Wright, April 1, 1957, Citadel, box 28, folder 6. He says "there are plenty of arguments on both sides," but it was the "slavery issue" that ultimately made the sectional conflict "irreconcilable" and war "the only way out."

45. Rembert W. Patrick, review of *The Coming Fury*, in *Pennsylvania Magazine of History and Biography*, July 1962, 366; Catton, *Coming Fury*, 80–81. On blacks as immigrants, see Peter Wood, *The Black Majority: Negroes in Colonial South Carolina from 1670 through the Stono Rebellion* (New York: Knopf, 1974); and Nathan I. Huggins, *Black Odyssey: The African American Ordeal in Slavery* (New York: Vintage, 1990).

46. Long to Catton, December 5, 1955; Catton to Long, December 8, 1955. Both in Catton Papers, Wyoming, box 9, 1955 folder.

47. Speech at Kansas State College, Manhattan, Kansas, October 11, 1957, Catton Papers, Wyoming, box 1.

48. Catton, *Coming Fury*, 81–82; speech at Oberlin College Alumni dinner, December 11, 1956, Catton Papers, Citadel, box 1, speeches file. *Narrative of the Life of Frederick Douglass, an American Slave, Written by Himself,* first came back into print in 1960, with a Harvard University Press edition prepared by Benjamin Quarles. Dudley T. Cornish, *The Sable Arm: Negro Troops in the Civil War, 1861–1865* (New York: Longman's, 1956). *American Heritage,* June 1956; Cornish to Catton, August 2, 1956; Catton to Cornish, August 7, 1956, Catton Papers, Wyoming, box 2, folder 3. Catton had written about black troops in the Union forces in 1864 to some degree, even quite movingly, in *Stillness*. See Catton, *Stillness*, 226–235, 249–253.

49. Dan Wakefield, "Civil War Centennial: Bull Run with Popcorn," *Nation*, January 30, 1960, 95–97; *Life*, January 11, 1960.

50. Anthony West, "The Hateful Legacy," *New Yorker*, January 12, 1957.

51. Editorial, "Misinformed Historian," *Baltimore Afro-American*, November 22, 1958; Sam Cornish, "Lingering in the Negro Museum," *Obsidian III: Literature in the African Diaspora* (Fall 1999–Winter 2000), 70.

52. Bruce Catton, "Names from the War," 1960, a commemorative copy, Catton Papers, Wyoming, box 3, miscellaneous folder.

53. Invitation to the White House from Mrs. Lady Bird Johnson for November 8, 1967; invitation to the White House from President and Mrs. Nixon for April 10, 1970; both in Catton Papers, Wyoming, box 6, miscellaneous folder. Catton's articles include "Focus on the Civil War," *Christian Science Monitor*, January 13, 1959; "Source of Strength," *Los Angeles Times*, January 20, 1958; "The Time Ethan Allen Got Mad," *Los Angeles Times*, May 4, 1958; "Full Speed Ahead!" *Los Angeles Times*, May 9, 1958; "Bravery Is Forever," *Los Angeles Times*, June 2, 1957; and "See America with Bruce Catton's Lifetime Travel Plan," *Los Angeles Times*, February 16, 1958. The above list is only a sample of the *Los Angeles Times* columns.

54. "Harvard Acclaims 14 with Honorary Degrees," *Christian Science Monitor*, June 13, 1957; "Fifty Artists Invited to Johnson Inauguration," *Christian Science Monitor*, January 15, 1965; "Vietnam: Johnson Wrestles," *Christian Science Monitor*, June 29, 1966; interview, *Bill Moyers Journal*, February 5, 1974.

55. On sales and royalties, see Sam Vaughn, Doubleday marketing plan, March 2, 1960; and Gerald Dickler, Catton's lawyer, to Catton, October 19, 1967; both in Catton Papers, Wyoming, box 12. The Dickler letter indicates that Sam Vaughn of Doubleday had estimated Catton's total accumulated royalties by 1967, not counting advances or paperback and book club deals, as "between $600,000 and $700,000." That figure is probably quite low.

56. Bruce Catton, "A Doom Was Taking Shape," *Life*, September 12, 1955, 168; interview transcript, *Bill Moyers Journal*, February 5, 1974. Some readers wrote to Catton about the wooden toy soldiers, showing their own interest in such collections. See Doris B. English to Catton, Sacramento, California, May 12, 1954, Catton Papers, Citadel, box 28, file 5. John Blum, interview with author, July 2010.

57. *Bill Moyers Journal,* February 5, 1974.

58. Catton to Kay Dixon, January 22, 1957; Catton to Beulah Dix Flebbe, April 16, 1957, Catton Papers, Citadel, box 28, file 6; "Asks First Class Citizenship for Negroes," *Chicago Defender,* May 29, 1961; speech at Berea, Kentucky, March 31, 1965, Catton Papers, Wyoming, box 6, speeches folder.

59. Bruce Catton, "The End of the Centennial," in *A Portion of That Field: The Centennial of the Burial of Lincoln* (Urbana: University of Illinois Press, 1967), 81–89.

60. On the Lost Cause as a racial ideology, see David W. Blight, *Race and Reunion: The Civil War in American Memory* (Cambridge, Mass.: Harvard University Press, 2001), ch. 7.

61. *Bill Moyers Journal,* February 5, 1974; Catton, "End of the Centennial," 90–91.

62. Excerpt of letter from Charles Morrow Wilson to Sam Vaughn, Doubleday, 1972, copy sent to Catton, Catton Papers, Wyoming, box 6, miscellaneous folder; Gertrude Wilson, "No Sacred Cows," *New York Amsterdam News,* January 23, 1962; *New Norfolk Journal and Guide,* February 11, 18, 25, 1961; Philip Toynbee, "A House Divided," *Observer* (London), March 13, 1966, 26.

63. "Address Delivered before the South Carolina Corps of Cadets, Faculty and Staff of the Citadel and Guests," Charleston, South Carolina, January 7, 1961, Catton Papers, Citadel, box 28, folder 4; "To the Sound of Trumpets," *Staley Journal,* April 1959, Decatur, Illinois, a dedication of a memorial room in honor of Benjamin Thomas, Catton Papers, Wyoming, box 6, miscellaneous file.

64. Catton, *Waiting for the Morning Train,* 199, 229.

65. *The American Heritage Picture History of the Civil War* (New York: Doubleday, 1960), 606; quote attributed to Alfred Knopf by John Blum, interview with author, July 2010.

3. "Lincoln and Lee and All That"

1. Lewis M. Dabney, *Edmund Wilson: A Life in Literature* (Baltimore: Johns Hopkins University Press, 2005), 11–26.

2. Dabney, *Edmund Wilson,* 20–21; Edmund Wilson, "The Author at Sixty,"

in Wilson, *A Piece of My Mind: Reflections at Sixty* (New York: Farrar, Straus and Cudahy, 1956), 214–217, 230–234.

3. Dabney, *Edmund Wilson*, 30–35. Wilson wrote in many places on and off about Hippolyte Taine, but see especially the chapter in Wilson, *To the Finland Station: A Study in the Writing and Acting of History* (New York: New York Review Books, 2003; orig. pub. 1940), 46–55.

4. Edmund Wilson, "Christian Gauss as a Teacher of Literature" (1952), in *The Edmund Wilson Reader*, rev. ed., ed. Lewis M. Dabney (New York: DaCapo, 1997), 51–53, 55.

5. Dabney, *Edmund Wilson*, 38–52. Gauss was of German ancestry and born in Michigan. In the 1950s he went to the American South and appears to have become involved as a civil rights activist.

6. Edmund Wilson, "War," in Wilson, *A Piece of My Mind*, 40, 49.

7. Wilson to F. Scott Fitzgerald, October 7, 1917, Grosse Point, Michigan; Wilson to Fitzgerald, December 3, 1917, France; Wilson to Stanley Dell, September 19, 1917, Grosse Point, Michigan. All in Edmund Wilson, *Letters on Literature and Politics*, ed. Elena Wilson (New York: Farrar, Straus and Giroux, 1977), 29–32, 34–35.

8. Wilson to Stanley Dell, December 29, 1917, May 19, 1918; and Wilson to Gilbert Troxell, September 18, 1918; both in Wilson, *Letters*, 35–37, 39–41. On Sassoon and Owen, see Paul Fussell, *The Great War and Modern Memory* (London: Oxford University Press, 1975), 90–105, 286–299; Pat Barker, *Regeneration* (London: Viking, 1991); Pat Barker, *Ghost Road* (London: Viking, 1995). For the poems, see Edmund Wilson, *Night Thoughts* (New York: Farrar, Straus and Cudahy, 1953), 4–7. Also see Dabney, *Edmund Wilson*, 53–68.

9. Wilson, *Night Thoughts*, 4–5.

10. Ibid., 4; Fussell, *Great War and Modern Memory*, 13, 17. Fussell takes the idea from a passage in Edmund Blunden, *The Mind's Eye* (1934), written eighteen years after the battle of the Somme, as Blunden remembers how all involved in the slaughter saw an end to illusion of meaning and purpose: "By the end of the day both sides had seen, in a sad scrawl of broken earth and murdered men, the answer to the question. No road. No thoroughfare. Neither race had won, nor could win, the War. The War had won, and would go on winning" (13).

11. The descriptions and memories of Wilson's return to New York were

first recorded in his *Journals*, vol. 3, quoted in Dabney, *Edmund Wilson*, 64. Wilson later more fully developed the same memories of return in his novel. See Edmund Wilson, *I Thought of Daisy* (Iowa City: University of Iowa Press, 1995; orig. pub. 1929), 225–227. Wilson, "The Author at Sixty," 221–225.

12. Wilson, "The Author at Sixty," 226–227. In the huge array of reviews and essays about *Patriotic Gore* that appeared in 1962, some delved at length into Wilson's affinity for Lincoln through his father's interests. See especially Kenneth S. Lynn, "The Right to Secede from History," *New Republic,* June 22, 1962, copy in Edmund Wilson Papers, Beinecke Library, Yale University, box 122.

13. Wilson, "The Author at Sixty," 227. William Herndon, *Herndon's Lincoln: The True Story of a Great Life,* 3 vols. (Springfield, Ill.: Herndon's Lincoln Publishing Company, 1888); Nathaniel W. Stephenson, *Abraham Lincoln and the Union: A Chronicle of the Embattled North* (New Haven: Yale University Press, 1918), series entitled Chronicles of America, vol. 29; and Stephenson, *Lincoln: An Account of His Personal Life, Especially of Its Springs of Action as Revealed and Deepened by the Ordeal of War* (Indianapolis: Bobbs-Merrill, 1922). In *Herndon's Lincoln,* a great deal of attention is paid to Lincoln's law practice, and Herndon famously collected voluminous oral-history testimony about Lincoln, not all of it flattering. Stephenson's books are relatively straightforward public-political histories of Lincoln's presidential years. Hence, Wilson's characterization of Stephenson's works as the "least sentimental" of writings about Lincoln is apt.

14. Lewis M. Dabney, "The Perspective of Biography: 1929, a Turning Point," in Dabney, ed., *Edmund Wilson: Centennial Reflections* (Princeton: Princeton University Press, 1997), 109–134; Wilson, *Axel's Castle: A Study of the Imaginative Literature of 1870–1930* (New York: Farrar, Straus and Giroux, 2004; orig. pub. 1931).

15. Wilson, "An Appeal to Progressives," in Wilson, *The Shores of Light: A Literary Chronicle of the Twenties and Thirties* (New York: Farrar, Straus, Giroux, 1952), 532.

16. Wilson, "Frank Keeney's Coal Diggers," "Detroit Motors," and "The Jumping-Off Place," in Dabney, ed., *The Edmund Wilson Reader,* 195–202, 203–219, 220–222, quotes on 219–220, 226–227.

17. Dabney, *Edmund Wilson*, 254–255. Louis Menand, in "Foreword," Wilson, *Finland Station*, ix–xii, considered it a singular example of "imaginative" history, and a "grand" if not a "great" book.

18. Wilson, *Finland Station*, "Introduction, 1971," xxi, and 115–116, 120–217. Also see Dabney, *Edmund Wilson*, 255–264.

19. Edmund Wilson, "Postscript of 1957," in Wilson, *The American Earthquake: A Documentary of the Twenties and Thirties* (Garden City, N.Y.: Doubleday, 1958), 570. See also Dabney, *Edmund Wilson*, 301–302.

20. Dabney, *Edmund Wilson*, 301–310, 334–337.

21. Wilson to Philip Vaudrin, April 21, 1947, and May 7, 1947, in Wilson, *Letters*, 608–609; Lee Grove to Wilson, October 9, 1958, and John R. B. Brett-Smith to Wilson, June 16, 1960, Edmund Wilson Papers, Beinecke Library, Yale University, box 53, folder 1433. In 1960, Wilson received an additional $1,000 advance on the Civil War literature book.

22. Wilson to John Dos Passos, September 8, 1952; Wilson to Mamaine Koestler, December 5, 1953; both in Wilson, *Letters*, 609–610.

23. Wilson to Felix Frankfurter, May 28, 1953, and December 14, 1957; Wilson to Arlin Turner, August 18, 1957, and August 31, 1957; Wilson to Chauncey Hackett, March 3, 1958; Wilson to John Dos Passos, April 30, 1953, *Letters*. All in Wilson, 610–614.

24. Dabney, *Edmund Wilson*, 363–364.

25. Daniel Aaron, *The Unwritten War: American Writers and the Civil War* (New York: Knopf, 1973), in series entitled The Impact of the Civil War, planned by Allan Nevins and edited by Harold M. Hyman. For another noted book that emerges as two books, the Introduction and the rest of the body of the work, see Perry Miller, *The New England Mind: The Seventeenth Century* (New York: Macmillan, 1939). The Introduction is "The Augustinian Strain of Piety," after which Miller proceeds to his real subject—the Puritans' theology, reason, and logic.

26. Wilson, "Postscript of 1957," 566–571.

27. Wilson to Alfred Kazin, July 8, 1961; Wilson to Daniel Aaron, October 11, 1961; Wilson to John Dos Passos, November 7, 1961. All in Wilson, *Letters*, 602, 605–607.

28. Jason Epstein, "Remembering Edmund Wilson," in Lewis M. Dabney, ed., *Edmund Wilson: Centennial Reflections* (Princeton: Princeton University Press, 1997), 137; Edmund Wilson, *Patriotic Gore: Studies in the*

Literature of the American Civil War (Boston: Northeastern University Press, 1984; orig. pub. 1962), xxxiii–xxxiv. On his own use of the term "anti-war morality," see Wilson to Robert Penn Warren, August 12, 1962, in Wilson, *Letters*, 620.

29. Wilson, *Patriotic Gore*, xiii–xvi.

30. Ibid., xvi–xvii; Wilson to Barbara Deming, April 11, 1962, in Wilson, *Letters*, 618.

31. Wilson, *Patriotic Gore*, xvii–xx.

32. Ibid., xxv–xxvi; W. E. B. Du Bois, *Black Reconstruction: In America, 1860–1880* (New York: Atheneum, 1962; orig. pub. 1935); John Hope Franklin, *From Slavery to Freedom: A History of American Negroes* (New York: Knopf, 1947); and Kenneth M. Stampp, *The Peculiar Institution: Slavery in the Antebellum South* (New York: Knopf, 1956).

33. Wilson, *Patriotic Gore*, xx, xxiii, xxxv.

34. Ibid., xx–xxii, xxxiv.

35. Ibid., xxxv–xxxvi.

36. The typical review of *Patriotic Gore* begins with a reference—often sighing or negative—to the Centennial's superficiality. Henry Williams, "Wilson Pierces Flapdoodle to View Civil War," *Peoria Journal*, April 28, 1962; "VHP," review in *Omaha World Herald*, April 29, 1962; review, *Economist*, August 18, 1962; Michele Murray, review, *Catholic Reporter*, October 19, 1962; Garry Wills, "The Lincoln Mythology," *National Review*, December 18, 1962; J. E. Morpurgo, "Patriots North and South," *London Daily Telegram*, June 29, 1962. All in Wilson Papers, Yale University, box 122, folders 2818, 2821, 2822.

37. Elizabeth Hardwick, "An American Royal Personage," *Harpers*, July 1962, Wilson Papers, box 122, folder 2823.

38. Richard Current, "Civil War Gore," *Progressive*, October 1962; Lewis M. Dabney, *Columbia University Forum*, Fall 1962, Wilson Papers, box 122, folders 2821, 2822.

39. Alfred Kazin, "Our American Plutarch," *Reporter*, May 24, 1962; Irving Howe, "Edmund Wilson and the Sea Slugs," *Notebook*, n.d. Both in Wilson Papers, box 122, folders 2818, 2822.

40. Wilson, *Patriotic Gore*, 108.

41. Ibid., 101–106, 115–117, 120, 122–123, 126, 130. For two recent examples of the resurgence of books on Lincoln as a writer, see Fred Kaplan, *Lincoln:*

Biography of a Writer (New York: Harper Collins, 2008); and Douglas L. Wilson, *Lincoln's Sword: The Presidency and the Power of Words* (New York: Knopf, 2006).

42. Conor Cruise O'Brien, "Sea Slugs and Slavery," *New Statesman,* June 22, 1962, in Wilson Papers, box 122, folder 2822; Wilson, *Patriotic Gore,* 329–334.

43. Malcolm Bauer, "Literary Critic Turns War Myth Breaker," *Oregonian,* April 29, 1962; John Alexander, "Civil War Debunker Sees Conflict as Part of a Process of Aggression," *Sunday Herald-Leader* (Lexington, Kentucky), April 29, 1962; Robert Penn Warren, "Edmund Wilson's Civil War," *Commentary,* n.d., in Wilson Papers, box 122, folder 2819, 2822. For a particularly astute appreciation of Wilson's understanding of myth, see David Donald, "Civil War Centennial's Most Absorbing, Important Book," *New York Herald Tribune,* May 6, 1962, in Wilson Papers, box 122, folder 2819. Donald was so fond of the book that he sent a manuscript copy of his review to Wilson. Daniel Aaron in 1973 opened his book *The Unwritten War* with his own brand of a Wilsonesque discussion of the competing "Federal" and "Secessionist" epics that fueled American writing about the war. See Aaron, *Unwritten War,* xiii–xix.

44. Dabney, *Edmund Wilson,* 437; Wilson, *Patriotic Gore,* title page, 397, 400–401; Sheldon Meyer to Wilson, November 23, 1960, in Wilson Papers, Yale University, box 53, folder 1432.

45. Wilson, *Patriotic Gore,* 397–400, 415; Warren, "Edmund Wilson's Civil War," in Warren Papers, Yale University, box 122, folder 2822. Wilson read two works by Stephens: *The Recollections of Alexander H. Stephens* (1910), and, under its complete title, the apologia *A Constitutional View of the Late War between the States: Its Causes, Character, Conduct, and Results Presented in a Series of Colloquies at Liberty Hall,* 2 vols. (1867 and 1870).

46. Wilson, *Patriotic Gore,* 415–425.

47. Ibid., 406–411.

48. Ibid., 434, 437.

49. Ibid., 435.

50. Alfred Kazin, "Remembering Edmund Wilson," in Dabney, ed., *Centennial Reflections,* 152.

51. Marcus Cunliffe, "The Despot's Heel," *Spectator,* June 22, 1962; Howe, "Edmund Wilson and the Sea Slugs," *Notebook;* Louis D. Rubin, Jr.,

"Edmund Wilson and the Despot's Heel," *Arts and Letters*, n.d.; Warren, "Edmund Wilson's Civil War," *Commentary;* and Marius Bewley, "Northern Saints and Southern Knights," *Hudson Review*, n.d. All in Wilson Papers, box 122, folders 2819, 2822.

52. Frederick Douglass, *Narrative of the Life of Frederick Douglass, an American Slave, Written by Himself* (Boston: Bedford Books, 2003; orig. pub. 1845); Harriet Jacobs, *Incidents in the Life of a Slave Girl, Written by Herself* (Cambridge, Mass.: Harvard University Press, 1987; orig. pub. 1861); Wilson, *Patriotic Gore*, xiii. It is useful to note Quarles's description of Douglass's varied writings, so similar to Wilson's of Civil War literature: "speeches, personal letters, formal lectures, editorials, and magazine articles." See Quarles's introduction in Douglass, *Narrative of the Life of Frederick Douglass, an American Slave* (Cambridge, Mass.: Harvard University Press, 1960; orig. pub. 1845), xiii.

53. Wilson, *Patriotic Gore*, 92–96; Douglass, "The Mission of the War," a speech first delivered in late 1863 and then many times in 1864, in Philip S. Foner, ed., *Life and Writings of Frederick Douglass*, 5 vols. (New York: International Publishers, 1950), 3:399–401; Douglass, *Narrative*, 89. For the name and location of the Washington, D.C., train station, see John Stauffer, *Giants: The Parallel Lives of Frederick Douglass and Abraham Lincoln* (New York: Twelve, 2008), 5–6. Wilson earlier explored the question of religious mysticism in Edmund Wilson, "The Union as Religious Mysticism," *New Yorker* 29 (March 14, 1953).

54. Randall Kennedy, "Omissions in Patriotic Gore," in Dabney, ed., *Centennial Reflections*, 221–223; "An Interview with Edmund Wilson," in Wilson, *The Bit between My Teeth: A Literary Chronicle of 1950–1965* (New York: Farrar, Straus and Giroux, 1966), 546–547.

55. Randall Kennedy, David Bromwich, Jed Pearl, and Daniel Aaron in Dabney, ed., *Centennial Reflections*, 224–230. Harvard's more composed Daniel Aaron somewhat lamely defended Wilson's sidestepping of Douglass, saying—inaccurately—that "no book" on the abolitionist "came out during the 50s, which says something about the limited racial awareness of the whole culture" (ibid.).

56. Toni Morrison, ibid., 230–231.

57. David Bradley, "A Great Man's Limitations," ibid., 233–235.

58. Ibid., 236–239.

59. Wilson to Robert Penn Warren, August 12, 1962; Wilson to Max East-

man, n.d., 1962, both in Wilson, *Letters,* 620–621; Wilson, *The Cold War and the Income Tax: A Protest* (New York: Farrar, Straus, 1963).

60. Wilson to Alfred Kazin, May 20, May 30, and June 2, 1962, all in Wilson, *Letters,* 619–620.

61. Edmund Wilson, *The Sixties: The Last Journal, 1960–1972* (New York: Farrar, Straus, 1993), 74–80.

62. Edmund Wilson, "An Interview with Edmund Wilson," *New Yorker,* June 2, 1962, 118–128. Also see Dabney, *Edmund Wilson,* 487–488.

63. Daniel Aaron, "Edmund Wilson's War," *Massachusetts Review* (Spring 1962), 570, in Wilson Papers, box 122, folder 5821; Donald, "Civil War Centennial's Most Important, Absorbing Book"; Warren, "Edmund Wilson's Civil War." On Wilson's enduring fascination with noncanonical literature, see Louis Menand, "Edmund Wilson in His Times," in Dabney, ed., *Centennial Reflections,* 261–263.

64. Wilson, *Patriotic Gore,* 139, 144; Bruce Catton, *U.S. Grant and the American Military Tradition* (Boston: Little, Brown, 1954), 187–189. Many reviewers and students of Wilson's *Patriotic Gore* saw the Grant chapter as its "center." See Morris Dickstein, "Edmund Wilson: Three Phases," in Dabney, ed., *Centennial Reflections,* 23–25.

65. Wilson, *Patriotic Gore,* 142–144, 148–149.

66. Ibid., 150–157.

67. Ibid., 152, 159.

68. Ibid., 790; Oliver Wendell Holmes, Jr., "The Soldier's Faith," address delivered on Memorial Day, May 30, 1895, at a meeting called by the graduating class of Harvard University, in *Speeches by Oliver Wendell Holmes* (Boston: Little, Brown, 1934), 56–64.

69. Quoted in Wilson, *Patriotic Gore,* 745–752.

70. Ibid., 788, 794; Mark Krupnick, "Edmund Wilson and Gentile Philo-Semitism," in Dabney, ed., *Centennial Reflections,* 73–74.

71. Wilson, *Patriotic Gore,* 755, 763.

72. Ibid., 795; Norman Podhoretz, "Edmund Wilson and the Kingdom of Heaven," *Show,* June 1962.

73. Warren, "Edmund Wilson's Civil War"; Wilson, *Patriotic Gore,* 669.

4. "This Country Is My Subject"

1. Baldwin to Mary Painter, September 24, 1964, Walter O. Evans Collection (private), Savannah, Georgia.

2. James Campbell, *Talking at the Gates: A Life of James Baldwin* (New York: Penguin, 1991), 93.

3. James Baldwin, "Why I Stopped Hating Shakespeare," *Guardian* (London), April 19, 1964, 21; James Baldwin, "Struggles Make Black Writer Say 'Amen!'" *Los Angeles Times*, November 8, 1964, T1.

4. Robert Penn Warren, *Who Speaks for the Negro?* (New York: Random House, 1965), 290–291; *Time*, May 17, 1963, cover and 23–27; Marvin Elkoff, "Everybody Knows His Name," *Esquire*, August 1964, 59–64.

5. Baldwin's yearning for love is a primary theme in most biographies of the writer. See especially Campbell, *Talking at the Gates*, 95, 110, 201–202. Also, in conversations and email correspondence, Caryl Phillips, who knew Baldwin well, said: "Probably more so than any writer I've ever met, he [Baldwin] craved affection." Email from Phillips to author, September 10, 2010. Campbell writes: "Baldwin was great at talking about love—he was capable of talking for hours about nothing else—but he was not always good at keeping it when it came to him" (95). On the theme of love in life and writing, also see James Baldwin, "The New Lost Generation," *Esquire*, July 1961, in James Baldwin, *Collected Essays* (New York: Library of America, 1998), 659–668.

6. The original title of Baldwin's most famous work, *The Fire Next Time*, was that of an essay, "Letter from a Region of My Mind," published in the *New Yorker*, November 17, 1962, 59–144.

7. James Baldwin, interview by Kenneth Clark, May 24, 1963, in *The Negro Protest: James Baldwin, Malcolm X, and Martin Luther King Talk with Kenneth B. Clark* (Boston: Beacon Press, 1963), 4–5; W. J. Weatherby, *James Baldwin: Artist on Fire* (New York: Donald I. Fine, 1989), 6–13.

8. James Baldwin, "Autobiographical Notes," 1955, in Baldwin, *Collected Essays*, 5–6; "Imagination," in Baldwin, *Jimmy's Blues: Selected Poems by James Baldwin* (London: Michael Joseph, 1983), 36. For Baldwin's famous critique of *Uncle Tom's Cabin*, see "Everybody's Protest Novel," in Baldwin, *Notes of a Native Son* (Boston: Beacon, 1955), 13–23. The admiration he had felt for *Uncle Tom's Cabin* in his youth was now long gone;

Baldwin called the book "a very bad novel" and full of "self-righteous, virtuous sentimentality." Baldwin's essay on Harriet Beecher Stowe probably had much to do with decline in interest in the book during the Civil Rights era, although Edmund Wilson may have revived it a decade later.

9. Baldwin, "Autobiographical Notes," 7–8; and Campbell, *Talking at the Gates*, 12–28.

10. Baldwin, "Autobiographical Notes," 8–9.

11. Countee Cullen quoted in Weatherby, *James Baldwin*, 24. On Delany, see Campbell, *Talking at the Gates*, 20–22; and David Leeming, *James Baldwin: A Biography* (New York: Knopf, 1994), 32–36.

12. James Baldwin, *Go Tell It on the Mountain* (New York: Signet, 1963; orig. pub. 1952), 19.

13. Leeming, *James Baldwin*, 24–25; Baldwin, *Fire Next Time*, 28–33.

14. Baldwin, *Go Tell It on the Mountain*, 167–191.

15. Baldwin, *Fire Next Time*, 38–51, 59–60; and see also Leeming, *James Baldwin*, 25–31.

16. James Baldwin, "Notes of a Native Son," in *Notes of a Native Son*, 92–98. On the New Jersey story, also see Randall Kenan, *James Baldwin* (New York: Chelsea House, 1994), 43–47.

17. Baldwin, "Notes of a Native Son," 94.

18. Ibid., 87–88; August Wilson, *Joe Turner's Come and Gone: A Play in Two Acts* (New York: New American Library, 1988). Harold Loomis is the central character of this drama. Born in the immediate post–Civil War South, he is ravaged by the Southern criminal justice system, chain gangs, and Jim Crow, and flees north to Pittsburgh with his daughter in search of his estranged wife. Loomis is nearly crazy with rage and fear, and all but unmanned by his experience. In Act 2 he achieves redemption of a kind.

19. Baldwin, "Notes of a Native Son," 106, 113.

20. Ibid., 108; Campbell, *Talking at the Gates*, 32–34, 40–42; Leeming, *Baldwin*, 53–55; Baldwin, "The New Lost Generation," *Esquire*, July 1961, in Baldwin, *Collected Essays*, 659–661.

21. Baldwin's essays on Wright are "Many Thousands Gone" (1951), in *Notes of a Native Son*, 24–45; and "Alas, Poor Richard" (1961), in James Baldwin, *Nobody Knows My Name: More Notes of a Native Son* (New York: Dial Press, 1961), 181–215.

22. James Baldwin, "The Discovery of What It Means to Be an American,"

New York Times Book Review, January 25, 1959, in Baldwin, *Nobody Knows My Name,* 3; Baldwin, "The New Lost Generation," 667; James Baldwin, "The Creative Process" (1962), in Baldwin, *Collected Essays,* 669–672.

23. Baldwin, "The Discovery of What It Means To Be an American," 3–4; Weatherby, *James Baldwin,* 62; Kenan, *James Baldwin,* 56–57; Baldwin, "Struggles Make Black Writer Say 'Amen!'"

24. James Baldwin, *Giovanni's Room* (New York: New American Library, 1959; orig. pub. 1956). Also see Campbell, *Talking at the Gates,* 101–104; Kenan, *James Baldwin,* 54–57, 80–81. *Giovanni's Room* was respectfully if awkwardly reviewed. The *New Yorker* said the topic of the homosexual "conflict" between "instinctual desires" and the "moral sense" was a "legitimate subject," but hoped that Baldwin would soon return to his "American subjects." See *New Yorker,* November 10, 1956, 220–221.

25. James Baldwin, *Another Country* (New York: Vintage, 1993; orig. pub. 1962), 36. *Another Country* was widely reviewed, but took some hard knocks. Naomi Bliven found it burdened with "novelistic fatigue"—too many scenes of characters "with the endless cigarettes that are lit and stubbed" (*New Yorker,* August 4, 1962, 69–70). For at attempt to ban *Another Country,* see "Chicago City Council Unit Votes No on Baldwin Book," *Baltimore Afro-American,* January 23, 1965, 17. Also see Campbell, *Talking at the Gates,* 154–158; and Robert Tomlinson, "'Payin' One's Dues': Expatriation as Personal Experience and Paradigm in the Works of James Baldwin," *African American Review* 33, no. 1 (Spring 1999), 135–148.

26. Baldwin to David Leeming, August 1965, July 1965, December 1966, Evans Collection, Savannah, Georgia; Baldwin to "Dear Mama," Corsica, 1956, letter provided by Caryl Phillips. In the letter to his mother, Baldwin addresses her as "baby" and "friend." The letter is worth quoting at even greater length. "At twenty . . . ," he says, "the undiscovered world lies before you. You are sure that you will conquer it. Ten years later, assuming you've survived—as many of my friends have not—you begin to be aware that it is your undiscovered self which is the challenge and that it is infinitely easier to conquer the world than it is to find out who you are. At twenty you imagine that you can make yourself; around thirty you see that you have already been made—for better or for worse; there are many things you can't do and some things you can do, some things which are

yours and many things which will never be yours. And the great, great effort is to swallow the cup and to swallow it, my friend, with joy."

27. Baldwin to Mary Painter, n.d. (likely 1958 or 1959); Baldwin to Painter, Peterboro, New Hampshire, the McDowell Colony, n.d. (but likely 1954); and Baldwin to Painter, Yad Mordecai, Istanbul, n.d. (1961?), Evans Collection, Savannah, Georgia.

28. Baldwin to Mary Painter, n.d. (likely summer 1957), Evans Collection, Savannah, Georgia.

29. James Baldwin, "Unnameable Objects, Unspeakable Crimes," *Ebony*, August 1965, online at www.BlackState.com. In its original version, this piece was called "The White Man's Guilt." See Baldwin, *Collected Essays*, 722–727.

30. From James Baldwin's novel *Just above My Head* (1979), quoted in Whitney Balliett, "Father and Son," *New Yorker*, November 26, 1979, 81–82; James Baldwin, "As Much Truth as One Can Bear," *New York Times*, January 14, 1962.

31. James Baldwin, "Lockridge: 'The American Myth,'" *New Leader*, April 10, 1948; and Baldwin, "The Negro at Home and Abroad," *Reporter*, November 27, 1951, in Baldwin, *Collected Essays*, 588–591, 604–605; Baldwin, "Many Thousands Gone," 31.

32. James Baldwin, "Faulkner and Desegregation," *Partisan Review* (Winter 1956), in Baldwin, *Nobody Knows My Name*, 117–123. And see Campbell, *Talking at the Gates*, 98–100.

33. Baldwin, "Faulkner and Desegregation," 124–126.

34. James Baldwin, "The Crusade of Indignation," *Nation*, July 7, 1956, in Baldwin, *Collected Essays*, 609–613.

35. Caryl Phillips, "The Price of the Ticket," *Guardian* (London), July 14, 2007; James Baldwin, Introduction, *Nobody Knows My Name*, xi–xiii.

36. James Baldwin, "Fly in the Buttermilk," *Harper's*, October 1958, in Baldwin, *Nobody Knows My Name*, 83–84. In this essay, Baldwin's analysis of the nature and purpose of segregation is quite similar to that of Robert Penn Warren in *Segregation: The Inner Conflict in the South* (New York: Random House, 1956).

37. Baldwin, "Fly in the Buttermilk," 85–97. On the Charlotte interviews, see Campbell, *Talking at the Gates*, 12–13; and Leeming, *James Baldwin*, 139–141.

38. Baldwin, "Nobody Knows My Name," 98–100. On the literary impact

and use of lynching in African American literature, see Trudier Harris, *Exorcising Blackness: Historical and Literary Lynching and Burning Rituals* (Bloomington: Indiana University Press, 1984), 69–84; Gladys Marie Fry, *Night Riders in Black Folk Memory* (Athens: University of Georgia Press, 1991), 110–169; and David W. Blight, *Race and Reunion: The Civil War in American Memory* (Cambridge, Mass.: Harvard University Press, 2001), 108–122.

39. James Baldwin, "The Dangerous Road before Martin Luther King," *Harper's*, February 1961, in Baldwin, *Collected Essays*, 638–645.

40. Ibid., 642; Baldwin to Mary Painter, n.d. (September 1957), Evans Collection, Savannah, Georgia.

41. James Baldwin, *No Name in the Street* (New York: Vintage, 2000; orig. pub. 1972), 69–74.

42. Ibid., 68–69, 79; Baldwin, "Dangerous Road before Martin Luther King," 641.

43. Baldwin, "Nobody Knows My Name," 104–109.

44. Ibid., 114–115; Irving Howe, "A Protest of His Own," *New York Times*, July 2, 1961, BR4; Charles Poole, "Books of the Times," *New York Times*, July 15, 1961, 17.

45. Baldwin, "Nobody Knows My Name," 109–110, 114; Russell Baker, *New York Observer*, November 21, 1963, 38.

46. Campbell, *Talking at the Gates*, 178–190; Kenan, *James Baldwin*, 87–103; Leeming, *James Baldwin*, 183–199.

47. James Baldwin, "They Can't Turn Back," *Mademoiselle*, August 1960, in Baldwin, *Collected Essays*, 636–637.

48. Studs Terkel, "An Interview with James Baldwin," July 15, 1961, in Fred L. Standley and Louis H. Pratt, eds., *Conversations with James Baldwin* (Jackson: University Press of Mississippi, 1989), 3–23.

49. Weatherby, *James Baldwin*, 180–196. On Baldwin at the legendary White House dinner, see Diana Trilling, "A Visit to Camelot," *New Yorker*, June 2, 1997, 55–60.

50. Claudia Roth Pierpont, "Another Country," *New Yorker*, February 9, 2009; Baldwin, "My Dungeon Shook: Letter to My Nephew on the One Hundredth Anniversary of the Emancipation," in *Fire Next Time*, 11–21; Robert Penn Warren, *Who Speaks for the Negro?* (New York: Random House, 1965), 290; Leeming, *James Baldwin*, 212.

51. Baldwin, "Dungeon Shook," 15–17.

52. Ibid., 18–21. The passage is from a Negro spiritual, "My Dungeon Shook."

53. Baldwin, *Fire Next Time*, 68–84.

54. Ibid., 76–79; Baldwin, "Notes of a Native Son," 100–101.

55. Baldwin, *Fire Next Time*, 90–97, 106–110.

56. Ibid., 88–89, 79–80, 113.

57. Ibid., 114–115, 132, 136.

58. Henrietta Buckmaster, "A Hard Look at Two Worlds That Cannot Live Apart," *Chicago Daily Tribune*, February 10, 1963, D2; Albert Murray, *The Omni-Americans: Black Experience and American Culture* (New York: Vintage, 1983; orig. pub. 1970), 158. For examples of Baldwin exploding at white liberals, see Weatherby, *James Baldwin*, 204–207, 215–216.

59. F. W. Dupee, "James Baldwin and the 'Man,'" *New York Review of Books*, February 1, 1963.

60. Baldwin, *Fire Next Time*, 132–133, 137, 141. On the impact and influence of *The Fire Next Time*, see Campbell, *Talking at the Gates*, 160–162, 168, 262–263.

61. Weatherby, *James Baldwin*, 203–204, 210–213; James Baldwin, "A Talk to Teachers," *Saturday Review*, December 1963, in Baldwin, *Collected Essays*, 681–683.

62. *Time*, May 17, 1963, 26; Howe, "A Protest of His Own."

63. Martin Luther King, Jr., "I Have a Dream," speech delivered in Washington, D.C., August 28, 1963; Baldwin, *No Name in the Street*, 140; Phillips, email to author, September 8, 2010.

64. "James Baldwin at Civil Rights Roundtable," video, August 28, 1963, www.YouTube.com.

65. This discussion of *Blues for Mr. Charlie* relies on Weatherby, *James Baldwin*, 247–255. Weatherby knew Baldwin at the time, in 1964, and uses many recollections of those months of the author's agony over the play.

66. Weatherby, *James Baldwin*, 273; George Shadroui, "Crossing Swords: James Baldwin and the Civil Rights Movement," www.intellectualconservative.com, March 7, 2008, 1–8; "James Baldwin, Debate at the Cambridge Union," video, February 18, 1965, www.YouTube.com.

67. "James Baldwin, Debate at the Cambridge Union"; Shadroui, "Crossing Swords," 3–4.

68. "James Baldwin, Debate at the Cambridge Union"; Weatherby, *James Baldwin*, 274–275.

69. Warren, *Who Speaks for the Negro?* Foreword.

70. Ibid., 30, 292.

71. Ibid., 277–280.

72. Ibid., 280–281.

73. Ibid., 291–292, 296.

74. Ibid., 290, 295.

75. Ibid., 298; Campbell, *Talking at the Gates*, 184, 157–158, 167–173; Phillips, "Price of the Ticket," 3; "Race, Hate, Sex, and Colour: A Conversation with James Baldwin and Colin MacInnes," July 1965, in Standley and Pratt, eds., *Conversations with James Baldwin*, 54. Campbell has, more than anyone else, researched the FBI's pursuit of Baldwin. The FBI opened its file on Baldwin in 1960 and did not close it until 1973. Director J. Edgar Hoover, ironically, took a personal interest in the agency's efforts to document Baldwin's homosexuality; the FBI's records repeatedly refer to their subject as a "pervert." See also James Campbell, "James Baldwin and the FBI," *Threepenny Review* (Spring 1999), 11. Baldwin's behavior could be quite volatile. One afternoon in Istanbul in 1966, he spoke with a young Turkish journalist, Zeynep Oral, in an interview that was full of wit, charm, and intelligence; yet that night at a restaurant, the drunken Baldwin shouted profanities at the same woman reporter, claiming that the singer in the establishment had "stolen" and "raped" *his* music by using African American melodies or lyrics. Oral left the restaurant in shock; the next morning a bouquet of roses was delivered to her home with Baldwin's apologies. Increasingly, the writer needed an ever-larger entourage to control his behavior, as well as his affairs. See Campbell, *Talking at the Gates*, 211–212.

76. Phillips, "Price of the Ticket," 1–4.

77. On the "slave novel" and the Ford grant application, see Campbell, *Talking at the Gates*, 134–136, 173–174. By the mid-Sixties, Baldwin was referring to the slave-novel project by a new title, "Tomorrow Brought Us Rain."

78. James Baldwin, "Inventory / On Being 52," copy provided to author by Caryl Phillips.

79. Phillips, "Price of the Ticket," 4.

80. For an initial effort to trace the extraordinary changes in scholarship about the black experience during the Centennial era and beyond, see August Meier and Elliot Rudwick, *Black History and the Historical Profession, 1915–1980* (Urbana: University of Illinois Press, 1986), 137–276;

Robert J. Cook, *Troubled Crusade: The American Civil War Centennial, 1961–1965* (Baton Rouge: Louisiana State University Press, 2007), 155–192.

81. Baldwin, "Unnameable Objects, Unspeakable Crimes," 2–3.

82. Ibid., 3–4.

Epilogue

1. Arnold Rampersad, *Ralph Ellison: A Biography* (New York: Knopf, 2007), 286–287, 496–497.

2. Ralph Ellison, "Tell It Like It Is, Baby," *Nation,* June 1965, 129. The book on tragedy Ellison was reading was Gilbert Murray, *The Classical Tradition in Poetry* (Cambridge, Mass.: Harvard University Press, 1927). Ellison said he was reading the final chapter, "Hamlet and Orestes," as he fell asleep the night of his dream.

3. Ellison, "Tell It Like It Is, Baby," 130.

4. Ibid., 130–131.

5. Ibid., 132–133.

6. Ibid., 133–134.

7. Ibid., 134.

8. Ibid., 135.

9. Ibid., 136.

10. Ibid.

Acknowledgments

While writing this book, I have amassed many debts that I now gratefully acknowledge. All four of the writers I examine here have long captivated my interest and imagination. I confess that as a teenager I began reading Bruce Catton with a zeal that never really ended, though it had many a hiatus. I used to pray for rain on my summer jobs so that I could get time off to read *Stillness, Hallowed Ground,* or *Terrible Swift Sword;* Catton's unsurpassed storytelling about the Civil War had much to do with my choice to become a historian. I quoted and used insights from Robert Penn Warren, Edmund Wilson, and James Baldwin in more than one of my previous works, but especially in *Race and Reunion: The Civil War in American Memory* (2001). In a sense, I might never have written that book without the model and stimulus of Warren's *Legacy of the Civil War.*

Wilson's *Patriotic Gore* is one of the great, confounding classics of American literature; I must have first read it in parts thirty years ago, and only now have digested every phrase of its overwrought brilliance. And James Baldwin's essays are, or ought to be, at the center of anyone's consideration of the legacies of slavery and the problem of race in modern America. I am grateful to those friends and acquaintances who shared their memories of where and when they first read *The Fire Next Time.* My first debt, therefore, is simply to the ideas and craftsmanship of these four magnificent writers. I hold each in awe, as I have striven to be their interpreter and critic.

Katherine Mooney gently prodded me to get serious about writing on Warren, and shared her own deeply hewn understanding of his complex genius. Conversations with Katherine's parents, Rex and Barbara Mooney, were also valuable for providing insights on Warren, as well as for sustaining my own sense of humor. I thank Blake Gilpin for reading my Warren chapter with insights from his own work, Peter Almond for his readings and our many collaborations, Tom Grace for inspiration and a good reading of my Catton, and Shawn Alexander for keeping me clear on Baldwin and providing many other sources of help. Richard Rabinowitz gave me a brilliant, critical reading of the Baldwin and Wilson chapters; his take on Wilson's embittered antiwar stance still makes me think. Skip Stout read the entire manuscript with the keenest skill for phrasing and interpretive turns. I am thankful for each of these readings; a writer is so very lucky to have friends who care.

I am especially grateful to four others who read and even inspired this work. Fitz Brundage and Gary Gallagher delivered careful critiques of the entire manuscript. Gary's remembrances of his own boyhood reading of Catton, as well as his astonishing knowledge of Civil War history, braced my confidence. Fitz is as good a historian as I know, and he expanded my own comprehension of what, indeed, I had written. Caz Phillips provided a kind of literary and personal friendship that one can only dream of; his stories of his own personal ties to Baldwin, his presence at the writer's death, the letters and documents he shared and gave to me—all made my chapter on Baldwin possible. Caz's own writings about Baldwin's art and career capture his friend "Jimmy" as few ever have. And without John Blum's hilarious and deeply insightful memories of Catton and Warren, as well as his readings of my drafts, this book would lack not only texture but purpose. John and Pamela have made New Haven home; thus the dedication page of this work.

At Yale University I extend thanks to several deans and provosts—Jon Butler, Chip Long, Peter Salovey, and Mary Miller—for their generous support of my research and writing. Jon is particularly special for his abiding friendship and as a model of a historian's historian. The late Frank Turner, beloved director of the Beinecke Library, took plenty of time to talk with me about Warren's relationship with C. Vann Woodward, as well as to chat about good history. The circulation librarians at the Beinecke and Sterling libraries endlessly served my needs in their customary professional style. Indeed, without the beautifully organized Warren and Wilson papers at the Beinecke, this book would not exist. At Yale's History Department I was extremely fortunate to teach a graduate course, "War and Memory," with my colleague Jay Winter, who has no peer in the study of the memory of the Great War. Jay made me rethink Paul Fussell and many other subjects; I learn something from him every time we talk. Ilan ben-Meier is as brilliant a Yale undergraduate as one will ever meet; his work as a research assistant for this book, especially in online sources, was absolutely pivotal in helping me to represent the critical reception—indeed, the essential meaning—of these authors and their major works. Ilan's mind and his zeal for ideas should be bottled and studied in a laboratory.

My colleagues at Yale's Gilder Lehrman Center for the Study of Slavery, Resistance, and Abolition, an institute that I direct, were crucial to my finishing this book. Melissa McGrath printed and organized Ilan's hundreds of pages of research. Tom Thurston gave valuable advice as a fellow historian, and Dana Schaffer simply does everything else to make my work, and that of the GLC, possible. I am also grateful to the many research fellows at the Center—especially Jim Walvin—who enrich my intellectual life in untold ways. To all the baristas at the Blue State coffee shop, I give thanks for their kind and daily attention to my needs throughout the summer of 2010.

I conducted my Catton research in two extraordinary and largely untapped collections. Jane Yates of the Citadel archives in Charleston, South Carolina, was a gracious and tremendously helpful host during my visit; she even opened on a Sunday for me. And I am grateful to Dean Bo Moore and the History Department at the Citadel for the opportunity to deliver a public lecture on Catton in December 2010, at the one hundred fiftieth anniversary of secession. Catton had been the speaker at the one hundredth anniversary. At the American Heritage Center, on the campus of the University of Wyoming in Laramie, John Waggener and Shawn Hayes were especially patient and helpful during my week-long immersion in their remarkable Catton papers. These two depositories of Catton materials are a goldmine that future scholars may soon discover. I am further grateful to Richard Blackett and to the Robert Penn Warren Center for the Humanities at Vanderbilt University for inviting me to lecture on Red Warren and the Civil War's legacies. And thanks to Joan Waugh for reading a chapter and for inviting me to speak on the book at UCLA.

In Savannah, Georgia, I am immensely fortunate to have access to the collections of my friends Walter and Linda Evans. The Baldwin letters in the Evans Collection were extremely valuable to this project. At the Huntington Library, in San Marino, California, I was privileged to hold the Rogers Distinguished Fellowship in Nineteenth-Century American History for 2010–2011, which enabled me to finish this book. My sincere thanks to Roy Riches, director of research, and to Susi Krasnoo and Carolyn Powell, for making my stay so enjoyable. Warm thanks, as well, to all the staff of the Huntington Library for providing a spectacular place to think and write. Many comrades among the Huntington fellows read or listened to this work, perhaps to the limits of their patience. An enduring thanks to: Erica Boeckeler, Jeannine DeLombard, Bill Deverell, Mary Fuller, Margaret Garber, Jennifer Greenhill, Steve Hackel, Helen and Dan Horowitz, Ted McCormick, Barry Menikoff, Bruce Moran, Marcy Norton, Tara Nummedal, Dan and Sharon Richter, Seth Rockman, Susannah Shaw Romney, Marni Sandweiss, Ron White, and Sean Wilentz. I extend very special thanks to Ken Warren, fellow Huntington writer, for his near-miraculous suggestion to use Ellison's story "Tell It Like It Is, Baby," which became the basis of my epilogue. Conversations with Ken immensely enriched this book. Pembroke Herbert, of Picture Research Associates, rendered her customary kind and creative assistance in my efforts to find photographs for this volume. Pembroke is one-of-a-kind in the world of visual sources.

I owe an enduring debt to my editor, Joyce Seltzer, at Harvard University Press. Joyce has achieved legendary status among history editors, and for more reasons than I can express. I thank her for her keen eye, her savvy mind about publishing and good history, and above all for her kind heart. I have learned, through tough love, that Joyce's friendship goes well beyond her sharp pencil. Harvard University Press is a great institution. I am grateful for Bill Sisler's confidence. Jeannette Estruth has been extraordinary in bringing every stage of this book to fruition with grace under pressure. Maria Ascher has been a critically skilled and supportive copyeditor. Phoebe Kosman is a terrific publicist. My agent, Wendy Strothman, has changed my writing career in countless good ways; I thank her for her extraordinary expertise about all aspects of publishing, and especially for her friendship.

Finally, Marsha Andrews endured countless conversations about this book's inscrutable subjects, as well as numerous lost weekends and other strains of knowing a writer who is never quite free from the work. For her soulful support, I give heartfelt thanks.

Index

Aaron, Daniel, 146, 147, 173, 285n55
Abolitionism, 34, 69; biblical narra-
    tives and, 167; blamed for the war,
    64; Douglass and, 167; "higher law"
    doctrine, 163; at Oberlin College,
    85, 115; Warren's literary attack on,
    38, 70–71, 78; Wilson's view of, 149
African Americans, 11, 19; Catton
    criticized by, 116, 117–118, 125;
    Centennial criticized by, 20, 109,
    116, 263n12; in Confederate army,
    65; journalists, 15–16, 17; violence
    against, 35; Warren's views of,
    39–40; writers, 164, 168–171. *See
    also* Union army, black soldiers in
Agrarians, 39, 40
All the King's Men (Warren), 41–46,
    73
America Goes to War (Catton),
    105–106
American Earthquake, The (Wilson),
    146
American Heritage magazine, 9,
    98–99, 101, 118, 119
American Revolution, 63
American Tragedy, An (Dreiser), 53
Andersonville Prison, 52, 72
Angle, Paul, 104
Another Country (Baldwin), 200, 202,
    203–205, 221, 289n25
Antietam (Sharpsburg), Battle of, 17,
    91, 110, 119, 178
Apologies to the Iroquois (Wilson), 168

Approach to Literature, An (Brooks
    and Warren, eds.), 40
Aristotle, 24
Arlington cemetery, 5
"Autobiographical Notes" (Baldwin),
    191
Axel's Castle (Wilson), 137, 144

Baker, Russell, 220
Baldwin, Barbara Ann, 188–189
Baldwin, David, 188, 198–199
Baldwin, Emma Berdis Jones, 188, 205
Baldwin, James, 7, 8, 9, 105, 172;
    in Africa, 223–224; Civil Rights
    Movement and, 183–185, 186, 221,
    232–233, 245; debate with Buckley,
    237–240, 248; early years, 188–193;
    fame of, 28, 186, 232, 242, 245; FBI
    file on, 244, 245, 293n75; on history,
    207–208, 211–212, 222; homosexu-
    ality and, 10, 28, 186, 200, 202–203,
    221, 289n24, 293n75; Negro history
    and, 209; "Negro problem" and,
    191, 233; in New York, 199–200,
    221; in Paris, 200–206; portrait of,
    182; race relations and, 187; reli-
    gion and, 192, 194–196, 227; in the
    South, 212–218, 221–222, 232; tragic
    sensibility and, 22–23; Warren and,
    240–244; at White House, 223;
    Wilson on, 164
Baldwin, James, works of: *Another
    Country*, 202, 203–205, 221, 289n25;

Baldwin, James, works of *(continued)*
"Autobiographical Notes," 191;
Blues for Mr. Charlie, 237; "The
Creative Process," 201; "The Dis-
covery of What It Means To Be
an American," 201; "A Fly in But-
termilk," 212–213; *Giovanni's Room*,
202–203, 289n24; *Go Tell It on the
Mountain*, 188, 192–193, 195, 200;
"Many Thousands Gone," 209–210;
"My Dungeon Shook," 224–225;
No Name in the Street, 217, 245;
"Notes of a Native Son," 8, 196,
198, 199, 207, 218, 227; *The Price of
the Ticket*, 247; "They Can't Turn
Back," 221; "Unnameable Objects,
Unspeakable Crimes," 248–249. See
also *Fire Next Time, The; Nobody
Knows My Name*
Bancroft, George, 22
Banners at Shenandoah (Catton), 121
Battlefields, 5, 91, 98, 106, 121
"Battle Hymn of the Republic"
(Howe), 19, 21, 96, 167, 209
Battle Pieces (Melville), 54–59, 77, 174
Beard, Charles, 64
Belafonte, Harry, 234, 235, 249
Bellow, Saul, 145, 172
Berryman, John, 145
Betts, Karl S., 11, 12, 13, 14, 109
Bewley, Marius, 165
Bierce, Ambrose, 145, 154, 177
Birth of a Nation (film), 83
Bismarck, Otto von, 151
Bit between My Teeth, The (Wilson),
168
Black Power Movement, 245
Blair, Mary, 137, 170

Blassingame, John, 248
Blue-Gray sentimentalism, 47, 52,
152, 187; Baldwin and, 229; civil
rights and, 15, 116, 236; Gettysburg
reunion and, 83; nationalism and, 4;
national mythology and, 3
Blues for Mr. Charlie (Baldwin), 237
Blum, John Morton, 105, 121
Bone, Homer T., 108
Border states, 52, 78, 110
Boynton v. Virginia, 14
Bradbury, Walter, 102
Bradley, David, 170
Brando, Marlon, 200, 234, 235
"Briar Patch, The" (Warren), 39–40,
76
Bromwich, David, 169
Brooks, Cleanth, 40, 62
Brother to Dragons (Warren), 60
Brown, John, 38, 69, 78–79, 159, 179
Brown, Sterling, 168
Brown, William Wells, 164
*Brown v. Board of Education of
Topeka*, 118, 213, 252
Buckley, William F., 105, 237, 239–240,
248
Buckmaster, Henrietta, 229
Bull Run, First Battle of, 14, 15, 222
Burns, Ken, 62, 121
Burt, John, 45–46

Cable, George Washington, 143, 144,
155
Campbell, James, 185, 244, 287n5
Canby, Margaret, 142
Capitalism, 137, 138, 139, 159
Capote, Truman, 105
Carmichael, Stokely, 241

Catharsis, 24, 27, 77

Catton, Bruce, 7–8, 9, 129, 152, 185, 206; "Catton touch," 90, 95, 96, 103, 104, 107; Centennial series, 102–103, 105–106, 113; Civil Rights Movement and, 110; on communism and democracy, 87–88; critics of, 104, 113, 116–118; as CWCC member, 11, 16, 109; early years, 81–84; fame and popularity of, 103, 119–122; historians' view of, 98, 100, 103–104; as journalist, 85–86, 100; Long as research assistant of, 100–103; Lost Cause tradition and, 112–113, 118, 122–124; military history and, 9–10, 25–26, 27, 119, 210–211; on mystery of Civil War, 96, 97, 98, 112; North–South balancing act of, 105, 110–113, 122, 126–127; portrait of, *80*; on race and slavery, 112–115, 124; readers' response to writing of, 95–99, 107–109; tragic sensibility and, 27; White House invitations for, 119, 120; World War II and, 86–87, 89, 273n13

Catton, Bruce, works of: *America Goes to War*, 105–106; *Banners at Shenandoah*, 121; *The Coming Fury*, 102, 111, 112, 113, 115, 153; "End of the Gallant Rebs," 116; *Glory Road*, 89, 91–93, 95, 102; *Grant Moves South*, 99; *Mr. Lincoln's Army*, 89–91; "Names of the War," 118–119; *Never Call Retreat*, 102, 120, 125; *Picture History of the Civil War*, 120–121, 126; *Stillness at Appomattox*, 89, 93–95, 99–100, 102, 108, 109; *Terrible Swift Sword*, 95, 102, 231; "The

End of the Centennial," 123; *This Hallowed Ground*, 100, 104, 107, 117, 203; *Two Roads to Sumter*, 103; *U.S. Grant and the American Military Tradition*, 175; *Waiting for the Morning Train*, 81, 124–125; *War Lords of Washington*, 86, 87–88

Catton, George R., 81

Catton, William, 103

Centennial, Civil War, 1, 2, 3, 10, 59; African Americans and, 76, 263n12; Baldwin and, 184, 186–187, 207, 219, 220, 236, 247–248; as banal wasteland, 74; battle reenactments, politics of, 14, 15; Catton and, 90, 95, 96, 100, 102–103, 105–106, 116, 123, 125; commercialism of, 27; Ellison and, 252; meaning of, 17; nostalgia of, 51; official opening of, 12, 125; Warren and, 59, 61; Wilson and, 145, 152, 153, 173

Centralism, of federal government, 161, 167

Chattanooga, Battle of, 44

Chesnut, Mary, 155, 157

Chickamauga, Battle of, 44, 119, 211

Chopin, Kate, 153

Christianity, 123, 130

Civil rights, 18, 64, 65, 90, 110, 120; Baldwin and, 183, 207, 221, 229, 232, 245; black militancy and, 238; "Bloody Sunday" beatings, 248; Centennial in contradiction with, 15, 116; Ellison and, 52; Freedom Riders, 221; "Freedom Summer" (1964), 123; Kennedy administration and, 13; King's "I Have a Dream" speech, 1–2; March on Washington,

Civil rights (continued)
183, 234–235, 236; Selma-to-Montgomery march (1965), 122; Warren
and, 76, 77, 79, 240–241; white
Southern opposition to, 67
Civil Rights Act (1964), 123, 183, 236
Civil War: brothers' war vision of, 12,
16, 21; "buffs" of, 106, 119; cemeteries, 26; fiftieth anniversary of, 31;
as intimate family history, 107–109;
literary and intellectual history of,
6, 143–144, 146; meaning of, 1, 3, 27,
54, 57, 106, 154, 171; moral responsibility for, 64, 75, 152; nostalgia for,
47, 62; in popular memory, 6, 22;
reenactments, 59, 222; songs of, 32,
95, 160; tragic vision of, 25, 51–52,
59; United States refounded by, 2;
in Warren's literature, 43–52; World
War I compared to, 4, 6. See also
specific battles
Cold Harbor, Battle of, 5, 72, 83, 178
Cold War, 2, 3, 9, 11, 27, 84; Baldwin
and, 248–249; Catton and, 111, 115,
119; Catton's commentary on, 87;
consensus of national unity and, 16,
73, 116; doctrine of progress and,
107; madness of, 142; nuclear weapons and, 228; race relations and,
185; tragic sense of history and, 223;
Warren's Civil War oracle and, 61;
Wilson and, 129, 134, 145, 146, 147,
152, 163
Cold War and the Income Tax, The
(Wilson), 171
Coming Fury, The (Catton), 8, 102, 111,
112, 113, 115, 153
Communism, 19, 61, 87–88, 138

Confederacy, 21, 110; Centennial
opening ceremony and, 12–13; Con-
federate army, 32, 43, 65; Confeder-
ate flags, 67, 249; legend of, 124,
125; in literature, 44; Montgomery
as cradle of, 217, 248, 250; women
diarists of, 155. See also Lost Cause
tradition
Congress of Racial Equality (CORE),
14, 222, 232
Conwell, Russell H., 5–6
Cornish, Dudley T., 115
Cornish, Sam, 118
Crane, Stephen, 99
Craven, Avery, 103
"Creative Process, The" (Baldwin), 201
Cullen, Countee, 192
Cunliffe, Marcus, 165
Current, Richard, 156

Dabney, Lewis, 139–140, 156, 160
Davidson, Donald, 36, 39
Davis, Jefferson, 44, 96, 103, 161
Davis, Sam, 62
Decoration Day (Memorial Day), 4,
82, 91, 99, 129
DeForest, John W., 143, 145, 155, 177
Delany, Beauford, 192
Delany, Martin, 164
Delbanco, Andrew, 54–55
Democracy, 86, 87, 134
Democrats, Southern, 11, 18
Desegregation, 13, 252
"Discovery of What It Means To Be
an American, The" (Baldwin), 201
Donald, David, 64, 70, 99, 174
Dos Passos, John, 143, 144, 145, 147
Douglass, Frederick, 210, 242; Bald-

win and, 225; *Narrative* of, 115,
166; Wilson and, 164, 166–168, 169,
285n55
Dowdey, Clifford, 110
Dreiser, Theodore, 53
Du Bois, W. E. B., 149, 208, 210
Dupee, F. W., 230

Eastman, Max, 171
Edel, Leon, 145
Eisenhower, Dwight D., 11, 86, 109,
120, 146
Elegiac mode, 58, 94, 231
Elkins, Stanley, 70
Ellison, Ralph, 7, 168, 201, 208,
251–252; *Going to the Territory*, 208;
Invisible Man, 49, 251; "Tell It Like
It Is, Baby," 252–257; on tragedy of
Civil War, 28–29
Emancipation, 25, 29, 109, 167, 187;
centennial of, 185, 224, 225, 229, 231,
235; legacies of, 114, 257
Emancipation Proclamation, 1, 16, 18,
19; Catton's commentary on, 125;
John Brown and, 38; legal limits of,
68; Wilson's critique of, 162
Emerson, Ralph Waldo, 38, 52–53, 143
"End of the Centennial, The" (Cat-
ton), 123
"End of the Gallant Rebs" (Catton), 116
Engels, Friedrich, 137
Everett, Edward, 92
Evers, Medgar, 184, 232, 237, 241
Evil, 10, 63, 79; as cost of good, 27,
56; in human nature, 24–25, 27, 53;
slavery as, 19; tragic sensibility and,
23; in Warren's writing, 40
Farmer, James, 241

Fascism, 86
Fate, 23, 27, 45, 107, 179; of African
Americans, 39, 66; history and, 42,
51; human making of, 60, 61; human
nature and, 65; ignorance and, 54;
mutual fate of blacks and whites,
231; of the South, 150; struggle with,
106, 125; tragedy and, 78, 112; war
and, 135; Warren on Civil War as
oracle of, 26, 61
Faubus, Orval, 67, 165
Faulkner, William, 22, 68, 75, 155,
210–211, 262n7
Fifteenth Amendment, 68
Fire Next Time, The (Baldwin), 8, 20,
23, 182, 241; on acceptance of his-
tory, 183; conversion experience in,
195; critical responses to, 229–231;
on Nation of Islam, 227; prophetic
mode in, 223–224, 248
Fitzgerald, F. Scott, 131, 133, 154
Fitzhugh, George, 154, 159, 179
"Fly in Buttermilk, A" (Baldwin),
212–213
Foner, Philip S., 166
Ford, Gerald, 120
Forrest, Gen. Nathan Bedford, 32, 34,
129
Forten, Charlotte, 154, 164
Fort Pillow massacre, 32
Fort Sumter, 13, 32, 55, 162
Fort Wagner, 5, 62
Foster, Alonzo, 108–109
Foster, Clarence, 108–109
Fourteenth Amendment, 68
Frankfurter, Felix, 144
"Frank Keeney's Coal-Diggers"
(Wilson), 138

Franklin, John Hope, 149, 248
Fredericksburg, Battle of, 72, 92, 178
Freedom Riders, 14–15, 16
Fugitive, The (poetry journal), 37
Fugitives, 36–39
Fussell, Paul, 4–5, 6, 135

Gauss, Christian, 131–132, 145, 280n5
Gettysburg, Battle of, 17, 33, 52, 92, 119, 211; Blue-Gray fiftieth-anniversary reunion (1913), 83; Cemetery Ridge, 26; centennial, 231
Geyl, Pieter, 64
Gilded Age, 26, 168, 179, 256
Giovanni's Room (Baldwin), 202–203, 289n24
Glory Road (Catton), 89, 91–93, 95, 102
Going to the Territory (Ellison), 208
Goldwater, Barry, 74
Go Tell It on the Mountain (Baldwin), 188, 192–193, 195, 200
Grant, Gen. Ulysses S., 50, 65, 72, 88, 123; Catton's writings on, 89–90, 93, 99, 121; *Memoirs* of, 157, 175; Mosby and, 154; Wilson and, 143, 145, 152, 174–177
Grant, Gen. Ulysses S., III, 11, 12, 13, 14, 109
Grant Moves South (Catton), 99
Grayson, William J., 154
Great Depression, 137–139
Great War and Modern Memory, The (Fussell), 4–5
Grierson, Francis, 143
Griffith, D. W., 83

Handlin, Oscar, 89, 90

Hardwick, Elizabeth, 153, 154
Harper, Frances Ellen Watkins, 164
Harwell, Richard, 75
Hawthorne, Nathaniel, 22, 52, 53, 79, 143, 154
Helper, Hinton R., 154
Hemingway, Ernest, 147
Henry, Aaron, 241
Heritage tourism, 31
Herndon, William, 136, 281n13
Higginson, Thomas Wentworth, 154
History, 46, 52, 61, 89, 207–208; belief in, 140; blindness of, 41; education and, 222; epic and mythic qualities of, 206; evil and, 25, 27, 51, 56, 59; fate and, 27, 42, 51, 56; horrors of, 4; irrationality of, 34; literature and, 131; poetry and, 35, 60; race relations and, 66–67; redemptive, 45; self and, 193. *See also* Memory, Civil War; Tragedy, in American history
"History Shows" column (Rogers), 15
Hitler, Adolf, 146
Holmes, Oliver Wendell, Jr., 69, 73, 79; in Ellison's dream, 254, 256; Wilson and, 144, 154, 174, 177–180
Homer, 63
Homosexuality, 10, 28, 186, 202–203, 289n24; Civil Rights Movement and, 221; FBI file on Baldwin and, 293n75
Hook, Sidney, 72
Horton, Robert W., 85, 86
Howe, Irving, 156, 165, 219, 233
Howe, Julia Ward, 96, 167
Huggins, Nathan, 113, 248
Hughes, Langston, 225
Human nature, 54, 65, 70, 75–76, 79;

dark view of, 72; evil in, 24–25, 27, 53; hope and despair in, 41; polarities in, 58

Hurston, Zora Neale, 168

Ideology, 24, 25, 54, 73; Melville's scorn for, 57; war and, 148; Warren's dislike of, 34, 38; of white supremacy, 9

I'll Take My Stand (Twelve Southerners), 39, 76

Industrialization, 158, 159

Innocence, American, 22, 46, 53; death of, 57; shattering of, 54; small-town, 82; World War I and, 134

"Interview with Edmund Wilson" (Wilson), 173

Invisible Man (Ellison), 49, 251

Irony, 4, 14, 34, 56

Jackson, Mahalia, 18

Jacobs, Harriet, 166

James, Henry, 53, 143, 206

James, William, 71, 72, 73, 270n61

Jim Crow: Baldwin and, 9, 185, 189, 196–197, 198, 206, 220; Centennial celebration and, 13; Lost Cause tradition and, 124. *See also* Segregation

John Brown (Warren), 38

Johnson, Lyndon, 119, 120

Johnston, Albert Sydney, 33

Jones, Peter d'A., 76

Jones, Walter, 12–13

Judson, Cassius, 83

Judson, Lyman, 83

"Jumping-Off Place, The" (Wilson), 138

Kay, Ulysses, 18

Kazin, Alfred, 75, 77, 147, 156, 164–165, 171–172

Keckley, Elizabeth, 164

Kennedy, John F., 16, 73; assassination of, 2, 183; Cold War liberalism of, 19, 223; King's appeal to, 17–18; race relations and, 13; Wilson and, 147, 172

Kennedy, Randall, 168–169

King, Martin Luther, Jr., 3, 12, 76, 186; assassination of, 245; Baldwin's meeting with, 215; as head of SCLC, 17; "I Have a Dream" speech, 1–2, 234–235, 236; Warren's interview with, 241

Knopf, Alfred, 105, 202

Koestler, Mamaine, 144

Korn, Jerry, 62

Krout, John A., 109

Ku Klux Klan, 15, 67, 113, 155, 170, 184

Lanier, Sidney, 174

Lee, Gen. Robert E., 29, 50, 63, 67, 123, 158, 257; Arlington residence of, 5; farewell address, 66, 149; invasions of the North, 95–96; as mythic figure, 62; surrender to Grant, 175–176

Leeming, David, 204

Legacy of the Civil War (Warren), 7, 23, 61–62, 67, 241; abolitionists criticized in, 70–71; critical reception of, 74–77; myths and, 60; on reality of war, 31; *Wilderness* compared to, 59; Wilson's invocation of, 151–152

Lenin, V. I., 140, 151, 158, 167

Lester, John, 130

Lewis, Lloyd, 90

Liberals, white, 115, 229, 230, 243

Lincoln, Abraham, 29, 96, 120, 281n13; as American institution, 152; assassination of, 253; attitudes toward slavery, 68; Baldwin on, 209; Catton on, 193; in Ellison's dream, 253–256; Emancipation Proclamation and, 16; Gettysburg Address, 2, 92–93, 134, 179, 252, 255–256; as ironist and pragmatist, 78; as mythic figure, 62; Southern views of, 33; Thomas as biographer of, 99; Wilson senior and, 130, 136–137; Wilson's views of, 143, 145, 149, 151, 153, 154, 157–158, 167

Lincoln Memorial (Washington, D.C.), 1, 17, 26, 234

Linkletter, Elihu, 83

Little Rock Nine, 107

Litwack, Leon, 248

Locke, Alain, 170

Logan, Rayford, 248

Long, Barbara, 101

Long, Everette Beach ("Pete"), 100–103, 113, 274n26

Long, Huey, 41, 73

Lost Cause tradition, 8–9, 16, 110; Baldwin's confrontation with, 210, 218; Catton as reconciler and, 112–113, 118, 122–124; Fugitive writers and, 37; as "Great Alibi," 66; mythic and tragic qualities of, 67; white supremacy and, 90; Wilson and, 149, 150

Lowell, Robert, 172

Lynching, 35, 47

Macaulay, Thomas, 91

MacLeish, Archibald, 19

Malcolm X, 186, 222, 226, 241, 248

"Many Thousands Gone" (Baldwin), 209–210

"March into Virginia" (Melville), 56

Marshall, Thurgood, 18, 19

Marx, Karl, 137, 138, 139, 140–141, 167

Matthiessen, F. O., 25

McCarthy, Mary, 142

McCarthyism, 146

McClellan, Gen. George B., 91

McCormick, Ken, 96

Melodrama, 31, 47, 172

Melville, Herman, 22, 24, 25, 52, 155–156; *Battle Pieces*, 54–59, 77, 174; tragedy as redemption and, 78; Warren and, 54–59, 70, 77, 78, 268n34; Wilson and, 143

Memory, Civil War, 6, 62, 69; Baldwin and, 207, 211; Catton and, 95, 110, 123, 124; literature and, 145; melodrama and, 56; mythic elements of, 58; pathos in, 65; reconciliationist, 21; slavery and emancipation central to, 3; Warren and, 33, 34, 56, 58, 59, 77

Mencken, H. L., 39, 130, 152

Meredith, James, 19, 232

Meyer, Sheldon, 155

Military-industrial complex, 86

Moby-Dick (Melville), 24, 25, 54, 55

Monaghan, Jay, 96

Montgomery Bus Boycott, 107, 214

Morgan, Edmund, 121

Morgan, Sarah, 155

Morpurgo, J. E., 153

Morrison, Toni, 169

Morrow, Edward R., 100

Mosby, John Singleton, 154

Moses, Robert, 241

Moyers, Bill, 121–122, 124

Mr. Lincoln's Army (Catton), 89–91

Muhammad, Elijah, 222, 226, 227–228

Murray, Albert, 230

"My Dungeon Shook" (Baldwin), 224–225

Mystery, of Civil War, 55, 96, 97, 98, 107, 112

Myths, 10, 158–159, 159–160, 177; artists' criticism of, 181; history and, 208; of segregation, 218–219; self-affirming, 34; tragic qualities in, 28; Warren and, 46

"Names of the War" (Catton), 118–119

Narrative of the Life of Frederick Douglass, an American Slave (Douglass), 115, 166

National Association for the Advancement of Colored People (NAACP), 12, 21

National Civil War Centennial Commission (CWCC), 11–14, 18–19, 20, 21, 109, 264n23

Nationalism, 3, 107, 147

Nation of Islam, 222, 226, 228

Nazism, 141, 146, 151, 165

"Needless war" interpretation, 111–112, 163–164, 277n43

Negro history, 1–2, 184, 186, 209

"Negro Revolution," 240, 242

Nelson, Donald M., 86, 87

Nelson, Truman, 76

Neo-Confederates, 13, 18, 110, 269n54

Never Call Retreat (Catton), 102, 120, 125

Nevins, Allan, 11, 16, 18, 19, 21, 98, 101; as CWCC member, 109; *Ordeal of the Union*, 99; White House invitation for, 120

New Republic magazine, 137, 138, 139

New York City draft riots, 47

Nichols, Roy, 104

Night Rider (Warren), 40

Nixon, Richard, 119

Nobody Knows My Name (Baldwin), 8, 207, 215, 218, 241; critical responses to, 219–220, 222; on "myth of America," 212

No Name in the Street (Baldwin), 217, 245

North, American, 94, 124; moral responsibility for the war and, 64; "Treasury of Virtue" and, 65, 68–69, 75, 152, 211; victory of, 3, 252

Nostalgia, 47, 51, 62, 109, 184; Catton and, 82; Confederate, 26; high tide of, 126; for Old South, 39; Warren and, 67

"Notes of a Native Son" (Baldwin), 8, 196, 198, 199, 207, 218, 227

Nye, Russell B., 99

O'Brien, Conor Cruise, 158

O'Connor, Flannery, 22

Official Record of the War of the Rebellion, 89, 102

Olmsted, Frederick Law, 154

"On the Slain Collegians" (Melville), 57

Ordeal of the Union (Nevins), 99

Painter, Mary, 183, 184, 204, 205, 216

Parkman, Francis, 91, 169

Patrick, Henry, 105

Patrick, Rembert, 113

Patriotic Gore (Wilson), 8, 23, 133, 141, 166, 171, 180–181, 256; African American critics of, 168–171; antiwar introduction to, 134, 147–148; Centennial and, 145, 152, 153, 155; critical responses, 173–174, 281n12; on legend and reality of Civil War, 129; Lincoln portrait in, 157–158; as literary history, 145–146, 154–155; on myths of Civil War, 158–159, 159–160; origin of title, 160–161; "sea slug" metaphor in, 148–149, 150; on Stephens, 161–164; writing of, 143

Patriotism, 11, 83

Pearl, Jed, 169

Penn, Gabriel Thomas, 31–35

Petersburg, Battle of, 58, 94, 107

Phillips, Caryl, 212, 245, 247, 287n5

Picture History of the Civil War (Catton), 120–121, 126

Pittsburgh Courier, 15, 20

Poore, Charles, 104–105

Populism, 41, 74, 88

Porter, Horace, 176–177

Porter, Katherine Anne, 53

Poverty, black, 2, 9, 218, 238

Powell, Adam Clayton, 241

Pragmatism, 71, 72, 75, 270n61

Prescott, Orville, 105

Price of the Ticket, The (Baldwin), 247

Progress, 83, 119; Baldwin's view of, 185–186, 210; Catton and, 107; myth of, 22; tragedy and, 24

Quarles, Benjamin, 166, 248, 264n25

Queen, Ellery (Manfred B. Lee), 97–98

Race relations, 14, 107, 241; Baldwin and, 187; Catton and, 113, 124; "Great Alibi" and, 65–66; Kennedy administration and, 13

Racism, 2, 9, 28, 64, 209; American self-righteousness and, 26; CWCC's efforts defeated by, 11, 109; defense of slavery and, 163; as disease, 216; traumas caused by, 238; in Union army, 114

Rampersad, Arnold, 251

Randall, James, 64

Ransom, John Crowe, 36, 37, 39

Reconciliationism, 14, 21, 111

Reconstruction, 2, 23, 121; Du Bois on, 149; failure of, 168; "Great Alibi" of South and, 66; in historical memory, 206; initial plans for, 102; North–South reconciliation and, 154; Warren's view of, 39; white supremacy and, 184; Wilson's view of, 150, 151

Redding, Saunders, 248

Religion, 24, 72, 74, 97, 140; African American churches, 194; Baldwin and, 192; Calvinism, 144, 159, 179; Civil War literature and, 144

Republican Party, 68, 74, 130, 162, 174

Robertson, James I., 18, 109

Robeson, Paul, 170

Rockefeller, Nelson, 17

Rogers, J. A., 15–16

Roosevelt, Franklin D. (FDR), 85, 146

Roosevelt, Theodore, 179

Rubin, Louis, 165
Russian Revolution, 136, 139, 140, 148

Sable Arm, The (Cornish), 115
Saint-Gaudens, Augustus, 26
Sale, Richard B., 33
Sandburg, Carl, 99, 100, 157
Schlesinger, Arthur, Jr., 64, 121, 223
Schwengel, Fred, 12
Secession crisis, 102
Segregation, 12, 13, 19, 78; Baldwin's
    analysis of, 218–219; in bus and rail
    stations, 14; Faulkner and, 210; in
    public schools, 118; racial tragedy of
    the South and, 214; Warren and, 39.
    See also Jim Crow
Segregation (Warren), 33
"Sense of the Past, The" (Warren), 53
Sesquicentennial, Civil War, 1, 7, 29,
    60, 65, 169
Sewall, Richard B., 23–24
Shaw, Robert Gould, 62
Shaw Memorial (Boston), 26
Sheridan, Gen. Philip, 83, 108
Sherman, Gen. William T., 68, 83, 122,
    144–145, 151
Shiloh, Battle of, 32, 33, 35, 44, 56, 83,
    211
Slavery, 1, 3, 21, 28, 109, 154, 209; Bald-
    win's planned novel and film about,
    246; Catton's views on, 112–115, 122;
    defenders of, 71, 154, 159, 162–163,
    165; destruction of, 2, 114, 115, 159;
    guilt about, 64; historians of, 23;
    images in popular culture, 233; in
    literature, 43; Northern attitudes
    toward, 68; slave cabins, 26, 52;
    slave narratives, 166; white factory

workers as slaves, 179; Wilson's
    view of, 150; writers born in, 164,
    167
Socialism, 136, 138, 142
South, American, 42, 94; battlefields,
    5; civil rights crisis in, 2–3; "Great
    Alibi" and, 65–68, 69, 75, 152, 211;
    memory of Civil War in, 34–35;
    modernization of, 154–155; moral
    responsibility for the war and, 64;
    resistance to desegregation, 13;
    struggle to face past of slavery, 42;
    tragedy and, 22; war dead in, 4, 5
Southern Christian Leadership Con-
    ference (SCLC), 17
Southern Review (journal), 40
Soviet Union, 11, 61, 142, 150–151, 173
Spotsylvania, Battle of, 67, 119, 178
Springer, Eric, 20
Stalin, Joseph, 140, 146
Stampp, Kenneth, 64, 121, 149, 248
States' rights doctrine, 71, 114, 161–
    162, 165
Stephens, Alexander H., 156, 160–164,
    165, 168, 180
Stephenson, Nathaniel Wright, 136
Sterling, Dorothy, 21
Stevenson, Adlai, 16, 19
Stillness at Appomattox (Catton), 8,
    23, 93–94, 102; popularity of, 89,
    99–100; readers' responses to, 95,
    97, 108, 109
Stone, Kate, 155
Stowe, Calvin, 159, 167
Stowe, Harriet Beecher: Baldwin on,
    288n8; *Uncle Tom's Cabin*, 159, 190;
    Wilson on, 143, 144, 152, 154
Stuart, Jeb, 3

Stuckey, Sterling, 248
Supreme Court, 14, 179, 180, 213
Sydney, Algernon, 24

Taine, Hippolyte, 131, 140
Tate, Allen, 36, 37, 39, 172, 173
Taylor, Richard "Dick," 154
"Tell It Like It Is, Baby" (Ellison), 252–257
Terkel, Studs, 222
Terrible Swift Sword (Catton), 95, 102, 231
"They Can't Turn Back" (Baldwin), 221
This Hallowed Ground (Catton), 97, 100, 104, 107, 117, 203
Thomas, Benjamin, 99
Thoreau, Henry David, 70, 78
Thornton, Elena Mumm, 142–143
Till, Emmett, 107
Tillich, Paul, 145
Tobin, Richard, 75
Tolstoy, Leo, 88–89, 94, 104, 272n12
To the Finland Station (Wilson), 139–140, 170
Tourgee, Albion, 153, 155
Tragedy, in American history, 22–28, 257; Baldwin and, 212, 222–223; Catton and, 103–104, 110–111, 124, 125; Civil War as oracle, 26; Warren and, 51–52, 59, 77–78
Trowbridge, John T., 154
Tuck, William, 109
Tuckerman, Henry T., 155
Turner, Arlin, 144
Turner, Nat, 179, 242
Twain, Mark, 48, 154
Two Roads to Sumter (Catton), 103

Ulysses S. Grant and the American Military Tradition (Catton), 89
Uncle Tom's Cabin (Stowe), 159, 190, 211, 287n8
Understanding Poetry (Brooks and Warren, eds.), 40
Union, preservation of: as "crusade," 178; destiny and, 159; emancipation and, 3; slavery and, 149; "Treasury of Virtue" and, 68
Union army, 47, 106; Army of the Potomac, 89, 90, 91, 93, 115; in literature, 49; racism in, 68–69; veterans of, 81, 82–84, 108, 126
Union army, black soldiers in, 5, 15–16, 63, 115, 125, 154; Fort Pillow massacre of, 32; in literature, 48
"Unnameable Objects, Unspeakable Crimes" (Baldwin), 248–249
Unwritten War, The (Aaron), 146
Updike, John, 105
U.S. Grant and the American Military Tradition (Catton), 175

Veterans, Confederate, 31–35, 129
Veterans, Union, 5, 81, 82–84, 99, 108, 126, 129
Vietnam War, 83, 120, 126, 223

Waiting for the Morning Train (Catton), 81, 124–125
Wakefield, Dan, 116–117
Walker, Wyatt Tee, 243
Wallace, Henry, 87
War Lords of Washington, The (Catton), 86, 87–88
Warren, Robert Franklin, 36
Warren, Robert Penn, 7, 10, 78–79,

151, 185, 206; *All the King's Men,*
41–46, 73; Baldwin and, 186,
240–244; "Briar Patch," 39–40,
76; Civil Rights Movement and,
240–241; Fugitive writers and,
36–39; grandfather of, 31–35, 58, 67,
129; on "Great Alibi," 65–68, 152,
211; Lost Cause and, 8–9; Melville
and, 54–59, 70, 77, 78, 268n34;
paradox and irony in, 71, 72–73, 78;
poems of, 35–36, 79; portrait of, *30*;
on prophetic significance of Civil
War, 62–64; tragic sensibility and,
22–23, 26, 28, 51–52, 77–78, 112; at
White House, 223; *Who Speaks for
the Negro?* 240; *Wilderness,* 46–51;
Wilson and, 172–173, 174, 180–181.
See also *Legacy of the Civil War*
Washington, Booker T., 39, 164, 213,
215
Weaver, Richard, 76
Wesley, Charles, 20
Wharton, Edith, 143
White Citizens' Councils, 67, 76
White supremacy, 9, 90, 184, 224
Whitman, Walt, 154, 155
Who Speaks for the Negro? (Warren),
240
Wilderness, Battle of the, 50, 83, 176,
178
Wilderness: A Tale of the Civil War
(Warren), 7, 46–51
Wiley, Bell, 11–12, 16, 109, 264n25
Wilkins, Roy, 21, 241
Williams, Madeline A., 13
Williams, Raymond, 23
Williams, T. Harry, 99
Williams, Tennessee, 172

Wills, Garry, 152
Wilson, Edmund, 7, 8, 10, 185, 206;
African American writers and, 164,
165–168; antiwar outlook of, 27,
146, 147–148; critics' views of, 156,
165, 168–174; early years, 129–132;
in Ellison's dream, 254–256; on
Grant, 174–177; Great Depression
and, 137–139; on Holmes, 177–179;
portrait of, *128*; race relations and,
164, 170; Southern sympathies of, 9;
tragic sensibility and, 22–23, 27–28;
at White House, 223; in World War
I, 132–135, 176; World War II and,
141–142, 146, 164, 171
Wilson, Edmund, works of: *The American Earthquake,* 146; *Apologies
to the Iroquois,* 168; *Axel's Castle,*
137, 144; *The Bit between My Teeth,*
168; *The Cold War and the Income
Tax,* 171; *To the Finland Station,*
139–140, 141, 170; "Frank Keeney's
Coal-Diggers," 138; "Interview
with Edmund Wilson," 173; "The
Jumping-Off Place," 138; *The Wound
and the Bow,* 140. See also *Patriotic
Gore*
Wilson, Edmund, Sr., 129–130, 131,
135–136
Wilson, Helen Mather Kimball, 130
Wilson, Woodrow, 132
Wood, Peter, 113
Woodward, C. Vann, 22, 74–75, 121,
169, 269n54
World War I (the Great War), 4, 6,
24, 280n10; Catton in, 85; Civil War
veterans and, 84; poets of, 57, 134;
Wilson in, 132–135, 176

World War II, 8, 78; public appetite
 for military glory and, 90; Wilson's
 view of, 141–142, 146, 164, 171
Worth, Eugene, 200, 203
Wound and the Bow, The (Wilson),
 140
Wright, Richard, 22, 168, 200, 208,
 230

Young, Whitney, 241